If I Had a Hammer

Margaret Hillyard Little

If I Had a Hammer:
Retraining That Really Works

UBCPress · Vancouver · Toronto

15 14 13 12 11 10 09 08 07 06 05   5 4 3 2 1

Printed in Canada on acid-free paper

Library and Archives Canada Cataloguing in Publication

Little, Margaret Jane, 1958-
    If I had a hammer: retraining that really works / Margaret Hillyard Little.

Includes bibliographical references and index.
ISBN 0-7748-1118-8

    1. Occupational training for women – Canada. 2. Poor women – Employment –
Canada. I. Title.

HD6059.6.C32R43 2005   331.4'2592'0971   C2005-900486-X

Canada

UBC Press gratefully acknowledges the financial support for our publishing program
of the Government of Canada through the Book Publishing Industry Development
Program (BPIDP), and of the Canada Council for the Arts, and the British
Columbia Arts Council.

This book has been published with the help of a grant from the Canadian
Federation for the Humanities and Social Sciences, through the Aid to Scholarly
Publications Programme, using funds provided by the Social Sciences and
Humanities Research Council of Canada.

Printed and bound in Canada by Friesens
Set in Stone by Artegraphica Design Co.
Copy editor: Joanne Richardson
Proofreader: Kate Spezowka
Indexer: Adrian Mather

UBC Press
The University of British Columbia
2029 West Mall
Vancouver, BC V6T 1Z2
604-822-5959 / Fax: 604-822-6083
www.ubcpress.ca

To my mother,
Lorna Margaret (Hillyard) Little
who, despite adversity,
insisted there was no such word as "can't"

Great Moments in Construction

1. The Carpenter

for Jacqueline Frewin

This too
   is camaraderie
to sit at midnight with the other woman
carpenter. We decided together
to kick the drywallers off the job
for gross incompetence
and have finished their work
in time for tomorrow's deadline.

Now we can sit
exhausted by a 16 hour day
drinking peppermint tea and laughing
over how we would act
if *we* had been stoned on this job.

I would have measured the space between nails,
you said and we giggled
   giddy with fatigue then
sat silent by the beam of a trouble light
admiring our work
proud of what we'd done,
proud
   we'd done it together.

– Kate Braid, "Great Moments in Construction,"
   excerpt, *Covering Rough Ground* (Vancouver: Polestar,
   an imprint of Raincoast Books, 1991), 44.

Contents

Acknowledgments / viii

1 Introduction / 1

2 Laying the Foundation / 14

3 The Everyday Lives of Our Heroes / 36

4 From Blueprint to Reality: Challenges at the Job Site / 72

5 Measuring Success / 118

6 "A Hand Up, Not a Hand Out": Let's Get Serious about Retraining / 138

Appendices / 144

Notes / 157

Selected Bibliography / 173

Index / 180

Acknowledgments

This book was truly a labour of love, a book of optimism written in a time of great pessimism. I began this book when Mike Harris and the Progressive Conservatives came to power in Ontario. I was overwhelmed. I decided that I could not simply continue my work on Ontario welfare policy. I needed an optimistic project. And so, when Mike Harris declared that he was going to give welfare recipients "a hand up, not a hand out," I started thinking seriously about what that might look like in its ideal form. This took me across the country, examining retraining programs from Voisey's Bay, Newfoundland, to Victoria, British Columbia. When I stopped in Regina and saw the Women's Work Training Program, I was hooked. It had so many of the key ingredients for success that I realized I could better explore the need for quality retraining programs by examining one specific program. Here before you lie the results of my discovery.

This research project would not have been such a happy endeavour without the very capable help of several research assistants. Sarah Miller, Sarah Riegel, Cheryl Auger, and especially Theresa O'Keefe were immeasurably helpful with the finer details of this project. Tina Burke, Julie Chatterton, and Catherine Mitchell transcribed the endless tapes of interviews. I am grateful to the Social Sciences and Humanities Research Council of Canada for a three-year Strategic Grant that funded this project and permitted me the luxury of following the participants at various stages through their retraining program. A Chancellor's Research Grant from Queen's University gave me research leave to write the first draft of the book.

I am thankful for the many helpful editors I had during the writing of this book. In particular, Kathryn Running's expertise was extremely helpful in the shaping of Chapter 1, and my carpenter pals Diane Kearnan and Patty Kenny provided me with useful carpentry details. My drumming pal, Jane Rodgers, put her professional editing skills to the test during the last hours of this project. My UBC Press editor Emily Andrew is a tour de force, completely unstoppable when she gets behind a project. I appreciate her commitment and her guidance. I also want to thank the two anonymous assessors who demonstrated great faith in the project and made very thoughtful suggestions.

There is such a strong support team behind this book. I was so fortunate to find an idyllic cabin in the woods to write the first draft. Marilyn Hood and Bob Greggs loaned me their little oasis, and Patty Kenny, who came up with this idea, watched over me from down the road. My students in Women's Studies and Political Studies at Queen's University are an endless source of inspiration and read an earlier draft of one of the chapters. My co-workers make it possible for me to enjoy teaching while trying to write and edit a book: Terrie Easter Sheen, Sue Hendler, Catherine Mitchell, Bonita Lawrence, Alison Goebel, Janice Helland, and Heather McKend. My writing buddy, Bonita Lawrence, shared all the joys and frustrations of writing and editing and taught me much about everyday racism.

I have two communities that round out my life. The Kingston Taoist Tai Chi Association keeps my body sound during the writing and editing hours at the computer. And a number of local music groups invited me to participate when I badly needed a diversion: the Two Margarets' Two Pianos, the Anvil Chorus, the Anahata Drummers, the Get In the Car Drummers, and the Porch Jammers. Thanks to my long-distance friends who also provided support at critical moments: Lykke de la Cour, Jennifer Ramsay, Malcolm Ramsay, Nicole Ramsay, and Michael Shapcott. I am truly blessed with friends who listened patiently as I talked endlessly about my plodding progress: Sandra Brooks, Deb Carr-Harris, Debra Easter, Elizabeth Greene, Jonathan Greene, Margaret Hooey, Betty Anne Howard, Diane Kearnan, Dovin Kearnan, Eleanor MacDonald, Grace MacDonald, Margaret McLauchlan, Theresa O'Keefe, Jane Rodgers, Sandra Woodhouse, and my dear cousin, Joanne Page. I give my heartfelt thanks to long-time friend Lynne Marks, who stands by me through thick and thin and is always only a phone call away. And to my father, Newton Little, and my late mother, Lorna Margaret Hillyard, who taught my two sisters (Laureen and Gwen) and me that girls can do anything they set their minds to. I am indebted to all of these people for believing in me.

This book could never have happened without the support and faith of everyone involved in the Women's Work Training Program. The coordinators, Valerie Overend and Denise Needham, made this all possible. Thank you for everything, for letting me tag along in every part of your life (not just your work life), for putting me up in your homes, for answering my tedious questions over and over again, and, most of all, for your big hearts, which made this retraining program a reality. Thanks, too, go to all the participants, all thirty of you whom I interviewed, for your patience, your generosity, and your genuine delight that I was going to try to write a book about you. I have learned more from you than I have ever learned from books. You were wonderful teachers.

Naturally, all errors of fact and judgment remain my own.

1
Introduction

Poor Women's Lives

This is a book full of heroes. It is about poor women – many of whom are single mothers, Aboriginal, or both – who have defied the odds to become apprenticing carpenters. To do so they have juggled childcare schedules, left abusive partners, kicked deadly drug habits, and done intensive retraining. Anxious at the beginning about handling a drill and afraid of heights, they now clamber up scaffolding and swing two-by-fours. I am in awe of their courage and determination. For three years I followed them as they learned first to build tool boxes and then to build two-story extensions to houses, concrete forms for industrial buildings, and more. During this time, they took me into their homes and into their lives, describing their fears, anxieties, and dreams of getting off welfare and providing a better life for themselves and their children.

This is a book for everyone who believes in possibilities. Two women who are journeyed carpenters in Regina, Saskatchewan, dreamt of teaching low-income women their skills. They scrambled for public and private funding and set up their dream apprenticeship program. For many important reasons, I believe the Women's Work Training Program is one of the best retraining programs for low-income women in the country. It is an intensive, long-term retraining program specifically designed for women, and it both teaches them to be carpenters and establishes a carpentry co-op that guarantees that, once apprenticed, they will have employment in an environment free of sexual harassment, in a company they own.[1] There were many trials and tribulations along the way. There were successes, too. Four women are now home owners and one of them actually built her own house. Five women have completed their requirements for Level 4 carpentry and have passed their Level 4 provincial exam; one of these women is possibly the country's first Aboriginal woman to achieve this goal.[2] However, none of these five has passed the interprovincial exam that would grant her a

Journeyperson Certificate of Qualification in the Carpenter Trade (carpentry journey papers).[3] The others are at various stages in their careers: some choosing to work full-time at carpentry and others choosing to do a mixture of work and schooling to upgrade their skills. And there are others who have yet to fully achieve their goals. Women in poverty are women who experience crises on a regular basis. Often these crises get in the way of their ability to sustain a commitment to an intensive retraining program. While these women may have left the program to turn their full-time attention to the current crises in their lives, most of them remain in contact with the other women in the program and wish to return once their lives have become more manageable.

In every way, the women in this book defy the current attack on the poor that describes them as lazy, dependent, and unworthy of help. Today's war on the poor is vicious and vitriolic. Politicians of all political stripes clamber over one another to be the chief warrior in this battle. This is both a discursive and a material battle. The rhetoric against the poor is inflammatory and incredibly damaging. Politicians and their pundits persist in perpetuating myths about "welfare cheats," "welfare bums," and "welfare queens." This discursive attack ignores the lived reality of the poor. It labels the poor as cheaters, when government statistics prove time and again that less than 2 percent of welfare recipients are convicted of welfare fraud.[4] It ignores the role of the global market in the perpetuation of inequities and instead blames poverty on bad individual choices. This appeal to rugged individualism also denies that many who receive welfare are also engaged in paid work with wages well below the poverty line.[5] It also ignores the fact that the poor may have dependants who may inhibit their free choice to work anywhere, anytime.

While all the poor are targets for this discursive attack, single mothers have been increasingly demonized. Although immigrants and youth have been accused of being lazy and dependent, single mothers have been viewed as the real hogs at the public trough. Politicians have asserted that single mothers are not merely lazy cheats but that they also spend all their welfare money on booze, prefer welfare to work, and have kids simply to get more welfare money.[6] Single mothers have always been considered morally suspect. They have been considered sexually dangerous creatures because they have failed to marry or stay married, and they have been charged with being irresponsible in their sexuality and their child bearing. This moral condemnation of single mothers has escalated during the last decade as politicians have willingly blamed single mothers for school drop-outs, youth gangs, and teenage drug use and pregnancy. And to further fuel the moral panic surrounding single mothers, this neoliberal rhetoric claims that the number of single mothers is increasing at an alarming rate and that, consequently, all of these moral problems are growing larger by the minute.[7]

Because of their childcare responsibilities, single mothers on welfare are now considered "dependent" upon the state, and neoliberals have vilified most forms of dependency. These critics do not appreciate the fact that single mothers are dependent because of their caring work and that the raising of the next generation is a selfless gift to society.[8]

Although there is much evidence to deny the myths about the poor, particularly those about single mothers, these lies persist. Generally it is believed that single mothers stay on welfare until their children are grown and have left home. In reality, an Ontario study found that 30 percent of single mothers leave the welfare rolls within five months and 50 percent leave within twenty months.[9] There is no evidence that welfare undercuts the work ethic. Single mothers work less because they have less education, poorer health, and younger children. Also, high unemployment, the increase in the number of low-paid jobs, and unaffordable childcare inhibit single mothers from finding work. Furthermore, it is a myth that women on welfare have large families, produce kids for money, lack parenting skills, and foster intergenerational welfare use. The truth is that the families of single mothers on welfare are smaller than what is reflected in the national average.[10] This refutes the claim that single mothers on welfare have more babies in order to receive more welfare money. There is also the belief that single mothers lack parenting skills. What is evident is that low-income single mothers lack resources that would support their parenting.[11] There is also a myth that welfare is a huge and ever-expanding, very expensive program that is responsible for the deficit and the country's faltering economy. According to the National Council of Welfare, only 6 percent of the entire Canadian population is currently on welfare, and the caseload has dramatically declined in recent years.[12] Meanwhile, in the last decade, the gap between the rich and the poor in Canada has greatly expanded.[13]

These unchallenged myths about the poor in general, and single mothers in particular, have provided a foundation of public approval that has permitted our political leaders to dismantle, without any outcry, what was already an inadequate, intrusive, and punitive welfare system. Over the last decade, most provincial governments have cut welfare rates, increased the policing of welfare recipients, restricted eligibility criteria, and begun to implement some form of workfare.[14] All of these legislative changes have deeply affected welfare recipients, but there is now evidence to demonstrate that single mothers have been hurt the most.[15] Because of a lack of adequate childcare, single mothers have not been able to supplement their diminished welfare cheques with part-time work to the extent that is possible for single able-bodied adults. Welfare fraud studies show that single mothers are one of the groups most harassed by the welfare fraud phone lines and follow-up investigations. There is also evidence to show that thousands of single mothers have been forced off welfare because of new

eligibility restrictions. In fact, during the first eight months of just one legislative change in Ontario, almost 9,000 single mothers lost their welfare
cheques.[16]

Workfare, which is gaining in popularity in Canada, creates a number of
new hurdles for single mothers. Increasingly, low-income single mothers
are defined as "workers" rather than as "mothers" and are expected to participate in paid work. Canadian welfare policies have always been ambiva-
lent about single mothers' paid employment. When welfare policy was first
enacted in this country in the early 1900s, the focus was on single mothers'
maternal responsibilities rather than on employment. Today, welfare policies virtually ignore the fact that these poor women are mothers and increasingly see them as gender-neutral workers. While mandatory, punitive
work programs have always been a part of welfare's history, it used to be the
case that single mothers were exempt because of their mothering responsibilities. Now, single mothers with children younger than school age are
increasingly expected to participate in workfare and retraining programs.[17]
This legislative change has forced mothers to juggle childcare, schooling,
and other parental responsibilities with menial jobs not of their choosing
and often miles from their homes.

Despite claims to the contrary, the real goal of these harsh welfare measures was to reduce the number of people on welfare. In this, the politicians
and administrators have been triumphant. While income disparity between
the rich and the poor continues to grow at an alarming rate, and while
increasing numbers of people are homeless, remarkably, our welfare caseloads
continue to diminish. Someday soon we will be forced to examine the impact of these welfare changes. We will need to determine the most effective
way of getting people off welfare – and keeping them off welfare. When we
finally come to ask these questions we will find that the answer is really
quite simple. Harsh welfare measures create greater misery, not greater employment. If we really want people to get off and stay off welfare, we need
to come up with retraining measures that effectively achieve this goal.

History of Women's Retraining in Canada
Retraining programs for low-income Canadians in general, and for poor
women in particular, have been few and far between. In fact, women have
rarely been the focus of public retraining programs. When we explore the
entire Canadian history of retraining women we find that it is dismal, with
only a few, brief moments when governments have demonstrated any inno-
vation in this area. During the twentieth century the Canadian state has, at
various times, been involved in the training and retraining of men. During
economic depressions, as well as war and postwar eras, the federal and provincial governments have financially supported programs to train and employ men. At the same time these governments have demonstrated incredible

ambivalence about women's participation in the workforce. They have encouraged women to do paid work when men were scarce, and they have restricted women's employment opportunities when men were plentiful. Even though the majority of women are involved in paid work today, the government has done very little to support these women as they juggle domestic and employment responsibilities. Although the federal government provides maternity leave, 39 percent of mothers are ineligible for this.[18] And despite promises to do so for more than a decade, the federal government has yet to implement a national childcare program. As a result, the majority of working mothers are unable to find affordable, high-quality public childcare for their children. These government policies, or lack thereof, gravely affect the economic opportunities of Canadian women. This section documents the role federal and provincial governments have played in the retraining of women in general and of poor women in particular. I specifically examine the government's support of non-traditional training because this is an avenue that can provide long-term economic independence for women.

For the most part, the federal and provincial governments have shown no commitment to providing Canadian women with retraining and/or employment; rather, women have been considered a reserve army of labour – one that can be drawn upon in times when men are not available but that can be ignored when able-bodied men are plentiful. During the Depression, women's unemployment was virtually ignored by government officials. It was during the Second World War that the federal government became active in apprenticeship training, and it was at that time that women were seen as a crucial national resource, worthy of being trained so that they could meet the unique employment demands of this era. Not only did this training focus on women, but it was also non-traditional training that prepared women for work in munitions factories, in aircraft hangars, and on farms. But with the end of the war, the focus returned to the need to employ all able-bodied men, and again women were all but forgotten.[19]

It was not until 1970 that the federal government first recognized women's training needs. In the Report of the Royal Commission on the Status of Women, Recommendation 82 called for training programs specifically designed for women, and these included non-traditional courses. And Recommendation 83 demanded that women be provided with postsecondary education that accommodated their family responsibilities.[20] Although neither of these recommendations was fully implemented, the Royal Commission did herald twenty-five years of some government attention to women's retraining, however minimal. In the 1970s, Canada's Manpower Training Program, despite its sexist title, provided some limited support for women's training. During the 1980s, the federal government established a number of retraining initiatives. In 1982, the National Training Act specified that a number of seats in training courses purchased by the federal government must be reserved for women. Three years later, the Canadian Jobs Strategy established two important initiatives for women workers: (1) re-entry training programs specifically designed for women and (2) the Designated Groups Policy, which identified women, Aboriginal peoples, disabled peoples, and visible minorities as equity groups with specific training needs. These two programs were very significant for women, and in one year alone more than 124,000 women participated in them, representing one-quarter to one-half of all the participants in these federally sponsored training programs and more than three-quarters of the designated groups participants.[21] In 1986, the minister responsible for the Status of Women endorsed a nineteen-point strategy to enhance women's training and education. Five years later, the federal government initiated a national labour force development strategy. As part of this strategy, the federal government established a national advisory board on labour and working groups to strategize about labour market adjustment. Through these policy initiatives, the federal government clearly recognized women's specific labour and retraining needs and adopted principles to improve gender equity in retraining. Despite this articulated concern about women's retraining possibilities, the federal government did not allocate significant resources for women's training during this period.[22]

Targeted training for women was only briefly available in Canada and difficult to gain access to at the very best of times. It is important to remember that the vast majority of recipients in federally sponsored training (whether it was federally purchased seats at community colleges or the subsequent Skills, Loans and Grants Program) were always men.[23] Yet these important policy directives in the 1980s and early 1990s did create a climate in which women's training needs were at least given lip service. This legitimized women's training and encouraged women's lobby groups and programs specifically designed for women. Women in Trades and Technology (WITT) served as a national and regional lobby organization that promoted women's non-traditional training and supported women in non-traditional employment.[24] Community-based organizations began to develop programs specifically for women and even for select groups of women (i.e., immigrant, Aboriginal, and low-income women).

Since the early 1990s, the federal government has withdrawn funding dollars from training programs, and while this has affected all workers and potential workers, it has most dramatically affected women. From 1990 to 1993, the federal money available for training programs declined by 48 percent. From 1990-91 to 1991-92, the federal government funding for training was cut by $100 million; however, over that same year, the training expenditures for women declined by $108 million. The programs that have been most successful in training women for jobs that can raise them out of poverty (i.e., women-only and bridging programs in non-traditional employment) have been the ones most severely cut.[25]

While the federal government never fully committed itself to women's training, in 1996 it withdrew from the field in four significant ways. First, it eliminated the Consolidated Revenue Fund training and employment support programs for women. According to Ursule Chritoph, an expert on women's retraining, this loss of funding for women's training "has had the single most devastating impact on women."[26] Second, the federal government devolved responsibility for training to the provinces and established agreements with all of them except Ontario. None of these agreements contains any equity provisions or equity guidelines. These agreements have resulted in a market-driven approach to retraining. The market, naturally, is not attentive to gender or other equity concerns and, consequently, public-funded retraining for women has virtually disappeared.[27] Third, the federal government decided to cancel the Designated Groups Policy. No longer are there any requirements for equity-based criteria in the public provision of employment training. Disabled peoples, Aboriginal peoples, and women are no longer granted any special attention when it comes to government funding of training programs. Fourth, in 1996, the federal government replaced the Unemployment Insurance Act with the Employment Insurance (EI) Act. Under EI policy fewer women are eligible for support. By 1999, the number of women receiving EI dropped to only 32 percent, down from 70 percent a decade earlier.[28] These EI changes also reduced the number of EI-sponsored women's training and employment services.[29] The current EI policy encourages provinces to finance only those who can adjust easily to a retraining program and then quickly re-enter the labour force. This means that there are few incentives for provinces to train women and others who have multiple barriers to employment.[30] This has drastically diminished the number of retraining opportunities available to women across the country. In Toronto alone, community-based training for women was reduced by 40 percent as a result of these federal policy changes.[31] And, according to experts in women's retraining, this is also happening in many other Canadian communities.[32]

These policy changes have devastated all women's training, including non-traditional training. The retraining programs that did lead women to relatively secure, well-paid jobs were the women-only and/or bridging programs that combined skills development in non-traditional employment with upgrading, counselling, and life skills. Non-traditional employment includes a broad range of trades skills for construction, manufacturing, fabrication and repair, and operations, as well as technical skills for computer and information technology and blue-collar work.[33] In the late 1970s and early 1980s, government bought seats in non-traditional training programs for women. When all of the seats set aside for women were not filled, the government deduced that this was because women were not interested in non-traditional training and abandoned its support. However, two national studies confirmed that these programs were particularly successful in preparing women to enter training in male-dominated jobs because they introduced them to new tools and equipment.[34] Women's groups argued the problem was not enough support rather than not enough interest. They complained that some of the gatekeepers of these courses (i.e., employment placement officers and teachers) actively discouraged women from participating in them. In addition, these courses tended not to be available to poor single mothers. The vast majority of these courses were not open to those on welfare, and there were no childcare provisions to aid single mothers.[35] Despite the limitations of the federal seat-purchase method of providing non-traditional training, its demise, along with other policy changes, has dramatically reduced opportunities for Canadian women to participate in non-traditional training.

While all women have suffered because of policy changes in the field of women's training, low-income women rarely got a chance to even consider any types of meaningful training. While poor single mothers who are considered worthy constitute one of the first groups to receive government aid, they remain one of the last to receive publicly funded retraining. Most provincial governments established welfare for single mothers in the early 1920s.[36] These welfare cheques were minimal, and only those deemed most deserving were eligible, namely, white Anglo-Saxon widows with more than one child. Because the payments did not begin to meet the real needs of single mothers, it was assumed that these women would supplement their cheques with paid employment. But welfare administrators were adamant that this employment should not interfere with their mothering responsibilities. In addition, administrators permitted only the most gendered employment. In fact, in the early decades of the policy, administrators insisted that single mothers refuse factory work in favour of domestic work such as selling pies, sewing, and laundry, even though the former paid substantially more than the latter.[37]

The retraining of poor women was not even considered until the 1980s. Up until 1985, welfare recipients, both male and female, were not permitted access to training programs; rather, welfare was considered to be a "passive" program, and retraining attention was focused on the "active" program – Unemployment Insurance. By the mid-1980s, the federal government encouraged agreements with the provinces that would provide training specifically for welfare recipients. As a result of these agreements, some provinces established retraining programs for poor single mothers that provided some short-term training and/or supplemented poor wages. Among the most ambitious projects were New Brunswick Works (NB Works) and the Self-

Sufficiency Projects in New Brunswick and British Columbia. These programs were specifically designed for welfare recipients, and the vast majority of participants were single mothers. Unlike most programs for welfare recipients, NB Works provided long-term training, thereby allowing women who were severely under-educated to gain academic upgrading and skills training that would enable them to compete for stable jobs at living wages. NB Works, which ran from 1992 to 1998, was a three-year program targeted at "employable" welfare recipients with less than a Grade 12 education. Participants, 84 percent of them female, were provided with allowances that were at least equal to their previous welfare cheques as well as a childcare allowance. They participated in a community workplace placement, followed by academic upgrading and training of their choice.[38] The Self-Sufficiency Projects, which ran from 1992 to 1995, did not conduct retraining per se but, rather, supplemented the wages of single mothers who were welfare recipients for up to three years, provided they were employed a minimum of thirty hours a week and remained off welfare. The purpose of these Self-Sufficiency Projects was to financially supplement the earnings of the participants for a certain period, thereby lifting these people out of working poverty. This supplement helped single mothers pay for childcare, transportation, and other employment-related expenses. It was assumed that the participants were being trained in employment-related skills while on the job. It was also assumed that these women would be able to find better-paying jobs once the program ended.

Unfortunately, most of these retraining and wage supplement programs specifically designed for poor single mothers did not lead to employment. The 1980s to early 1990s was a period of high unemployment, and poor single mothers, despite some retraining or supplements to their wages, generally could not find permanent employment. NB Works participants found that they were not able to complete their educational goals before the program disbanded. And some participants of the Self-Sufficiency Projects had difficulty finding employment and were concerned that they would not be able to meet their childcare and other employment-related expenses once the supplement to the poorly paid job ended.[39] Consequently, these programs did very little to remove single mothers from poverty. Instead of the government investing in job opportunities so that single mothers could see a light at the end of the retraining tunnel, it abandoned the entire project. Today there is virtually no training program in Canada specifically designed for poor single mothers.

With few retraining programs now available to low-income women, these people are forced to compete with others who have more resources and often more education for those training programs that do exist. The new federal-provincial agreements can require participants to pay up to 100 percent of the costs of the program, with the average amount being half of the cost.[40] Obviously, this is prohibitive for low-income women. Also, most provinces consider student loans to be income that is to be deducted from the welfare cheque, therefore making many low-income women receiving postsecondary education ineligible for welfare.[41] While most women have to juggle domestic responsibilities with their attempts to retrain, low-income women have fewer resources to cushion the strain of these competing duties.

What is clear from this analysis of the history of women's retraining is that women continue to get the short end of the stick. "Women get fewer opportunities than do men for job-related training; they get fewer hours of training; they face more barriers; and what they do get goes primarily to those already at the top."[42] Despite fewer opportunities, women make heroic efforts to get what little training is available. Enrolment figures in postsecondary education shows that women outnumber men. Women, on average, graduate with more debt than do their male counterparts.[43] Studies of women in retraining programs illustrate that they put in long hours getting their education, followed by more hours of unpaid domestic work, all to ensure a better life for themselves and their children. This suggests that women want postsecondary education and training and that they do their best to achieve it, despite the lack of government attention to the issue.

Women continue to experience much greater poverty than do men. This is partly the result of a very gendered economy. Traditionally female jobs pay less than do traditionally male jobs. The majority of female workers remain in a narrower range of occupations (i.e., clerical, services, sales, and managerial work) than do male workers. In addition, women make up the majority of the part-time work force.[44] Consequently, many women work at dead-end, low-paying jobs. The average female wage is still approximately 70 percent of the average male wage. One way to attain women's economic equality is to achieve a more equitable distribution of women and men through all occupations and pay levels. Some of women's current poverty would be alleviated if women had "good" jobs – jobs that provide adequate salaries, job security, decent pensions and benefits, and opportunities for advancement. Training for non-traditional employment is one of the ways that women can gain the necessary qualifications to compete for these "good" jobs.

If we do not train women for non-traditional jobs, then we can expect fewer women to hold "good" jobs in Canada. Today, women make up 58 percent of the workforce but occupy fewer than 10 percent of the trades, technicians, and technologists in Canada. Although women represent more than half of all student enrolments at colleges and universities, the proportion of women enrolled in technology and trade programs had shrunk from 1 in 18 students in 1983 to 1 in 27 by 1989.[45]

Non-traditional retraining that specifically focuses on women can meet the specific needs and concerns of participants. Women need to be encouraged to enter non-traditional training programs. These programs need to be readily available and publicly funded. Support services need to be available and male workers must be re-educated in order to enable women to enter harassment-free workplaces once they have completed their training. A women-only space for initial training, female role models, a variety of learning techniques, counselling, and support services that meet women's familial responsibilities and challenges would all make it possible for women to learn new skills in a positive and encouraging environment. This would, in turn, grant women more employment choices and more self-fulfillment.

Case Study: Women's Work Training Program, Regina, Saskatchewan
I have been frustrated for years about the lack of training opportunities for poor single mothers. I have met women who have trained to be data-entry clerks, receptionists, and retail assistants. Many of these women juggled childcare arrangements, public transportation schedules, and family crises in order to complete a training course, only to find there was no work available at the end. Others, the "lucky" ones, found jobs that were part-time and minimum-wage and that did not financially improve their lives. Even the "success" stories were discouraging because these women had moved from welfare poverty to working poverty.

Non-traditional retraining simply provides better opportunities for low-income women. And despite the diminishing government funding, there remain a few innovative retraining programs around the country specifically designed to initiate women into non-traditional employment. I researched these, travelling to various sites and interviewing women trainers who have been committed to these programs for a long time. In the midst of this research I visited the Women's Work Training Program in Regina, Saskatchewan. Here I met two women, Valerie Overend and Denise Needham, who had trained to be carpenters when they, too, were poor women on their own. They were determined to provide other low-income women with the opportunity to do the same. Because of their own experiences, they were well aware of the barriers that poor women face when training and seeking employment. They met and dreamed their ideal training program and then turned it into a reality.

If I Had a Hammer explores why I believe the Women's Work Training Program is one of the best retraining programs for low-income women in the country. Over three years I travelled four times to Regina and met with the organizers, participants, government administrators, and funders of the program. For the most part I stayed at the homes of the two coordinators – Valerie's house in town and Denise's ranch in the country. I saw how important it was to them to make this program work and how they both sacrificed their health and time with family and friends in order to give every ounce of themselves to this endeavour. But above all, I spent the majority of my time in Regina with the women participants. I met their children, partners, and friends. They told me about their heartaches and their small triumphs. I interviewed them at their worksites and in their homes. In order to make this as comfortable for the participants as possible, I used an open-ended interview style, focusing on one particular theme with each visit. This interview style encouraged the women to "tell their stories." I hoped that this approach would be particularly useful when meeting with Aboriginal women, who come from traditions that respect storytelling and oral history. These women participants have been intimately involved in the creation of this book. Right from the beginning, they were excited about having their struggles and achievements recorded. In most cases the interviews were tape-recorded and then transcribed.[46] The participants read the previous transcript and edited it before proceeding to the next interview. They signed research agreements at every stage of the interview process and were assured that they could use either their name or a pseudonym. They were also guaranteed that I would not use any portion of the interview without their written consent. They offered advice on what subjects they believed I should cover, on how the book should be organized, and on what types of photographs should be included. I have been overwhelmed by their support and interest in this project. And I am indebted to them for sharing their joys, fears, and doubts throughout their retraining program. I am more proud of them than I can express. I fear that I, in their circumstances, would not have found the courage to defy the odds and keep on hammering.

Chapter 2 introduces you to Denise and Valerie and explores the structure of the program. Chapter 3 examines the many barriers to retraining that the women participants faced on a day-to-day basis. Racism, violence, lack of education, and the everyday reality of poverty are very real barriers to these women becoming journeyed carpenters. Chapter 4 examines the flaws in the program and the issues that have to be addressed in order to understand the many challenges to running a successful retraining program for low-income women. We see how racism, sexism, class inequities, and homophobia challenge both the women participants and the coordinators. Chapter 5 explores the keys to a successful retraining program. Here I argue that we need new measures to determine exactly what constitutes a successful program. Simply counting the heads of journeyed carpenters at the end of the program does not adequately assess the program's effectiveness. Any notion of success must also assess how the participants view themselves and their opportunities both during and following the program. Chapter 6 addresses how retraining programs that provide real opportunities for low-income women could be set up across the country.

There are many reasons why I chose the Women's Work Training Program as the best example of non-traditional training for low-income women. Many of the women participants were single mothers on welfare – a group that is rarely targeted for intensive training that leads to "good" jobs. Two-thirds of the participants are Native (either status or Métis), again a group that receives very little attention in non-traditional retraining. Few of the women had much in the way of employment experience or skills development. Many had not finished high school. Almost every one of the women had at least one major challenge in her life besides the everyday difficulties of living in poverty (e.g., a drug or alcohol addiction, an abusive partner, mental health issues, a childhood of sexual or physical abuse, a violent or abusive past history, children with learning difficulties, etc.). The coordinators of the program have experienced some of these difficulties themselves. They understand that low-income women, who often have many crises in their lives, require a retraining program that is free from harassment, that is flexible, that is long-term, that comes with secure funding, and that facilitates gaining secure employment at the end. This is more than a retraining program. Attached to the program is the Regina Women's Construction Co-operative. After forty-six weeks of training, women can apply to join the Co-op. Through the Co-op women can gain their on-the-job trade time in a women-only workplace – a feature that no other women's non-traditional retraining program provides.

The women learn a lot more through this retraining program than simply how to handle the tools of their new trade. Retraining programs are usually assessed according to their retention rates: How many women stayed with the program from start to finish? How many women had carpentry jobs at the end of the program? How many women remain carpenters two years after they complete the program? While retention is important, these criteria do not begin to measure the success of a retraining program for low-income women. As you follow the progress of these women you will see that, along with carpentry skills, they acquire self-esteem and develop communication skills. They reassess and sometimes leave abusive relationships; they find new coping strategies for dealing with challenging children, and much, much more. The real success of this program can be read on the faces of these women. So, read on and meet these "heroes of their own lives."[47]

2
Laying the Foundation

In the Beginning ...

One of the first rules of carpentry is that a house is only as good as its foundation. The same can be said for retraining programs. A program that is hastily organized and insensitive to the real needs of the participants will simply not open the door to long-term employment. As Chapter 1 illustrates, most of the retraining programs designed for low-income women have been short-term, providing only a narrow range of skills, which, for the most part, have not led to well-paying jobs. At best, low-income women were redirected into dead-end part-time jobs with few benefits or opportunities for advancement. The majority of these jobs were in the service sector, a female ghetto for women workers. In other words, the foundation of retraining programs for low-income women had a major crack in it, and the structure could not hold.

Two women in Regina, Saskatchewan, with years of carpentry experience, were determined to build a different type of retraining program for low-income women. It all began with a chain letter. Denise Needham became a journeyed carpenter when she and her husband divorced and she needed to support herself financially. While living in Buchanan (a small town in rural Saskatchewan) in the late 1980s, she received a chain letter for women. "You were supposed to send a dollar and write down something about your dreams, and Valerie had written her name, address, and phone number, and she wrote ... that she would love to do nothing better than work with a group of women training them how to do carpentry ... I didn't get the million dollars back ... but I kept Valerie's name," recalls Denise.[1] Two years later, Denise moved to Regina. She immediately called Valerie and said she wanted to come over to talk about Valerie's dream. "I was astonished that someone I'd never met remembered what I'd written more than two years earlier in a chain letter," says Valerie.[2] They met for the first time at Valerie's house and talked about their mutual dream.

In talking about their dream, they realized the possibilities of working together. "We were incredibly different," recalls Denise. "Valerie was interested in the big picture, the dream, and I was worried about toilet paper, the nitty-gritty." Although they had never met previously, there were some common threads in their life stories. Both women are white, from middle-class backgrounds, and had fallen into poverty when their relationships ended. Denise came from small-town Saskatchewan. Her father had been a fighter pilot during the Second World War and later followed his father's footsteps and became editor of the local newspaper. Denise grew up to be a self-starter. She has an abundance of energy, a strong work ethic, and a powerful belief that the individual can conquer all odds. Her partner describes her as "a diamond in the rough," for Denise tells it as she sees it, swears as colourfully as any male carpenter, and is most comfortable in baggy jeans and a lumber jacket. Denise began carpentry when she and her husband bought a fixer-upper farmhouse in rural Saskatchewan. "He went in to work all day and would tell me what I could do before he left in the morning. I would tear down walls, do all kinds of things – but finally, I decided to get some real training in this," recalls Denise. So she packed her daughter off to daycare and began a carpentry apprenticeship. She was the first woman to complete her apprenticeship at Palliser Institute in Saskatchewan, for which she received a letter of acknowledgment from the premier of the day addressed to "Mr. Dennis Needham."[3] When Denise came out as a lesbian, and she and her husband amicably divorced, she put her new-found carpentry skills to work. In the early 1980s, Denise taught women's carpentry in Moose Jaw. In the late 1980s, she moved to Regina and decided to set up her own women's carpentry company, hoping to employ women apprenticing carpenters. As well as owning her own carpentry company, with her partner she also owns and operates the Two Spirit Guest Ranch near Regina Beach. In 1992, she received the Woman of Distinction award from the Regina YWCA.

Valerie was brought up in Regina and had two babies before her abusive relationship ended. "The options looked pretty grim – any of the 'typical' jobs women could get would not go anywhere. That's why I made the decision to get my journey papers," recalls Valerie. "To me, learning a trade means you can raise your family in dignity."[4] As she learned carpentry, she became very active in encouraging other women to join the trades. For more than a decade, she has been an extremely active member of Women in Trades and Technology (WITT), a national non-profit organization that provides research, education, and support for women in the non-traditional trades and technology sector. As well as holding various executive positions in WITT, she has established and coordinated workshops to introduce school-aged girls to the non-traditional trades and technology. Following on this successful program, Valerie has guided the establishment of a similar program designed specifically for Native girls. She also regularly teaches an exploratory trades course to women at the provincial technical institute. She has a background in community development, is trained as a life skills facilitator, and is committed to matters of social justice and equity. She sits on the board of numerous trade organizations and is the only woman on the Provincial Apprenticeship Board and the Carpenters' Trade Advisory Board. As a result of her commitments, she has received both local and national recognition, including the Governor General's 125 Medal for community volunteerism. She is nationally known and respected as a skilled advocate for women in the trades. She knows all the important government players on a first-name basis, she can persuasively lobby both government and the private sector for funding, and she can mediate and alleviate conflict. Above all, she is relentless in her pursuit of real opportunities for women in the trades.

Together, Valerie and Denise make a powerful partnership. In the fall of 1991, they ran their first women's carpentry retraining program. During the first program, they trained sixteen women. "We then started a second program and trained a second group. The Carpenters' Union bought all the tools and found the location for the shop: all we had to do was concentrate on teaching," recalls Denise. "It was great fun – teaching with Valerie. But it ended and that was it. We packed up our bags and I went back to my own carpentry company."

Denise hired one of the participants in the program to work for her carpentry company. "The problem [with our retraining program] was that there was no work experience attached: the women had to go out and find their own," explains Denise. As study after study demonstrates, the major problem with training women for non-traditional work is retention. Women gain the skills and then they go out to all-male working environments. They experience harassment, isolation, and lack of support. Thus many of them leave the field.[5]

If they had a chance to do it again, Denise and Valerie knew that they wanted to include a work component, a way to keep women working in the field once they had the basic skills. In 1995 they got their chance. Marion Proctor, the deputy minister of labour for the provincial government, was in charge of New Careers, which provided training for people on welfare. Most of the training was in construction, and the participants were almost all men. "Marion was a strong feminist and she asked Val to establish a program for women," recalls Denise.[6]

In February 1996, Valerie and Denise's dream became a reality. That month, sixteen women entered the Women's Work Training Program for the first time, with the hope of completing a four-year carpentry apprenticeship. With first-year funding in place and the hope of more to come, the coordinators and the sixteen participants picked up their tools and laid the foundation for a retraining program unlike any other in Canada.

Structure of the Women's Work Training Program

Valerie and Denise carefully developed a program that would meet the needs of low-income women. They incorporated the best features of successful retraining programs aimed at helping women interested in non-traditional work. Also, based on their own experiences and insights, they included some unique features in the program to make it more possible for low-income women to participate and succeed. These are outlined below.

Prerequisites are minimal, but they are an essential part of the screening process used to determine who is prepared to participate fully in the program. In order to qualify for the program, participants must be women, unemployed, seventeen years old or more, have Grade 10 math, be Saskatchewan residents with valid Saskatchewan health cards, and "have a positive attitude towards physical work."[7] If the women do not have the math requirement, the coordinators will help them acquire it so that they can join the program. Women with children are required to make childcare arrangements. On their application forms, mothers must explain not only their childcare arrangements but also their back-up plan for when these arrangements don't work.

The coordinators were adamant that this program be available to as many low-income women as possible. Initially, posters were displayed at women's centres and a number of public locations. Several local government agencies played a role in the recruitment process. In fact, almost three-quarters of the participants were recruited through career services for people on welfare. Another 20 percent discovered the program from the federal Human Resources Development Corporation offices.

Interested candidates receive written information about the program. This information explains that all successful applicants must have a commitment to participate in the life skills component of the program, to respect all other participants and their learning styles, to be alcohol- and drug-free while at the shop and job site, and to seriously consider joining the Co-op after one year of training. If interested, the candidates attend a half-day group orientation session at the shop where the goals of the program are further clarified and the women meet the coordinators and visualize the program. At this session the candidates complete self-check lists that they keep to themselves and a personal history and current information form that they submit. Denise and Valerie also conduct personal interviews with each candidate to further screen the applicants.[8] This careful screening process helps ensure that the participants chosen are well aware of the commitment they are making to dramatically alter their futures.

Demand has been much greater than the program allows. Those who qualify are put on a waiting list in case an opening emerges later in the program. All of the women are low income and almost everyone was a welfare recipient before joining the program. The majority of the thirty participants interviewed were low income mothers, and one-third were single mothers.[9] Twenty of the thirty participants (66 percent) were Native, the vast majority being status and only three being Métis. Initially, the coordinators expected that only 30 percent of their participants would be First Nations and Métis women, a proportional representation of the Native population in Regina. "Three or four months [after the program began] 95 percent of the women walking through the door were Aboriginal women," explains Valerie. She believes this is partly due the program's location within the inner city, where the majority of Native urban women live.[10] It also became clear that Aboriginal women were spreading the word about this unique retraining program to their friends and relatives. The program included three sets of sisters, sisters-in-law, and first cousins, most of whom are Aboriginal.[11] Perhaps this also speaks to the very few training programs available for Native women and these women's strong desire for any opportunity to alleviate the intense poverty they face on a day-to-day basis.

Funding for such innovative training programs is always a challenge. The program is divided into six phases representing six different educational components. This allows funders to commit financially to one specific phase of the program or to one set of skills development rather than to all aspects of the long-term project (see Table 2.1). In this case, the Saskatchewan government, a New Democratic government headed by Premier Roy Romanow, strongly supported the program. The provincial government provided the lion's share of the funding for Phases 1 and 2, which represent the first year of the program for all the participants. This provincial funding of $261,000 was a significant commitment. Phases 3 through 6 of the program, which include the Co-op, were funded by the federal government ($95,000), the Saskatchewan government ($190,000), and the Women and Economic Development Consortium ($194,900) (see Appendix A). As Chapter 1 illustrates, this funding was established at a time when both the federal and provincial governments were dramatically withdrawing financial support for retraining programs. Even in the best of training times, most government-funded training programs lasted for only six weeks to six months. The Saskatchewan government promised almost 100 percent of the funding for the first year of the retraining program for low-income women. This established an important financial base. Following this, the coordinators had to arrange funding from a number of provincial, federal, and private sources. In the second year, a steering committee of all the funders was established so that each could understand his/her relationship to the overall project and to the other funders. "It was virtually unprecedented to have

Table 2.1

___

Six phases of the Women's Work Training Program

Phase 1	Phase 2
20 weeks Level 1 carpentry theory and shop Life skills Math skills	26 weeks Work experience 4 days per week on site 1 day per week in classroom/shop/life skills Training in electrical, plumbing, finishing, framing Women take Level 1 exam
Phase 3	**Phase 4**
52 weeks Training in business management, production shop Specialty training in barrier-free construction Eligible for Level 2 carpentry at provincial technical institute	52 weeks Business training Home and workplace renovation for accessibility Some women move to positions as crew chiefs Some women begin taking Co-op board roles and public speaking
Phase 5	**Phase 6**
52 weeks Eligible for Level 3 training at provincial technical institute Leadership training and mentoring Home and workplace renovations More advanced business skills	52 weeks Eligible for Level 4 training at provincial technical institute Eligible to write journey exam in carpentry At end, able to move into instructional, supervisory or management positions with Co-op

all funders sit down together on a regular basis and to brainstorm ways to support the training program without gaps," explains Valerie.[12] This unique funding arrangement demonstrates a real concern for low-income women, the strength of a carefully designed program, and Valerie's persuasive lobbying skills.

One of the keys to successful funding arrangements for this retraining program is the close association between it and Saskatchewan Women in Trades and Technology (SaskWITT). SaskWITT is a non-profit organization that began in the 1970s with a mission to encourage and assist in the education and successful employment of women in trades, technologies, operations, and blue-collar work. Valerie and Denise both have a close association with this group. The Women's Work Training Program is one of many programs that SaskWITT has sponsored. As a result, SaskWITT, with its long and credible history in the area of women's retraining, provides a strong alliance for the fledgling retraining program, making it easier to gain access to financial and community support.[13]

Many of the features of this program are similar to those in other WITT training programs. The program recognizes that there are many barriers common to low-income, marginalized women that inhibit their participation in the workforce. These include lack of affordable childcare for their children, lack of family support for work outside the home, conflicting demands of home and job, poverty (resulting in lack of money for transportation and other work-related expenses), and low self-esteem (which keeps women in undervalued and underpaid jobs). In addition to these barriers, there are others that are specific to the building trades. Women wishing to enter non-traditional trades encounter barriers to information and to knowledge about what is available or possible. They may not have a realistic understanding of the physical requirements of the trade and/or they may not believe that they can meet them. Often they lack self-confidence because they lack role models. Fear of harassment in the workplace can also be a barrier. Finally, the lack of academic and experiential background for the trades makes that area seem utterly formidable to most women.

This retraining program attempts to alleviate the real barriers to low-income women's participation in non-traditional training and employment. Almost all the participants are on welfare when they enter the program. Valerie establishes agreements with social assistance administrators to ensure that their policies will cover the necessary costs associated with a woman's participation in the program (i.e., clothing, transportation). Also, borrowing from the WITT model, this program is a women-only training space. During the initial phase of the program, all of the instructors are women, and, for the remainder of the program, wherever possible women are hired as instructors, supervisors, and crew chiefs. Training is given in a supportive environment that encourages women to develop sensory, motor, language, math, and science skills required for the job. All of the women interviewed said that the women-only environment was vitally important to their success in the program. "Great! Women teaching women! I wasn't intimidated by anyone," explained one participant. Another said, "I think it was good because the women and I were nervous enough using tools for the first time without having hecklers. Some men, not all, have negative attitudes towards women doing non-traditional trades."[14] In an all-female environment women can make mistakes, admit their intimidation in the face of certain equipment, and encourage each other as they learn to develop their new skills.

Carpentry apprentices must complete four levels of theoretical training and 7,200 hours of trade time. The training program is carefully designed to do this, offering six distinct phases of learning (see Table 2.1). In addition, there are three separate intake groups of sixteen participants each; one group begins in each of the first three years of the program. This means that this training program has women at different stages in their carpentry education, which permits women participants to mentor each other (see Table 2.2). The first phase of the program is an intense twenty weeks, during which participants do technical schooling, some hands-on carpentry, and some life skills work. To begin this introductory phase the women must sign a contract that states very clearly that they are committed to the program. Denise explains, "I say to the women, I want you to marry me for five months and I want the focus to be here, and everything else has to fit in around that. I want you to put yourselves first, and in order to do that I'm expecting you here everyday."[15] Participants initially commit to a two-week probationary period. At the end of this period the coordinators and the respective participants discuss any difficulties with their arrangements (i.e., childcare, transportation, addictions) that interfere with their participation in the program. If they pass the two-week period, participants may then recommit to completing the first phase of the program.

Training begins at 8:00 a.m. and ends at 4:00 p.m. (see Appendix B for the daily routine and for participant guidelines). Any appointments are to be scheduled after 4:00 p.m. Participants are expected to phone Denise first thing in the morning to explain any absence or lateness. Unexcused absences result first in a verbal warning, then in a written warning, and finally in dismissal. Any unexcused absence of four days results in automatic dismissal.

Given that the participants are low-income, virtually all that is required to participate in the program is provided for them. Even calculators, safety goggles, and pens and paper are available. In addition, once the women turn in their receipts to their welfare or Employment Insurance worker,

Table 2.2

Timelines for new intakes in Women's Work Training Program

Intake	1996	1997	1998	1999	2000
1	Phases 1 and 2	Phase 3	Phase 4	Phase 5	Phase 6
2		Phases 1 and 2	Phase 3	Phase 4	Phase 5
3			Phases 1 and 2*	Phase 3	Phase 4

* Intake 3 started in May 1998, so Phase 2 extended into 1999 and Phase 3 extended into 2000.
Source: Valerie Overend, *Foundation for Success: The Story of the Women's Work Training Program in Saskatchewan* (Regina: SaskWITT, 2001), 12.

they are reimbursed for the money they spend on their steel-toed work boots. Childcare, however, is not covered by the program; the participants must attempt to make arrangements with their welfare or Employment Insurance worker to cover licensed daycare, but this can be difficult to obtain. Most of the participants choose to have family members care for their children, but they do not receive financial compensation for this childcare arrangement.

The shop is located in the same building as the classroom, which allows "for lots of trips to the tool crib to take out the 'tool topic of the day.'" Activities in the shop are project-based and provide time for the participants to have hands-on experience with each tool taught in this phase of the program. Participants are able to take projects home if they pay for materials, and they can get the materials free if they find them in the scrap bin. In this way some of the women are able to provide many presents for their children.[16]

Math and life-skills classes occur daily during Phase I. Every attempt is made to alleviate women of their math anxieties. The math classroom provides a supportive environment wherein the women all encourage one another. Wherever possible the math problems are applied to real-life situations. Quizzes occur regularly, and participants must receive 70 percent in order to continue on to the next math section. "The women's confidence builds as they begin to see themselves passing quiz after quiz," explains Denise.

In Phase 1 of the program, the life-skills component is taught by a certified life-skills coach for two hours every morning. Since the 1970s, life-skills courses have been commonplace in retraining and literacy programs designed for marginalized groups. The inclusion of a life-skills component in this retraining program acknowledges a holistic style of learning, one that recognizes that an appreciation of the whole person – someone who comes with a history and current struggles – is critical to the success of this and other adult learning programs.[17] The goal of life skills is personal development. In the Women's Work Training Program, life skills are applied to five areas of a woman's life: self, family, community, leisure, and job. This includes discussions about self-awareness, self-responsibility (such as problem solving and assertiveness training), and strategies for self-guidance (goal setting, future planning, and budgeting). One of the unique features of this program is that life skills incorporate trades concepts, tool terminology, and occupational references at every turn. As Valerie explains, "Every icebreaker followed this theme; every activity or role play took place in a construction environment; every example of conflict resolution, problem solving, or goal setting was modelled after similar situations of women who had gone before them."[18] In particular, the life-skills coach focuses on promoting independence, problem solving, and communication skills that can be applied in the workplace and in all other aspects of one's life. Every day begins with a morning "check-in," which encourages communication by having participants describe their state of mind and energy level. During this time, participants speak about family problems, relationship issues, and conflicts or tensions between them. Participants also learn about community supports and how to gain access to them through life-skills sessions. And attention is paid to Native cultural issues. For example, in an initial life-skills class, all the participants smoked sweet grass, and they all participate in a sweat lodge event during the program. Cultural differences between white and Native women with regard to childhood experiences, family responsibilities, and community obligations are addressed. (See Chapters 3 and 4 for a discussion of racism and cultural differences.)

Many participants find life skills the most difficult component of Phase 1. Here, women face and reflect upon many difficult experiences in their lives – experiences that may affect their self-confidence and their ability to trust and/or work with others. Abuse, incest, and drug and alcohol addiction are all revealed during the life-skills sessions. As a result, these sessions are often emotionally draining; however, they are also where the women really come to understand and support one another. Some women said they detested life skills and complained bitterly. "I'm very shy; I don't like spilling my life story to a group of women I hardly know," explained one participant. But almost all agreed that learning life skills was important. In fact, even the women who had the strongest complaints against the life-skills component insisted that it was essential to the program, and that they would not eliminate it if they were in charge. "With life skills I was reborn. Getting all the garbage within me out. It gave me a whole new life – with hopes and dreams," explained Zena. More than one woman said she used the life skills she had learned in class in her home situation. "I have all of my family sit around and I insist that everyone has a chance to talk about what is bothering them," said Zena.[19] "I would never have been able to work out the difficulties between myself and my boyfriend if it wasn't for life skills. It taught me that we can have differences and, as long as we can communicate about them, we can find a solution," explained one woman.[20]

The life-skills component of Phase 2 occurs approximately once every two weeks. Usually the participants have to come to the shop on Fridays for updates and team-building activities, and this is when the life-skills sessions occur. Life skills are also integrated into the activities on the job site. Most job sites hold a "check-in" circle every morning, where the participants air issues and, if necessary, resolve them. Sometimes the life-skills facilitator visits the site and is involved in the circles; sometimes other staff or lead hands carry out this function.[21]

The program also includes a component that aids women to develop strong, healthy bodies. Instructors introduce the participants to physical fitness programs at the local YMCA, as well as to Tai Chi, an ancient Chinese set of movements that promotes health and reduces stress. Women are also encouraged to think about their eating habits and other behaviours that might inhibit their ability to develop strong, healthy bodies.

During Phase I, women are introduced to the tools of their new trade. Teaching methods include group lectures, one-on-one instruction, shop demonstrations, guest speakers, and job-site visits. Above all, the instructors give the women a great deal of time to familiarize themselves with these tools. It is an all-sensory education. The participants develop a familiarity with and appreciation of the touch and feel of industrial materials, the smell and noise of the tools and machines, and the visual impact of a well-finished product. The program is designed to give women time to tinker. As Marcia Braundy, an expert in non-traditional training, explains:

> Tinkering is an absorbing, self-paced, exploratory type of learning, which has as its goal to work and play with an object until an increased awareness and understanding of the essence of the object emerges. Women traditionally practise tinkering in the kitchen or sewing room, so ... it is more a matter of facilitating the transfer of an already learned skill to a new application. Through mechanical tinkering, an intimate familiarity is developed wherein theoretical concepts are grasped, information is processed, and a power relation is established: the tinkerer gains mastery over a complex, inanimate object.[22]

As well as being provided time with new tools, participants are given time to learn how to develop and use their bodies in new, very physical ways. As the women continue the program, they discover how their bodies are becoming stronger, more flexible, and more enduring.

During this phase, participants are encouraged to think about their own life goals. Studies have shown that few women receive proper career counselling.[23] One of the exercises that the participants engage in during the first week of the program is a lifecycle exercise. In this, the women are asked to draw their lifeline, to think about the goals they have in their life, to place on their lifeline events that have helped or hindered their achievement of their goals, and then, on the "future" portion of the line, to write what they want to happen. This exercise shows many women that they can move beyond simply accepting what befalls them and take some control over their lives.

The course is taught according to relational learning principles. Research on learning styles shows that 80 percent of the population in our Western culture are relational learners.[24] And in non-traditional courses 93 percent of the women and 60 percent of the men are relational learners.[25] Despite these figures, most students are taught as though they are mental learners, learning primarily by lectures and debates. Relational learners need to make connections, value relationships, and relate personally to the material being taught. Relational learners need to have a dialogue with the instructor, to be able to ask questions, to interact with the tools and their peers. In order to meet these learning needs, the training program attempts to connect new material to something already known, to connect one idea to another, and to create an environment in which participants feel respected, liked, and trusted by one another. Often the participants will learn a theory in the classroom in the morning and then apply it in the workshop in the afternoon. Moreover, given that the classroom is merely a few steps from the workshop, it is possible to stop classroom activity at any moment, should the participants be having trouble with a particular concept, and go into the workshop and apply it. The coordinators encourage group work, both in the classroom and in the workshop, which also benefits relational learners (who like to learn in a social setting rather than in isolation).

Carefully designed evaluation components are integral to the entire phase. Participants have weekly math quizzes along with other small tests to help them build their knowledge base and to realize small victories along the way. Participants are also encouraged to keep "learning journals" in order to record their personal struggles and successes, providing added perspective upon and insight into their efforts. Throughout the course there is time set aside for participants and instructors to verbally evaluate their efforts.

At the end of twenty weeks of this program, when both their bodies and their minds have been challenged, the participants write the provincial Level 1 carpentry exam. Upon passing the exam, the participants begin Phase 2 of the program, which involves 26 weeks of on-the-job training. At this point, the women can close the books and just concentrate on developing their new carpentry skills. Life skills continue, but only once every two weeks. In between life-skills sessions, the women are expected to put what they have learned into practice. At some job sites, the women agree to have a quick life-skills session first thing every morning or at the end of each day; at others, they have a life-skills session whenever a difficulty arises. During Phase 2, life-skills sessions focus on building effective communication, team building, group cooperation, and accepting differences. The women work in groups at various worksites, and it is vital that they learn how to work together effectively. During this second phase, they renovated a variety of buildings for non-governmental organizations. They built a Habitat for Humanity house and renovated a food bank, a community church, the local YMCA, and a gay and lesbian community centre. During this phase, Valerie and Denise were able to hire Sharon Murray, a woman who had been in the first women's carpentry training program in 1991. While mentoring the women, she took a six-week upgrading course and, subsequently, wrote and passed her interprovincial exam to become a journeyed carpenter in 1998.

Completing Phases 1 and 2, the women achieve their Level 1 carpentry certificate and can then apply to join the Regina Women's Construction Co-operative for Phase 3. Phases 3 through 6 each last 52 weeks. During each of these phases, the women spend seven weeks a year at the Saskatchewan Institute for Applied Science and Technology (SIAST), Moose Jaw campus, gaining the necessary training for the Levels 2, 3, and 4 carpentry certification, respectively. At the end of each term at the provincial technical institute, the participants write an exam that grants them their next level of carpentry expertise. Their time at SIAST is challenging. The Moose Jaw campus is about one hour away by car, so the women have to be on the road by 7:15 a.m. and are not home before 5:00 p.m. at the earliest. Once home, the women have a large amount of homework to complete before the next day. For those who are mothers, especially single mothers, it is difficult to juggle childcare and other family responsibilities with their training. During this phase of the training the participants usually pull together, take turns driving, and help each other with homework and assignments.

During the seven weeks at SIAST, the participants receive Employment Insurance at 60 percent of their normal wages. To financially support the participants through this period, the program helps to finance transportation to the institute, student fees, and school supplies. The program also pays for tutors (up to three hours per week) should the participants desire them. Sometimes the tutors are senior participants in the program, and the tutoring creates additional wages for them.[26] Clearly, the participants have to make a financial sacrifice in order to undertake the training at SIAST.

The SIAST experience is also difficult because it is the women's first introduction to a male-dominated carpentry environment: the majority of students in the classroom are male, and all of the instructors are male. The women from the Women's Work Training Project attend SIAST in groups so that they are able to support each other when they meet harassment or discrimination. While the SIAST experience is challenging for all, it was particularly difficult for the first group of women who enrolled. They complained about how hard the transition was from an all-female environment, where the pace was slower and the instructors were more supportive. The second group of women to attend SIAST were better prepared because of the feedback from the first group. Also, seven women attended in the second group. Given that the class had a total of twelve students, "This means women out number[ed] the men – A FIRST IN CANADA!" boasted Valerie in a newsletter. "This time the guys are chumming with the women, because the women know more!! Many of the guys have only done commercial work so they are at a disadvantage at school. The women's wide range of renovation experience is coming in very handy."[27]

SIAST presents the participants with a sense of what the carpentry trade is like outside their training program. For some, this provides them with contacts who encourage them to seek work outside the Co-op. For others, this reminds them of why they prefer the Co-op as a place to learn their new skills. It is certainly unique to this program that it can boast that, "with the exception of 21 weeks of apprenticeship training through SIAST in Moose Jaw, all courses are taught and supervised in-house by journeyed and otherwise qualified women through the five years of the program."[28]

As well as taking a term at SIAST, during Phases 3 through 6, the women work at the Co-op. During their Co-op time, they receive business management training, production shop skills, specialty training in barrier-free construction, and the traditional on-site training they would receive as apprenticing carpenters. At the end of Phase 6, the women are eligible to write their journey exam and to receive their Journeyperson Certificate of Qualification in the Carpenter Trade (journeyed carpentry papers). This is the only women's training program in Canada that provides the opportunity and support for women to become full-fledged journeyed carpenters.[29]

The Regina Women's Construction Co-operative was established in June 1997 and is a unique feature of this women's non-traditional retraining program. But what is also significant and unique about the co-op is that it allows the women to receive the necessary training to achieve their journeyed carpentry papers within a female work environment. Studies that follow women through non-traditional retraining find that they experience a great deal of harassment on the job site, causing many women not to complete their apprenticeships.[30] The Co-op alleviates this problem.

The Co-op has received a number of grants. The major funders have been the federal government, the Saskatchewan government, and the Women and Economic Development Consortium (WEDC), which is supported by contributions from six large companies and is administered by the Canadian Women's Foundation. The WEDC grant is for five years, but the bulk of the money was allocated for the first two critical years, when the Co-op was attempting to establish itself as a viable business. Specifically, this grant paid for the salary of a full-time business manager for three years and the part-time salaries of legal and accounting services for the full five years. The provincial government also granted funds to the Co-op for job-site training, business training, marketing, Internet linkup, some rent, and some bookkeeping (see Appendix A). When the Co-op started, it was supported 100 percent through grants; however, within two years, half its money was being secured through its construction contracts. The federal government contributes wage subsidies of $5,000 a year per woman during her first year of employment in the Co-op.[31] The Co-op has established a niche market, specializing in renovations that provide accessibility to all, and this has helped it become financially viable. In addition, participants have manufactured a number of products, such as children's picnic tables and folding Adirondack chairs, for the local market. Participants have not only constructed these products but also been responsible for their promotion. Both of these products have sold well in Regina, and this has encouraged the women to think of other products that they could build and sell. All of these activities help to financially support the Co-op and the participants.

Transportation is one of many barriers that low-income women face when attempting to participate in a retraining program. In the program under discussion, a number of strategies evolved to help alleviate this problem. Some women who had vehicles picked up others en route to the program. Denise arranged for transportation from the shop to the job sites and back again at closing time. Also, the program encouraged and financially supported women who were interested in obtaining their drivers' licences.

Throughout the program, wages were constantly an issue. In Phases 1 and 2, the women received training allowances provided by the provincial government; those previously on welfare had their allowances topped up if they were less than what had been provided in their previous welfare cheques. Provincial social services monitored their clients closely and gradually reduced supports when the women's wages improved. However, even during Phases 3 and 4, provincial social services provided some assistance for dental care, prescription drugs, and even childcare services for those who could not support all of their dependants on the Co-op wage. "The whole key was that they never made less money than social services could provide for them on welfare," explains Valerie.[32] For the first six months upon joining the Co-op, the women were eligible for wage subsidies of $5,000, after which their wages were based on Co-op finances. Given that the Co-op was a new business, money was tight and not on par with the industry at large. When the Co-op first began, the women earned $5.60 an hour, the provincial minimum wage, but this was quickly raised to $7.00 an hour (considered to be the starting wage in the industry).[33] From there, women receive raises both when they complete a new level of carpentry at SIAST and according to a regular schedule for evaluations. While wages are below those in the construction industry, it is important to remember that, before the program, the majority of women received welfare and, if they leave the program, they will be eligible for Employment Insurance (EI). Generally, EI will provide them with more training opportunities, more employment prospects, and more financial resources than will welfare.

A routine schedule of evaluations that is linked to wage increases has been established. Valerie, Denise and other instructors who are employees of the Co-op are responsible for instructor evaluations, one facet of the process that assesses technical skills. As well, peer evaluations are conducted by members of the Co-op, concentrating on employment skills. Consequently, the women learn to assess both the strengths and weaknesses of their peers' work for the Co-op. Initial acceptance as a Co-op member depends on a minimum score, with a probationary period allowed for improvement. Subsequently, the overall scores on peer evaluations will determine the rate of a wage increase. But the results are still poor wages compared to what women with their experience would receive at another construction company. "It's a Catch-22. Many of the women wouldn't make it right now at a mainstream company. They don't work fast enough. They don't have the confidence to work on their own," explains Denise. "And we're a new company – we won't get the contracts if our prices are not competitive. So I have to estimate low and pay the women below what I'd like to."[34] As a result, the women have moved from welfare poverty and have joined the working poor.

Job sites are selected according to their relevance to the carpentry curriculum. These sites have offered a range of work, from such minor jobs as retiling a bathroom and putting up a backyard fence to such major jobs as: building a Habitat for Humanity house; renovating a garage into a seniors' home; putting an extensive two-storey addition onto an old house; building a computer room at the local YMCA; reconstructing walls, floors, and building bars at a local community centre; making an ultra-modern executive office centre out of a warehouse; and making rooms, homes, and offices accessible. Supervisors on the job site provide leadership and instruction, and ensure that all the work meets trade as well as occupational health and safety standards. At each project one of the participants is responsible for ensuring that health and safety standards are met throughout the job.

The program has a high level of evaluation in order to ensure that the participants are learning and reflecting throughout their journey. They are tested in both theory and practical application. In order to receive a Level 1 carpentry certificate, the participants have to successfully complete the provincial Level 1 exam at the end of their first twenty weeks of the program. This exam accounts for 50 percent of their final standing, the other 50 percent being determined by their course work; participants must receive an overall average of 60 percent or more. In addition, Co-op members are involved in peer evaluations to help determine promotion and pay increases.

A final characteristic of this retraining program is the high level of cooperation that is required. Unlike a classroom setting, which generally emphasizes individual work, this retraining program emphasizes collective work. The working environment at the Co-op naturally requires that the participants work in groups on the job site. Because the participants in the Co-op are not merely employees but also owners, they are responsible for a lot of management and business decisions, which requires collective decision making. Some women work easily in pairs and groups and enjoy making decisions together; others prefer to work alone, find it stressful to match their working style and pace with someone else, and find collective negotiation difficult.

Unique Features of the Women's Work Training Program
While the Women's Work Training Program has borrowed many of the successful aspects of previous non-traditional retraining programs for women, in a number of ways it is the first of its kind in Canada. There are six aspects of this program that make it unique among other non-traditional training programs for women: its duration, its relationship with the Regina Women's Construction Co-operative, its ability to provide its participants with continuity vis-à-vis the workforce, its flexibility, its female mentorship, and its racial diversity. All of these features respond to the unique needs of low-income, marginalized white and Native women.

The majority of non-traditional retraining programs for women are about six months long. These programs provide an initiation to various trades information, but they do not permit women to move beyond the introductory level. Two examples of these innovative programs originate on the Sunshine Coast in British Columbia and in North Bay, Ontario. The former provides trade skills, life skills/academic upgrading, and work placements. The nine-month program includes two work placements of seven weeks each. Students learn construction, industrial first aid, small engine repair, physical training, math, and personal growth. This program has been successful partly because it provides not merely technical skills but also life skills and academic upgrading. The latter program, SKILTEC, which was in operation from 1982 to 1995, provided thirty-two to forty weeks of training for seriously disadvantaged women in North Bay. This integrated program combined employment-related skills, basic math and communications learning, hands-on and theoretical trades instruction, and the production of saleable commodities. One of the reasons this program was successful was that it employed the women to manufacture a product to market standards and it paid them a wage while they did so.[35]

The Women's Work Training Program has adapted many of these successful traits but, unlike the other programs, it provides women with *five* years of integrated training. It takes women from an introduction to carpentry through all levels of apprenticeship and ultimately provides them with an opportunity to achieve journey carpentry status. Each phase builds upon the previous one. The initial training incorporates concentrated teaching and supervision. Over time this tapers off as the participants gain work skills and become self-motivated. This is the only long-term apprenticeship program of its kind.[36] And the long-term nature of this training program is absolutely vital to its success. Often low-income, marginalized women lack self-esteem; such a program gives them a chance to develop skills and confidence at their own pace. Often, this process involves major changes in the women's personal lives. Not surprisingly, this all takes much time and support – something not available in short-term training programs. As one participant explained, "Building a house is easy, skill-wise. Believing we can do it is another thing."[37]

One of the reasons the retraining program can sustain itself financially over this five-year period has to do with the creation of the Co-op. As women gain their carpentry skills, they become more responsible for the successful operation of a member-owned self-sufficient business. The Regina Women's Construction Co-operative incorporated in August 1997 with eleven members, all of whom had been trained through the Women's Work Training Program. The Co-op was formed to create jobs and income for its members. Given the skill level of the members, the Co-op is not automatically self-sufficient; however, its members do earn enough through construction contracts to cover their own wages and benefits. Outside funding covers the wages of the business manager and overhead costs. Within a year and a half of incorporation, the Co-op boasted eighty-three clients and a gross labour income of more than $65,000.[38] Starting from scratch, with no previous business knowledge, the Co-op members established bylaws, policies, and procedures; and they elected a board of directors that eventually made governance decisions for the direction of the Co-op (see Appendix E).

The Co-op segment of the training program is an ambitious one. "We are working to empower women who have never been part of a self-managed business. In fact, their experiences in the work force have basically been in disempowered positions working for low wages," explains Valerie.[39] It is hoped that once the women graduate with their journey papers in carpentry, some of them will assume leadership positions within the Co-op as project managers, office managers, and training assistants. Already, a number of women have expressed interest in taking on these positions once they graduate. As members of the Co-op at various levels of carpentry, the women are expected to take leadership positions in what is essentially *their* company: each member owns shares and has one vote at Co-op meetings. The members elect a board of directors that hires a construction superintendent and business manager. Initially, Saskatchewan Women in Trades and Technology (SaskWITT) had a stewardship role with the Co-op, managing and guiding its members in all decision making, helping them to gain confidence so that they could manage financially on their own.

Because an all-women's construction co-op is unique, its members have been invited to a number of public events. The Co-op has conducted a number of basic home repair clinics, and its members help to teach other women in the Regina area about basic carpentry skills. Denise and Sherry flew to Toronto to attend a Canadian Women's Foundation meeting to represent the Co-op. This created a number of firsts for Sherry – it was the first time she had flown in a plane and the first time she had spoken at a national press conference. Another Co-op member, Pat, has represented the Co-op on the Saskatchewan Women in Trades and Technology Board. She has also been hired to help supervise Girls Exploring Trades and Technology (GETT) and Indian Métis Girls Exploring Trades and Technology (IMGETT). These are one-week camps, whose purpose is to introduce Grade 7 and Grade 8 girls to a variety of careers in trades and technology. Instruction is provided by a pool of female role models who work in a variety of related occupations. Co-op members have also been invited to participate in career fairs for youth, career days for Aboriginal youth, a business forum in Saskatoon, and several conferences for cooperatives.[40]

The Co-op has also made links with other women entrepreneurs and the co-operative movement. For instance, it established an advisory board of women entrepreneurs from the Regina community. This advisory board meets with the Co-op members on a monthly or bi-monthly basis, offering the women business advice. Heather Hamilton, a Co-op member, attended the Canadian Co-operative Association national conference and regularly attends a local co-op organization in an effort to learn more about running a cooperative enterprise and to bring that information and advice back to the Co-op. Because of the Co-op's interest in innovative housing, Heather also went to Saskatoon to visit and make a report on straw-bale house sites.

The Co-op also helps to ensure that women remain in the field of carpentry. The literature on women in non-traditional training reveals that women often leave the industry because of a hostile work environment. Retaining women in the field after they complete their training has always been a concern.[41] The Co-op helps to alleviate this problem.

Women face distinct problems regarding work and family responsibilities. These have been taken into account in the multitude of training programs developed since the 1970s. But very few of these training programs provide the women with continuity vis-à-vis the workforce.[42] The Co-op provides this continuity. The women continue to work alongside other women, developing their skills both in the classroom and at the job site.

The flexibility of the Women's Work Training Program makes it unique among non-traditional retraining programs. Because most retraining programs are for a short, intense amount of time, full participation at every moment is essential. But a long-term five-year retraining program is able to accommodate women's needs to withdraw at various stages. Participants receive certification at the end of each phase, and this permits them to leave at any point in the program with skills and carpentry hours that are recognized by the industry. Thus participants can leave, join the industry, and later decide to return to the program. This has allowed some women to have the experience of building on a reserve or working in a large industrial construction company, and then come back to share their knowledge with the other women. The only disadvantage in returning is that, as in any other workplace, they will have lost their seniority in the Co-op.

The ability to leave the program is ideal for low-income, marginalized women who have to face a number of obstacles to participating in full-time training and work. When a child is ill, having difficulty with school, or otherwise requires attention, a single mother is usually forced to choose between the child's needs and her work responsibilities. Even women with partners tend to do the lion's share of childcare and familial duties, thus finding it difficult to balance the multiple roles of breadwinner, mother, and spouse. Some women have left partners during the training program or have renegotiated relationships with abusive or difficult partners. Native women, in particular, often have strong extended familial ties and, as a result, additional responsibilities. Some of the women have needed to care for a recently widowed brother and his children, take in a daughter's children, or shelter a sister from an abusive relationship. Also, a number of women have personal challenges, such as prior alcohol or drug addiction, abusive (ex)partners and/or unstable housing accommodation. These challenges can thwart a woman's ability to participate fully in a retraining program. The Women's Work Training Program recognizes the crises that low-income women face and permits them a certain degree of flexibility so that they can deal with the challenges that plague their lives.

Although women are generally expected to arrange their responsibilities around work time, the program provides them flexibility to arrive late, leave early, and so on, in order to meet other pressing obligations. Women are also able to arrange leaves of a few days or a few months in order to concentrate full-time on whatever crisis might have arisen. "I like to think that a woman who enters our doors can return at any time and we will find a way to accommodate that," says Valerie. "They never have to leave feeling that they've failed themselves and their friends and co-workers because they know they can return."[43]

Another feature of the flexible nature of the program involves the fact that women start the program at different times. In all, there were three major entry points: the first intake was February 1996; the second was February 1997, and the third was May 1998. This staggered intake permits women who need to leave the program for some reason to return to it and resume their training with a new group of women. For example, one woman, who was living in an abusive relationship, left halfway through the first phase of the program to deal with that situation. When she returned, she joined another group of women who were in the first phase of the program. She had some previous knowledge from her initial introduction to the program, and this gave her great confidence in relation to the new women. Thus, instead of feeling like a failure and lagging behind the other women, she was actually in a position to take a leadership role. These staggered entry times permit women to mix with other women at different levels of the program. This gives them confidence that they, too, can succeed in this program because they have daily evidence that others, who are just like them, have done so.

The staggered entry points also create potential mentors for each new group of women joining the program. Because members of the Co-op and Phase 1 and 2 participants share common work space, the women are always surrounded by others who are willing to offer support, advice, feedback, and expertise. Women who are more advanced in the program become lead hands for a crew of less skilled participants. The women share not merely carpentry skills but also advice on how to manage the provincial technical institute experience, which participants consider a big challenge. As they become better acquainted, they advise one another on parenting and relationship challenges. Again, this is unique to the program. It is rare that women get to meet and befriend other women at various levels of trade apprenticeship. Too often a woman is on her own, learning her skills in an all-male environment with only men to turn to for help. But in this case the women can ask for advice from the female coordinators of the program, a female life-skills coach, a female lead hand, or another woman who is one level ahead of her. This also bridges the huge gulf between participant and instructor. In most other non-traditional training programs, the participants are all at the same level, with the female instructor being the ultimate expert. For a participant it can often be intimidating to ask the instructor questions for fear of seeming ignorant. It is often easier to ask these same questions of women who are only a bit more advanced in the training programs. This can build the self-esteem of women at different levels of the program and can also create a strong bond between them. They all learn that they can help one another, and that they don't have to rely entirely on the instructor for all the answers.

The most challenging unique feature of the program is the racial diversity of its participants. Two-thirds of the thirty participants are Native (seventeen are status and three are Métis) and one-third (ten) are white. For many of the women, this is the first time they have worked with women of a different racial background. Cultural differences in work habits, family responsibilities, and communication styles constantly arise as women attempt to understand one another. There is much misunderstanding. For instance, the white women often do not understand why the Native women have to care for so many extended family members (something that obviously interferes with their training). And Native women are sometimes envious of the material resources available to white women due to greater family resources. Cultural differences between Native women and predominantly white supervisors and coordinators of the program also arise, creating power inequities with powerful historical resonances. For instance, only one of the staff members is a person of Aboriginal ancestry. She was hired as a life-skills coach but, because the job was part-time, she was forced to leave after her term. There are no other Aboriginal life-skills instructors available who have knowledge of the construction industry, nor are there any Aboriginal women with journeyed carpentry status.[44] This means that white people have the ultimate power in the training program, and there are moments when the Aboriginal women feel that the white leaders favour the white participants. Instructors have attempted to integrate Aboriginal culture into the retraining program. All of the participants honour and participate in certain Aboriginal rituals, such as a sweat-lodge event and a sweet-grass ceremony, and have toured an Aboriginal exhibition at the provincial museum. Yet racism and racial misunderstandings continue to persist throughout the retraining program. These problems require more attention, education, and negotiation than the retraining program has so far permitted. (For a more detailed discussion of this feature of the program, see Chapter 4.)

Conclusion

Two women had a vision to create the best non-traditional retraining program for low-income women they possibly could. With their own carpentry skills they built the foundation. Borrowing from other non-traditional retraining programs for women, they created a program that was women-only and combined life skills and academic upgrading with on-site training. But Valerie and Denise dreamed a larger dream. They were not content with what was offered by other non-traditional training programs for women, and they designed one that included more positive features. It was long term, and had a co-op, built-in flexibility, and female mentors. And it attempted to meet the needs of a racially diverse, low-income, marginalized group of women. The foundation was carefully designed and very strong. But a house needs walls, windows, and doors to become a home. It is the participants, the women themselves, who struggle every day to make this training program really work.

3
The Everyday Lives of Our Heroes

It makes no sense to draw up the blueprints for a house until the needs of the residents are known. The same can be said for retraining programs. In order to develop a successful retraining program for low-income women, it is absolutely vital that the architects and the instructors fully appreciate the everyday lives of the participants. Low-income women's lives are full of struggle. Against all odds, the women in the Women's Work Training Program have determined to not only become economically self-sufficient but also to have a career. Most of them couldn't imagine this before they entered the program. The majority of these women grew up, and remained in, grinding poverty. Most of them have experienced sexual and physical violence. Most of them have also encountered intense racism and hatred. Most of them have been survivors of generations of colonial exploitation and marginalization. Some of them were shuffled from home to home because their parents, survivors of the residential school system, lost their purpose. Many have also battled major drug and alcohol addictions. A few have lived on the streets, selling their bodies in order to eat. They are survivors in the true sense of the word. And every day they make Herculean efforts to participate in this unique retraining program.

The first day I met these women in their workshop, it was obvious that they were defying all odds by their very presence. A new group of women had joined the retraining program that week and they were busy making their toolbox, using the skill saw for the very first time. Besides learning to use these tools, they had many other things on their minds. Some were anxious about the childcare arrangements they had made – unsure that they would be able to juggle their mothering responsibilities with this intensive program. Others had never worked before and were uncertain they could meet the demands of full-time retraining and employment. Some had never befriended a white woman or a Native woman – having come from very distinct racial communities within Regina. Most had debts that constituted a constant background noise as they listened to the teacher's instructions. And almost all of them were wracked with self-doubt, scared to dream that the future could hold anything but continued hardship and worry.

It is these women who make this retraining program a success. Every day they dramatically alter their life course by simply participating in this program. This chapter introduces you to these women. As I interviewed them in the workshop, on the job sites, and in their homes I became a part of their lives, and they of mine. I was invited for supper, for a beer, to weddings, and to graduations. I have met their children, their partners, and their friends. They have shared their fears, their dreams, and their confidences. I am deeply honoured that they trusted me with so many personal details of their lives.

In total, I interviewed thirty women – each of whom was present at the worksite during my four visits over a three-year period. Those participants who joined and then quickly left the program in between my visits were not part of the interviews. I interviewed seventeen participants one time only, thirteen participants more than once, and some as many as four times.[1] Anyone familiar with low-income women will know that they are often transient. It is virtually impossible to track low-income women over an extended period because they move frequently, often do not have access to a phone, and often room with others in between insecure housing arrangements. Where possible, I attempted to contact women I had previously interviewed who had left the program. Where this was not possible, I attempted to collect information about their circumstances from other participants of the program. I visited Regina four times during this period in order to conduct these interviews. Because I interviewed the women over a three-year period I was able to follow them through different stages of the program. Through our conversations I watched them struggle with the various challenges in their lives and in the program. I audio-taped each interview and, at subsequent interviews, handed the women their previous transcripts so that they could edit them for errors and omissions.

With regard to the women who had left the program, I initially attempted to send them their transcripts by mail in the hope that they would edit and return them to me. I gave this up after the first round of interviews because I found it to be an unsafe practice.[2] The editing process was in place for all but the fourth interview. The participants did not edit these final interviews because I did not return to Regina when the program disbanded.[3] At each interview I told the women that anything they said could be stricken from the transcript. When editing the transcript they could decide to delete or alter any personal details they did not wish to share. They could choose to use their real name, a pseudonym, or to remain anonymous. They also completed a written survey about violence, in which they remained anonymous.

I have followed their wishes, with the exception of choosing to make some of the more intimate details of their lives anonymous even when they did not ask me to do this.[4] Above all, I did not want to do anything that might have harmed the tremendous trust they placed in me.

These women were highly involved in the development of *If I Had a Hammer*. At various stages of the project they advised me about what topics I should cover in the interviews and what themes the book should include. They presented their opinions and the details of their lives in the hope that others could learn from both the successes and the challenges of this retraining program and that more such programs could be made available to low-income women across the country.

Barriers to Retraining

The barriers to low-income women's participation in a retraining program cannot be exaggerated: they are simply colossal. The fact that any low-income woman continues to return to the shop and pick up her hammer week after week is nothing short of a miracle. Against all odds these women continue to be a part of this program. And it is these odds, these barriers, that I explore in this chapter. While there are many barriers to low-income women's participation in retraining programs, there are six in particular that have deeply affected their life choices.

Race

It is impossible to spend time with these participants without noticing how profoundly their racial identity has affected all aspects of their lives. For the Native women in the program, it is profoundly obvious that their daily lives, from childhood through adulthood, have been deeply marked by the devastating impact of centuries of colonization.

In particular, all of the Native participants have been harmfully influenced by the residential school system. For a full century Native boys and girls were wrenched from their families and their communities. In some cases, they never saw their families and communities again. These schools repressed their language and culture, and taught them extremely negative attitudes towards sex, intimacy, and love. In sum, the residential school experience was soul-destroying, and Aboriginal communities are still dealing with the consequences.[5]

Native women in the program spoke about how the residential school system had personally affected their lives. "My mom and dad went to residential schools and they never got over it," explains one woman. "Weekends were drinking binges for them ... They were chronic alcoholics and I raised my sister and brother."[6] Because their biological parents were unable to parent them, many of the Native women were raised by other family members. As Emily, for example, explains,

I was born in Saskatoon and raised on a reserve for a few years when I was a kid until my great grandmother died because my mom didn't raise me. And then I was passed back and forth, here and there, quite a few years actually until I was about 15, then I left home and said no more passing me about, I'm going on my own. And I've been on my own since.[7]

Residential schools and the colonial environment generally condemned Native women as "squaws" – lazy, drunk, and sexually promiscuous/available. These images have promoted the sexual exploitation of Native women and have deeply affected Native women's self-esteem. While prostitution can be a rational choice for low-income women with few opportunities to feed themselves or their families, one woman understood her experiences of prostitution to be a result of colonialism, which had robbed her of her dignity and self-worth.

I did horrible things to myself. I abused my body. I worked as a hooker, as well as the drugs. You know, I did a whole lot of things to hurt myself. I just didn't know where I stood in society, but now I know. I'm an Indian and there is good in our ways, in our Native ways.[8]

This woman spoke about the uphill battle to find value in her life and in her Aboriginality. She still struggles with alcohol and drugs. She still deals with an abusive partner with whom she has a turbulent, on-again-off-again relationship.

The difficult lives that Native women experience deeply affect their ability to focus on themselves and their aspirations. The Native women interviewed spoke about the many deaths in their extended family. One Native mother with four children explained how the recent death of her baby brother was both a barrier to and a sense of support for her participation in the program.

I just about quit because my brother killed himself. He was living with me at the time. I think that was the turning point of my life, that's when I knew it was because of him that I'm doing all this. He would have been so proud of me. That's why I finished school and that's why I started working here.[9]

Another Native woman said that, during her first six months in the program, she had to attend six family funerals. "The day that I came to orientation, my cousin passed away, and that was the beginning of the deaths."[10] And another woman had been widowed three times before entering the program.[11]

A few of these women have also experienced the devastating colonial practice of having their children taken from them and placed for adoption or foster care. Native scholars commonly refer to the incredible number of Native babies who were snatched from their homes during the 1960s as "the sixties scoop." Some scholars believe that this baby-snatching phenomenon was more destructive than the residential school system.[12] While in the residential school system, Native children learned that everything Native was bad and dirty, but at least they were aware that there were other Native children in the universe. Many of the Native children taken from their homes in the 1960s were placed in white homes and had no reference point from which to gather any information about their Native heritage. They were simply robbed of their cultural identity. Shirley recalls being raised in a foster home from the time she was four years old: "I was always cleaning the house, or mending clothes, or ironing or taking care of kids. It was a hard life."[13]

The colonial practice of defining Native identity has also deeply influenced the way these women view themselves and their connections to others. For centuries, the Canadian government has actively determined who was and who was not Native. In their attempts to destroy and assimilate Natives, government officials denied many people Native status. "If they did not live Indian enough lives," federal officials rejected their status. Those deemed Métis by the white government were not only denied their Aboriginality but were also forced off reserves and given land in isolated places where they could not recreate another community. This land, which was foreign to the Métis, was, for the most part, sold to whites. Consequently, the Métis of western Canada became disenfranchised and isolated.[14]

This history of the government's creation of Métis and status Indian identities has affected participants in the Women's Work Training Program. Of the twenty Aboriginal women interviewed, seventeen described themselves as treaty (or status) Indians and three as Métis. Of the seventeen status Natives, six had lived on a reserve for the majority of their lives, while eleven had lived an urban existence. But even those who lived urban lives spoke of a strong connection to a local reserve. Many visited their reserves during holidays, and others relocated to them during the summer months. The three Métis women did not have as strong a connection to reserve life as did the status women, even though they had a powerful sense of their Métis identity. They spoke of their identity as distinct from that of status women. Whereas several status women had received retraining and educational money from their bands, the Métis women did not have this kind of access to resources. The Métis women spoke of living between the white and the Aboriginal worlds, being fully accepted by neither. These racial distinctions replayed themselves throughout the retraining program and are discussed in greater detail in Chapter 4.

An examination of the other barriers to low-income women's participation in this retraining program shows that racial identity intensified each of them. Even though white and Native women faced all five of the following barriers, the latter experienced them to a much greater degree than did the former.

Motherhood

One crucial barrier in these women's lives is also their greatest source of pride and identity: motherhood. Twenty-three of the thirty women interviewed are mothers; thirteen are single mothers, and seven are raising children other than their own (i.e., nieces, foster children, their partner's children from a previous relationship, and grandchildren). In sum, these thirty women are currently caring for and financially responsible for sixty children. This does not include grown children who are financially independent or children who live with relatives or in foster care. Even knowing these figures, it is difficult to capture the magnitude of this mothering responsibility, which is compounded by the fact that these women are low-income and have few economic resources upon which to draw. Quality childcare, restaurant meals, and laundry services would significantly help these mothers juggle their paid work and mothering responsibilities, but these services are all luxuries that they cannot afford.

Motherhood has greatly affected these low-income women's life stories. Many became pregnant in their late teens and left high school as a result. Their later attempts to upgrade their education were often interrupted by other pregnancies. And, because of their intense mothering responsibilities, their employment history tends to be sporadic and short term.

These women have a lot invested in motherhood. Often, given their difficult lives, parenting is the one thing that makes them feel good about themselves. As a result, they carry tremendous guilt about leaving their children for any length of time. Some admit they spoil their children, trying to make up for the hard things they cannot change about their lives. Ginny, a twenty-four-year-old single mother describes with delight how she bought her two-and-a-half-year-old son hockey equipment to outfit him from head to toe. "I can't believe I bought him all that stuff ... He can't stand on his skates but he loves hockey."[15] And another woman, who was neglected by her alcoholic parents when she was a child, is adamant that she can only remain in the training program if her husband stays home full time with the children. "I am determined that we will be there for our children – they won't be raised by somebody else," she explains.[16]

Colonization has created further anxiety for Aboriginal mothers. If Native women are believed to be poor mothers, then this provides an excuse for the state to remove their children and place them in residential schools and foster homes. Many of the Native women interviewed spoke about how mothering was their most important responsibility. Those who had experienced neglectful childhoods were adamant about being exceedingly attentive to their children's needs. Although low-income mothers are often criticized for their parenting abilities, Aboriginal mothers are criticized even more. The long history of colonial prejudice makes it very apparent why the Native women I interviewed were particularly concerned to prove that they were good mothers, and why they vowed that their children's needs came before their own.

Motherhood, for Native women, is particularly demanding partly because they have so many children requiring their love and attention. Studies have documented that Aboriginal communities in Canada have the highest population growth. As Native scholar Kim Anderson explains, in Native cultures new life has always been considered precious. "Children were always welcome, and because women were esteemed for having children, pregnancy was a natural part of the sexual cycle."[17] Given this cultural heritage, it is not surprising that, of the women interviewed, the Native women bore and raised more children than did the white women. On average, the Native mothers interviewed had 2.6 children (with one woman having raised eight children, and two women having raised five children). In comparison, the white mothers interviewed had 1.8 children on average, ranging from five children to none. What is perhaps more telling is the number of white women who remained childless. Forty percent (or four out of ten) of the white women did not have children, whereas only 15 percent (or three out of twenty) of the Aboriginal women did not have children.

Many women in the program have the extra burden of being single mothers. Pat, who was among the first group of women to begin the training program, recalls that everyone was a single mother in her group. "I don't remember anyone in there who was actually married with their kids. They were either separated or they were just seeing somebody but they all had kids and were all alone," she recalls.[18] Historically, single motherhood was unheard of in Native communities. Native scholar Kim Anderson explains that "children were accepted into large kin-based or clan-based communities, with all the supports that accompanied this."[19] Unfortunately this extended care network is not as available as it once was. It is true that most of the Native single mothers interviewed did turn to sisters, mothers, and partners for temporary childcare in a way that the white mothers did not. If an Aboriginal woman had to stay late at work, she could usually call an extended family member to take care of her children. Interestingly, Native single mothers' permanent childcare arrangements were very similar to those of the white single mothers in the program. Both groups relied on after-school programs as well as public and private childcare centres.

Many of the Native mothers are raising not only their own children but also those of extended family members. Cheryl, who is forty-four and status Indian, recalls her early mothering years when she raised six children. She remembers all too vividly the death of one of her babies. She also recalls another time when she and her children were homeless and sleeping outside. Cheryl is adamant that none of her children will ever be homeless, as her current living arrangements demonstrate: "I live in a little, two-tiny-bedroom house. And I've got my son and my daughter-in-law. My other grandchild and my other son and my other grandchild came and camped last night. And I have my daughter-in-law's brother and his baby there."[20]

Rhonda M., also status Indian, explained that seventeen people are financially dependent upon her. She and her partner support two houses side by side on the reserve. Some of her children live with her and some of them live next door.[21] Her sixteen-year-old daughter and her grandchild live in the second house.

These extended family ties create a number of demands that interfere with women's participation in the retraining program. For instance, one week when I interviewed Rhonda M. she had received a very small paycheque, and this concerned her. "I need all the money I can get for my family," she said. But she had missed two days' pay that week because she had taken her grandson to the Saskatchewan Penitentiary to visit his mother. "She [the boy's mother] has been away from him for four years, so every chance we get I like them to be together. I couldn't find anyone else to take him because it takes three months for the security clearance."[22] Another woman took an extensive leave from the program to take care of her brother and his children when her sister-in-law died in a tragic car accident. Valerie Overend, one of the coordinators of the retraining program, is very aware of the tremendous familial demands placed upon Native women.

> I was married to a Native man and know a lot about his sisters and the differences between men and women on the reserves ... It is an absolute fact that the Native women receive less support and they have bigger demands ... The more successful they become, the more demands that they have put on them ... I mean, they're surrounded by needy people.[23]

At other times extended family members were a tremendous help to the women in the program. Some women relied upon their sisters and mothers as pinch-hit babysitters when their regulars couldn't make it. Others had their young children move in with other family members, especially during the summer months when the children were home from school, which enabled them to stay in the program.

It is a tremendous achievement to juggle this intensive retraining program with the extensive demands of mothering. Many of the participants spoke about their elaborate organizational schemes, which keep the home fires burning while they are training to be carpenters. One single mother with two children explained what has to happen every evening in order to make the morning rush possible.

> When I come home, I make supper, clean the house at the same time, and usually try to get my youngest to sit at the table and practise her alphabet or numbers or something. After supper is homework and then they must get their clothes all laid out for school tomorrow and then story time and bedtime. Then I make the lunches, tidy up and do my own homework.[24]

Rhonda H. lives forty minutes away in Vybank with her partner; two of her own children and two of her partner's children live with them part-time. In order for Rhonda to be at work on time, she rises at 5:30 a.m. and drops the children off at the daycare at 6:30 a.m. before heading in to town. "Yes it's a big rush and it's a fight in the morning with the girls," she says. But the biggest challenge is making certain that the children are picked up by 6:00 p.m. when the daycare closes. "Many days we have meetings or we're working late or whatever and my mom picks them up."[25]

Another mother with four children explained her morning schedule as follows:

> My oldest son, he helps get my two older ones, my six- and eight-year-olds, ready and he gives them breakfast. I let my baby sleep and I get him dressed while he's in bed and then just ship him off like that. We leave the house by 7:15; my one daughter though has to run down the street to my cousin's house because she goes to a different school than my other kids.[26]

The fact that her daughter went to a different school than did her other children was a great source of anxiety for this mother.

> Just a couple of weeks ago, the school sent home their letters of warnings that men are trying to call kids and that's why she [her daughter] was out of school for about four days because I didn't want her to walk by herself to school. I just told my babysitter to just let her stay home until I feel it's OK. I have a phone call into the school and I hope she can change to the other school with my other kids.

Many single mothers worry about how their participation in the program affects their children's school attendance or time after school. Lorie, a single mother with five children, is particularly concerned about her fifteen-year-old son. "He's got like a 50 percent school attendance. When I have to be at the worksite at 7:00 a.m. I can only hope he goes to school. When we move to another job site and I don't have to be at work until 8:00, I'm hoping that then I'll be able to keep an eye on him."[27] Other mothers worry about leaving their children in their home unattended for a brief time. Shelley worries about her two children coming home alone after school, when her husband is out picking her up from work. "I hate leaving her [daughter] alone but it's only for five or ten minutes. But she knows how to open the door, let herself in, lock the door right behind her, grab a snack and she usually watches TV or something. And I always ask her, 'How long have you been home?'"[28]

Pat's constant worry is her son. As a single mother she is solely responsible for both her daughter and her son. Her son has an attention deficit disorder, is hyperactive, and is on Ritalin. At one point, Pat discovered that her ex-partner was taking her son's medication and selling it on the street. The training program attempted to accommodate Pat's needs.

> Denise and Val sat down with me and helped me arrange my schedule where I could take off from the shop for an hour or so and go get him [her son], take him home. I don't think any other program would do something like that. Like they knew I wanted to stay but they also knew that he was more important and if I had to I would leave. But I didn't want to, I wanted to stay.[29]

Pat particularly appreciated the advice and support of Val, a single mother who had raised two children, one of whom had an attention deficit disorder. At another time during the program, Pat found her son becoming unmanageable and abusive. With the help of the program's instructors, she decided to have her son temporarily placed in a foster home. He has since returned to her home and is doing much better but remains a constant source of anxiety. Pat spends a lot of her free time meeting with teachers, social workers, and social service providers – all in an effort to keep her son in school and under control.

A number of women have moved several times during the program in order to be closer to childcare arrangements or extended family. Pat explained:

> I've been through a few changes [since the program began]. I've been through a few different childcares and I moved to a few different areas. The one area I was in was a big problem because the bus didn't go anywhere near there ... The winter was terrible ... I had to pull my daughter, who was three years old, by sled.[30]

But now Pat's life is made easier by the fact that she lives a mere fifteen-minute walk from the workshop and only a couple of blocks from her sister's house. "I take my kids to my sister's in the morning and then I make the fifteen-minute walk here [to the shop]. That's my quiet time. I usually wear a walkman and shut the world off. My few minutes alone – that's all I get to think, where I don't have to work and I don't have to have the kids with me."[31]

Most of the mothers find it impossible to put their own needs above their children's – even for a limited amount of time. Rarely could they voice their own needs, as Lorie did when she said, "For the last quarter of a century I've been basically a caregiver. Well, I like being a caregiver, but now I'm doing something that I enjoy doing and, for the first time in my life, I've put my needs above my children's. Not so much my four-year-old – I'll still be a wuss for him – but the older boys."[32]

While most of the mothers spoke of their concerns for their children, they also continually emphasized that they could only do this retraining program because they knew it would make their children's lives better in the long run. Rhonda M. explains her rationale for continuing.

> The one important change in my life since I've joined this program is that I've realized that this has to be almost number one in my life. Because it's something that's not going to only help me financially but in a lot of other ways. That's a major change. When I was going to university my family, my children, and my grandchildren came first. But I have to realize that, if I really want to help them and make my life a lot better, I've to go do it. I've got to kind of put them aside.[33]

Some women who were concerned about how the retraining program would affect their family life were surprised to see the positive results. Shelley was pleased about how the program affected both her son and daughter.

> My daughter actually told me that she wants to be a carpenter now. And I brought little pieces of wood home, little blocks of different shapes and stuff, and both of them were out in the yard this summer just playing with them. She wanted to make a bird house ... I can't bring my toolbox home because they're both in there, hitting stuff, It's cute, it's really cute.[34]

It is clear that some women are taking pride in being role models for their children. Still, the struggle between the time needed for the retraining program and mothering responsibilities is difficult. Some women have quit or have temporarily withdrawn from the program because of their mothering responsibilities. For instance, Evelyn, a mother raising four children and one grandchild, withdrew briefly when her teenage children began to experiment with drugs. "My sixteen-year-old has a little girl. But it took something in her life to make her straighten out ... She landed in the hospital; she was really sick from taking drugs ... It was very stressful." Evelyn didn't feel she had her children's support for this retraining program, and that added to her stress.

> I was trying and trying [in this program] and the children weren't trying and I felt like I was doing it all for nothing. And then I remembered that I'm doing it for myself. They don't want to be a part of the way I'm going, and they can do what they want and find out the hard way, the way I did. So I just said, I'm just going to go to work and forget about everything until I get home and deal with it [then]. And that's what I did.[35]

Eventually, Evelyn left the program for a second time because she found it impossible to juggle the stress of her rebellious teenage children with her intensive retraining program.

This retraining program has deeply affected the women's home lives. In some cases male partners have increased their domestic responsibilities in the home so the women could participate in the program. This is the case for Shelley, who describes her own childhood as difficult. Deeply traumatized by the residential schools they were forced to enter, her parents turned to alcohol for relief. They were rarely home to attend to her needs, and it was Shelley's grandmother who generally stepped in to care for her. "I had a childhood until kindergarten. I remember playing in kindergarten," she recalls. "Grade 1 was different. I grew up then." Shelley is adamant that her own children will never be neglected, and she and her husband have promised that one of them will be home full time until the kids are in school. So now, her partner is a full-time parent.

> Childcare is number one. If I didn't have [my husband], I wouldn't be here, plain and simple, because I'm so protective of my kids. I figure if I can't watch them, the only other person I trust to watch them would be [him]. And he has lovingly given up his career temporarily while I start mine.[36]

Shelley explains their new domestic arrangement: "He does the sheets, I do the clothes, but he does everything else: he pays the bills, he does errands, grocery shops – he's great. I come home to a beautiful clean house, supper. Yes, if I need anything, I ask him and he's wonderful."[37]

Unlike Shelley, most of the ten mothers with partners continue to do the majority of the domestic work while they participate in the training program. Diane explained how she and her husband worked out the domestic chores: "He pays the bills and other things. I do the groceries because I can just look in the cart and tell I have seventy dollars worth of groceries there. I don't need a calculator. He makes his own lunches and I make the kids' lunches." Diane describes herself as a very organized person, and her daily schedule was very detailed.

> I get up before everyone else and have a nice bath: it is my quiet time in the day. Then I throw in a load of laundry, I dry it when I come home from work while I make supper. And then there's vacuuming and floor scrubbing, that all just fits into the evening. But it's not a problem. I'm the kind of person who does fifteen things at once.[38]

Diane's husband works as a disk jockey on one of the local radio stations. When she first started the program he was "the morning guy" on the radio. Everyone got up early and he was home before the children came home from school. But six months later he became "the afternoon guy," and Diane's job at the time required her to be at work at 7:00 a.m. "We haven't really seen each other since this new schedule began," she explained. "He doesn't get home until 7:00 p.m. now and I am out of the house before 7:00 a.m."[39]

Not surprisingly, given the demands of motherhood and the training program, a number of the women have complained about difficulties with their boyfriends or partners. One single mother said she broke up with her boyfriend because there simply was no time for him. "We just didn't have time for each other. He was busy and whenever he had time I was busy ... It was high maintenance to take care of that relationship and I just couldn't do it any more," she explained.[40] Another mother said that she and her husband split up for a month because she was in the retraining program: "He was feeling low self-esteem because I'm making money and he's not."[41] To add to her anxiety, her husband did not want to look for a job because he didn't want to leave the children with a babysitter. This made the woman feel quite guilty about the retraining program. Eventually, the tension between the two parents was too great and they separated. This separation caused financial worries for the mother. The father had left her with the phone bill and other debts that she could not afford to pay. She was terribly distraught about all of this, and she took an extended leave from the program to get her home in order.

Even the women who are single have caring responsibilities. All four single women live with their parents. Michelle's mother has been ailing for years, so, generally, Michelle drives her to appointments, buys groceries, cleans the house, does yard work, and makes meals. Milarin and Charlene, sisters who live with their parents, often babysit their niece, who lives with them. And Heather lives separately from her family but is very close to her grandparents and attends weekly to their needs.

Violence
Up until recently, domestic violence has rarely been connected to issues of

poverty and retraining. And yet emerging studies demonstrate a high correlation between poverty and violence against women. The 1994 Statistics Canada national study of violence against women illustrates that most women experience violence, and that poor women experience twice as much violence as do non-poor women.[42] Another study reveals that Aboriginal women's rate of spousal homicide is eight times higher than that for non-Aboriginal women.[43] These statistics demonstrate the impact of colonialism. Aboriginal men and women have been subjected to the violence of colonialism, have internalized it, and have suffered a loss of self-esteem and self-worth. As a result, Aboriginal men and women are steeped in a culture of violence in which they are both the victims and the perpetrators.[44]

There is very little scholarship on low-income women and violence in Canada.[45] The American research, which is far more extensive, has shown in study after study that low-income women experience significantly higher levels of violence than do more privileged women. In nearly all of the American studies that address this issue, well over half of the women on welfare reported that they had experienced physical abuse by an intimate male partner at some point during their adult lives, and most also reported physical and/or sexual abuse in childhood. These women also reported high levels of violence and abuse from current male partners (between 19.5 and 32 percent).[46]

The experiences of the women interviewed reflect similar findings about low-income and Aboriginal women's experiences of violence. They had experienced verbal, physical, sexual, and psychological abuse. They had been raped at gun point, thrown down stairs, and put in situations where they feared for their lives. They spoke about the violence they had experienced as little girls and as adult women. The Aboriginal women talked about the violence stemming from white culture – a violence that was a daily part of their lives. They also spoke of how centuries of oppression and forced assimilation had promoted violence within their communities. During the three years in which I interviewed the participants, one woman's brother committed suicide, the sister-in-law of two sisters in the program died when she fell out of a speeding truck, and others dealt with their own or other family members' alcoholism and the abuse/violence associated with it. Violence is an integral part of these women's lives. With the exception of *three* women (two white and one Métis), every one of the women interviewed had experienced significant levels of violence in her life.

The violence stemming from white culture creates further inequities for Native women. During the interviews Native women spoke about how they have been harassed and how they have endured catcalls when walking to or from job sites. On the job site more than one white customer accused the Native women of stealing. These same Native women were accused of stealing at a local corner store. In the latter case, the white foreperson was able to defend the Native women and the issue was dropped. What this speaks to is how Native women are considered sexually available or guilty simply because they are Native. The white women interviewed had not encountered any of these experiences of violence, harassment, or suspicion on the job.

As a result of colonization, violence is epidemic in Native communities both on and off the reserve. Colonization is, in and of itself, a violent process. Both the federal government and the church instilled violence into Native children, who were placed in residential schools and foster homes where they were often deprived of love and abused physically, sexually, and psychologically. Abused Native boys and girls grew into adults who abused or accepted abuse as a normal part of a relationship. This violence has destabilized and destroyed homes, families, and communities.

The impact of the colonial legacy of violence cannot be overstated. Aboriginal men, impoverished and robbed of their land, "have exerted their anger in the only arena of power they were given by the colonizer: the power to dominate Native women and children." The introduction of alcohol and drugs has exacerbated this violence. "The violence that has become a 'way of life' for many Native women has crippled their well-being," explains Native scholar Kim Anderson.[47]

The mainstream images of Aboriginal women only support and incite this violence. There is a long popular history that depicts Native women as lazy, drunk, and sexually available. Native princesses, a variation on a theme, are overtly sexualized in a way that young white girls generally are not.[48] Because Native women are assumed to be sexually promiscuous they are "inherently rapeable," states anti-racist scholar Sherene Razack.[49] And a Native woman who is drunk is considered fair game for men's violence and is deemed particularly unworthy of help. All of these popular images make it extremely difficult for Native women to negotiate a place for themselves that is free from violence. They make it difficult for Native women to establish spousal relationships based upon mutual respect and autonomy. These images also make it difficult for Native women to assert that they have a right to safety and to assume that police and hospital services will attempt to protect them from serious harm.

Certainly, the Aboriginal women in this retraining program have witnessed and experienced significant levels of grief and violence within their homes, their families, and their communities. As Native writer Lee Maracle states, "it is nearly impossible for Native men to cherish the femininity of Native women. They have grown up in a world in which there is no such thing as dark-skinned femininity. There is only dark-skinned sensuality."[50] One woman, Karen, was widowed twice by the time she was thirty-five. Another, Emily returned to her home reserve as an adult but left again with her one-year-old son when her uncle was murdered.[51] This violence, which is part of Native urban and reserve life, has resulted in Native women being more transient than white women. In their attempts to protect their children from violence, many have been forced to leave their communities.

Childhood experiences of abuse and neglect were rampant among the women in this retraining program. Forty-three percent of the women who answered the anonymous violence survey said they had been sexually abused as a child (see Appendix D, Section B, Question 4). One Native woman describes her childhood on the reserve:

> I was molested as a child. And I had a pretty rough life with my mother, too. I looked after all my siblings. My mother would leave me on a Sunday night and she'd come back Friday. I used to haul water, wash diapers, cook and clean. If the house wasn't clean Friday Night, I'd get a licking. I never had very much of a life.[52]

Another woman recalls how physical violence was an integral part of her family life.

> One time my Dad grabbed me and gave me a good shot in the ribs and I just kind of fell over ... My brothers were all there getting their lickings on the side and I just couldn't breathe ... And then one time he did it one too many times to my brother and my brother ended up in the hospital. My Dad came up to me and he went down on his knees and he told me, "Hit me" ... And I told him, "I don't want to be like you." And he cried.[53]

She also remembers other violent incidents, where she, as well as other family members, had to go to the hospital to recover.

Sharon Murray, hired as a foreperson for the program, is well-known and liked by the participants. She has visited their homes, met their families, and been a confidante to many of them. Sharon has lived through a ten-year relationship with a former partner who was abusive and an alcoholic, so she is personally familiar with the difficulties of dealing with a loving yet abusive person. On more than one occasion, Sharon has counselled women to leave their abusive partners.

> Generally I ask them what does he do that still makes you happy and how important is that to you. I generally just encourage them to assess the situation – not to leave. But one night I said to ____ "Do yourself a favour and phone the police," but she said, "No, that means he'd go away" ... I know that that is a lot of the reason that she's not at work – dealing with this abuse.[54]

The anonymous violence survey supports Sharon's belief that the vast majority of the participants have experienced abusive relationships. More than half of the respondents had a partner who destroyed or took their possessions and prevented them from seeing their friends or family. And more than 70 percent acknowledged that a partner verbally and physically abused them. The severity of the violence experienced is also worth noting. More than half said a partner had cut, bruised, choked, or seriously harmed them. And more than one-third said a partner had used a gun, knife, or other sharp object to threaten them (see Appendix D, Part A).

The rate of spousal violence increases among the Native women participants. In Sharon's estimation every Native woman in the program, with the exception of one, is *currently* dealing with an abusive relationship. They may or may not be living with the abuser; they may or may not be economically dependent upon him; he may not even be their current partner.[55]

The women have used whatever resources are available to deal with these difficult situations. A number of them have charged their abusive partners or ex-partners with assault. Others have gone to a counsellor or therapist to strategize about abusive partners. And still others have attempted to avoid the abusive partner by staying at someone else's home and by avoiding public places. One single mother recalls an abusive relationship that she finally found a way to leave: "He would be high on coke [cocaine] and he would do stuff to me like as in experiments for him or something ... He would burn me on my legs and stuff ... to see how much tolerance I had or to see if I had the guts to leave him." When she attempted to leave him, he would show up at her family home and threaten her mother until he found out where she was. Terrified, the woman saw only one solution:

I just couldn't take it any more, so I stabbed him in his sleep ... He crashed out and I knew he was drunk and his body was really tired, so I got up and I grabbed my knife ... you could just hear all the blood hitting the bed. And I was out the door and I went across the alley and I phoned a cab and an ambulance and the cops and I took off.

The man recovered and has threatened her several times since, but the woman says she feels safe now because her brothers and father know about the situation.[56]

Both previous and current experiences of violence affected the women's ability to fully participate in the program in many ways. Violent traumas can cause depression, low self-esteem, and health problems. According to US studies, abused women have higher rates of depression and drug/alcohol abuse than do non-abused women. In one American study, drug and alcohol problems were reported by 19 percent of currently abused women and 10 percent of non-abused low-income women. The same study found that 54 percent of the abused women had "severe depression" compared to 32 percent of the non-abused women.[57] The women in the Women's Work Training Program reflect many of the findings published in the earlier studies about violence and health. According to the anonymous violence survey, 22 percent of the women in this retraining program felt depressed daily or once a week and 36 percent said they had no energy daily or once a week (see Appendix D, Section E). Of the thirty women interviewed over a three-year period, seven said they had dealt with, or continue to deal with, long-term alcohol and drug abuse issues. All seven of these women had experienced significant abuse either as a child, an adult, or both.

This experience of violence can interfere with a woman's ability to participate in retraining programs or paid work. American studies have shown that as many as 40 percent of currently abused women are prevented from participating in education and training by their abusive partners. A Chicago study of female workfare participants who were currently in abusive relationships reported that 8 percent of them were prevented from going to school or work by their partners, 2 percent were subject to telephone harassment at work by their partners, and 1.7 percent were harassed in person at their worksites by their partners.[58] Job training and welfare-to-work programs in the United States report male sabotage of participants as the greatest single barrier to moving women from welfare to work.[59] Consequently, it is not surprising that low-income women in abusive relationships in the United States have reported higher spells of unemployment, more job turnover, more absenteeism, and more reliance upon welfare than have non-abused low-income women.[60]

Literacy expert Jenny Horsman argues that previous and current violence dramatically affects a person's ability to learn. As a result of this violence, students are often afraid to trust their teachers or peers, lack assertiveness, have difficulty with communication skills, and lack the ability to set goals.[61] According to the anonymous violence survey, 14 percent of the women have been harassed by their partners at work while participating in this retraining program. Twenty-one percent said their partners were jealous that they might meet someone new at work (even though they seldom worked with men). And 14 percent said their partners were worried that they might become lesbians because they were working in a women-only environment (see Appendix D, Section C, Questions 16-18).

Violence and abuse have interfered with the ability of a number of these women to concentrate on and participate in the retraining program. Some of the women mentioned that flashbacks continue to be a problem, disrupting their sleep and sometimes interfering with their ability to work. According to the anonymous violence survey, 29 percent of the respondents said they had intrusive memories while they were at work. In addition, 14 percent said they had trouble concentrating at work because of stresses that occurred in their homes either daily or once a week (see Appendix D, Section E). "Flashbacks are a big part of my life," explained one woman. "When they happen sometimes I have to go, I have to leave and I have to cry and there is no way around it. You can't do that in front of customers. But I just go off in a corner and I'm OK. Other women in the program, I know they have to stay home when they can't cope."[62] In one case, a single mother with three children did not last a week in the program because of her recent experience of violence. When interviewed during one of the three days she attended the program she stated that she had been raped seven months earlier. She had become agoraphobic as a result of her trauma and had rarely left her home since the sexual assault. Nevertheless, she saw the retraining program as a chance to move forward with her life:

> In the last seven months, I haven't been outside of my home for more than a couple hours at a time. Yesterday I made it through the morning and I went home at noon. I felt good and I was reading through this [carpentry] book and I was using my brain again ... I got up this morning and there was a purpose to have a bath and get dressed ... I feel alive! I feel like a caterpillar turning into a butterfly.[63]

Despite her enthusiasm, the woman found the sudden change from being house-bound too difficult. Donna Thomson, the life skills coach, recalls this woman's difficulties:

> Well, her mother tried to commit suicide the very first day of class, so she missed the first day of school. Then she came to the second one but she wasn't able to make it through the whole day. I don't think she came the Thursday and Friday at all. And then the following week she didn't show up again and then she called and said, "You'd better fill it [my spot] with somebody else. I just can't leave the house."[64]

This is just one woman's experience of violence, but it illustrates how violence can severely impede a woman's ability to retrain.

There is now some evidence that low-income women experience increased levels of violence when they attempt to work or participate in retraining programs. Often, low-income women's partners are also poor and their self-esteem is fragile. Women earning an income and having a social life outside the family home may threaten their partners. This was the case for one woman, whose attendance record was sporadic due to her partner's jealousy. After several months, she left the program because her partner felt threatened. When things calmed down on the home front, she returned, but again her partner became difficult. "He calls the women I work with dykes. He's jealous of them and he's jealous because I like this work," she explains. "I tried to fix the fence at home but he said it was 'a man thing.' He got mad because the neighbours might see me doing a man's job."[65] Other women in the program said they were worried about her and witnessed her coming to work bruised after a weekend at home. Although she turned to the coordinators and the other women in the program for support, eventually she left the program for a second time because she simply could not handle the increased conflict in her life.

According to Jenny Horsman's research on violence and learning, it is very common for women to stop and start training programs due to their past experiences of violence.[66] Certainly the violence in their lives disrupted the women's attendance at this retraining program. Some of them said they had to pick up in the middle of the night and take their children to a shelter or to a relative's home. Valerie recalls other times when the women had "to leave without their children to protect themselves, even more heart-breaking because when they went back in daylight to get the kids they would be accused of abandoning them and would need to fight to get them back." As Valerie explains, "For some women these were daily events, for some they were cyclical; but over half of those who were in relationships knew the warning signs and lived on the edge of fear for some part of their home lives."[67]

Other women reported that their partners were jealous of the training program and the friends they were making. One woman had a partner who followed the crew to every job site and spent the whole day watching.[68] Partners seem particularly upset about the women getting together for a drink after work on Friday nights. One woman's husband threatened to beat her co-workers if she socialized with them on a Friday night.[69] Another woman said her partner was envious of the accreditation she was achieving through the program. Although he worked in construction, he did not have any papers. She recalls when her second-year carpentry apprenticeship card came in the mail. "I was so excited and proud. I was flashing it around in front of him, showing it off, so he hid it on me because I was getting carried away."[70] This woman remained in the program despite her partner's jealousy, but she learned to be quiet about her achievements.

Several women spoke about conflict between themselves and their spouses over the money they earned in the program. Several male partners frequently showed up on payday so that they could get the cheque immediately. In other cases, the partner took the rent or food money and left the woman to cover the bills. Denise Needham recalls the many times that the women got paid on Friday and then came into the shop on Monday asking for an advance on their next paycheque because they couldn't feed their children. "It's overwhelming to see how the men in their lives control the money that the women have earned through hard, hard work."[71]

While the program has escalated domestic conflict for a number of women, it has also given them skills to enable them to deal more effectively with this conflict. A number of women have reassessed their relationships as a result of the program. Some have left abusive partners; some have decided to live separately from their partners; and others have established limits around certain unhealthy behaviour. Pat feels that the program helped her to re-examine a previously abusive relationship.

> I didn't realize that verbal abuse was actual abuse before life skills. And then I realized that, hey, he used to do that to me ... I was scared to go out in public with him because I was scared he would call me down and stuff like that in front of other people and it was so humiliating that I just couldn't go out ... I think that really brought my self-esteem down.[72]

Because of her experiences and the knowledge she gained from life skills, Pat now feels that she is more able to help other women. Many women spoke about how their friendships in the retraining program helped to break the isolation they felt when dealing with an abusive partner. Some of the women confide in each other about their difficulties with abusive partners. And a number of the women create safe houses for one another – allowing a workmate to secretly stay at their houses for a while so the abusive partners cannot find them. This is outside the parameters of the program, but it suggests the tremendous solidarity that these women feel for one another.[73] Together, they are helping each other break old patterns of jealousy and abuse.

Previous Employment

Another barrier to women's participation in the retraining program is their limited experience as paid workers. For seven of the thirty women interviewed, the program was their first job. Most of them left school around Grade 11 and have since been trying to complete their high school education. Eleven of the thirty women had been on welfare all their adult lives. But the majority of them had a scattered career of short-term employment interrupted from time to time by the birth of a child. Of course there are exceptions to every rule. Four had some university or community college training that they did not complete. And one of the women has a doctorate.

For the most part, these women's job experiences have given them little hope of climbing out of poverty. The vast majority of their employment has involved short-term, service sector work (e.g., secretarial work, reception work, and waitressing). This work provided only minimum wage with no hope of advancement or job benefits. Only two of the women described their previous employment experience as in any way self-fulfilling; the rest had not enjoyed their work, where they had been harassed, given low pay, and had virtually no support or friendship from their co-workers.

A number of women spoke about the harassment they encountered while working at minimum-wage, part-time jobs. One woman said her boss consistently directed racial slurs towards her. Another said her boss made her change light bulbs, but only on the days she wore skirts. "He never paid me on time. He'd always say that he gambled the money away. He would bang his fist on the table and scream in my face and make me cry."[74]

A number of the women had done odd jobs in the carpentry and construction trades with family members. Some, as children, had been encouraged to learn to use a hammer and other carpentry tools. Others, as adults, had worked with their fathers, brothers, or male partners doing construction jobs. The literature on women in non-traditional trades suggests that it is easiest for them to adjust to non-traditional training and employment.[75]

Postsecondary education was simply impossible for most of these women. The legacy of the residential school system has made many of the Aboriginal women distrustful and fearful of schooling.[76] For this reason, a number of the participants in the program never went to high school. And many have juggled young children and endured poverty while returning to school to get their high school diplomas. The horrors of residential school left one woman with little desire to go to high school: "I just never went to high school. I got out of that residential school as fast as I could – after Grade 5." Out of school at thirteen, she moved off the reserve and into Regina to live with her mother and care for the younger children. "I was thirteen when I went to visit her and then I got raped and then I had my own baby nine months later." Two weeks after the baby was born she was kicked out of her mother's house and had to fend for herself. "I did odd jobs like house cleaning, babysitting – anything to feed the baby. And I got welfare."[77]

There was one clear exception to this rule. One woman had a doctorate. She had encountered a number of health problems while doing postdoctoral work and sessional lecturing: "Teaching is a phenomenal amount of work. And the publish-or-perish pressure. It was just too much stress and I was starting to have health trouble. I started having trouble concentrating and ... I realized I just can't do this work any more."[78] She then went to work at the local casino until it closed down. When she entered the retraining program she was on Employment Insurance for the first time in her life.

Another woman with a high school diploma attempted to train as a graphic artist at the local community college while she worked full time. "I didn't end up getting my certificate – I was short a couple of classes but I couldn't do it anymore... I didn't want the school to suffer but then if I didn't work I couldn't pay for anything so I ended up quitting school and continuing with work," she explained.[79]

Often pregnancy interfered with the women's ability to continue their educational upgrading. Rhonda H. was one of the lucky ones who got a chance to try university, but she could not stay once she became a single mother: "I was going to university and I was waitressing part-time and I got pregnant so I quit university because it was just too hard, and I went back to waitressing full-time and then I took my maternity and then I went back to waitressing again and then I had my second baby. They're twenty months apart."[80] As a single mother with two babies under two years old, Rhonda H. could no longer consider university a possibility.

Many of the women straddled the divide between welfare and paid employment. It was often very difficult to trace their employment history. They were very much a reserve army of labour, working when childcare arrangements and a job were available and then falling back on welfare when a baby was born or their job disappeared. They had absolutely no job security. Delphine described her employment history: "It's always been a job, unemployment, a job, unemployment, just back and forth, back and forth."[81]

These women often complained that welfare regulations made it difficult to pursue training or paid employment. As one single mother explained, "Welfare didn't really help me ... Every little job, even babysitting, I would claim it and I was using the money to go for computer classes at school. The more I tried to get off of welfare, the deeper I got dragged in ... By the time I paid my transportation and daycare and everything, I was in the hole."[82]

Another woman was frustrated that welfare wouldn't let her retrain. "I wanted to upgrade but they wouldn't let me. As long as I had a job, they were happy and they'd subsidize the wages but absolutely no chance to upgrade."[83]

The employment history of these women was also affected by personal tragedy. One woman stopped working and started drinking when her baby died of crib death. Another gave up her job and returned with her three-year-old twins to Regina (where her family lived) when her husband was murdered.

More than one-third of the women had no paid employment experience and had been on welfare all their lives. The majority of these women were Aboriginal single mothers with virtually no resources, little education, and few family contacts who would help them enter the workforce. With children to raise, they had viewed paid work as impossible. One woman explains why she went on welfare when she was a single mother at sixteen: "I was brought up in a single-parent home and my mom had nine children so she could have worked but it was too strenuous on her so she was on welfare ... Welfare is all I've known. I felt like I couldn't get a job because you needed Grade 10 or you needed some kind of experience. I just felt trapped."[84]

Diane worked at a number of service jobs before her children were born. Since then she and her children have relied upon her husband's income. She has been frustrated for some time because she has wanted to get into the workforce but had been unable to find anything. "I am a stay-at-home mom with no skills. I went to the government and demanded them to explain why there are retraining programs for those on UI, those on welfare but no funding for parents like me – who want to work but need skills."[85] These situations were typical of the women participants in the Women's Work Training Program.

Money, Debts, and Grinding Poverty
Another significant barrier to participation in a retraining program is the grinding poverty most of these women experience. Almost all of them know what it is like to live without food at the end of the month, to be unable to pay the regular bills, and to be anxious about money on a daily basis. This is the reality of low-income women's lives. Some of the women in the program do not have phones; some have insecure housing that changes frequently; most do not own a vehicle. Most of the women are very anxious about outstanding bills. One woman worries about her $20,000 student loan, while another worries about how to get her winter clothes out of storage:

> I've got bills coming out of my ears. I don't let it worry me any more, I guess. As long as my kids have food, then we manage to survive somehow. I've got to get two of my kids winter jackets because when I moved off the reserve I stored my stuff – all the winter clothes. [But now] I can't afford to pay the storage to get it back.[86]

When middle-class women experience a period of poverty they can usually rely upon family and friends to ease the financial stress. This is generally impossible for low-income women. Sharon Murray, one of the forepersons for the program, compares her previous circumstances to those of the women in the program. As a single mother she knows what it is like when money is tight. "I've been broke many times and I've had to go to my parents and say, 'Listen, I really need some help right now.' But these women can't do that."[87]

Native identity has also deeply affected the amount and types of resources available for the women. As any poverty report will state, Native men and women experience far greater poverty and unemployment than do all other racial groups. For instance, Aboriginal people in cities are more than twice as likely to live in poverty than are non-Aboriginal people.[88] As a result, the Aboriginal participants in this retraining program have fewer resources to draw upon than do the white participants. Of the ten white women interviewed, two experienced financial help from their parents and one from her grandparents; as a result, one of these white women was debt-free, two received cheap rent, and one's family had given her a gift of a second-hand truck. None of the Aboriginal women had family members with such economic resources; rather, their families viewed them as the ones with the economic resources because they had a steady (albeit minimal) income. Consequently, these women spoke of constant requests from family members for money and food.

This grinding poverty can result in feelings of helplessness and hopelessness, especially if combined with a childhood of abuse. It is little wonder that many women turned to drugs and alcohol as a way of coping. One Aboriginal woman explains her hard economic times: "I completely gave up on everything ... I was right down to nothing and me and my husband were getting a divorce. It was a really bad year for my family ... I lost a lot of people in our family that year ... That's when I went back to drugs and alcohol."[89] Another woman recalls her experiences of homelessness: "Back then I had no place to stay. Welfare wouldn't put me up anyplace. They said they wouldn't give me my cheque for my rent because they said that I wasn't looking for work. So me and my son and my cousin had to sleep out on 13th Avenue, where there's a bowling lane. That's where we slept, and it was cold." This single mother finally found work as a chambermaid and waitress, and then another crisis befell her. "I had my third baby. She would have been eighteen now, but I lost that baby. She was two-and-a-half-months old when she died of crib death. And then I sort of just went really crazy and started drinking a lot."[90]

A white single mother explains her past: "I've been through my addiction with drugs. I have had my house burn down twice. I have had my kids go with their father. I have had to move many, many times because I couldn't afford the rent. My twenties was one battle after another."[91] Still another recalls her hard times: "I just saw no way forward. I stopped working and I started doing crime – B and Es [break and enter], stealing cars, drinking, not caring about nobody or nothing, not having a place to sleep and not worrying about it." When she became pregnant at twenty-three she changed her life. She went to Alcoholics Anonymous and began to care about herself. The Women's Work Training Program has given her another reason to change her life. "I just love carpentry and I love the learning – this gives me another reason to stay away from the bottle."[92]

The transition from welfare to employment is a costly one. Women, other than those who are status Indian, lose their drug benefits. Welfare can provide a higher income because welfare rates take into account the number of dependants, whereas wages do not. Also, once they pay for childcare and transportation, low-income women often find that it is financially disadvantageous to leave welfare, even though welfare payments are well below the standard poverty line.[93] Despite all attempts to provide a living wage for these women, the wages in the program remain relatively low compared to those in the construction industry. As a result, many of these women have moved from welfare poverty to working poverty. A number of the women in the program live without telephones. A few go without food on a regular basis. Financially, it would be better for a single mother with four or five children to remain on welfare than to participate in this retraining program. However, despite the financial sacrifices, these single mothers persist in participating in a program that, in the long run, can change their financial circumstances. Eventually, when they have earned their Journeyperson Certificate of Qualification in the Carpenter Trade (journeyed carpentry papers), they will make a good industrial wage. But three or four hard years of financial sacrifice are necessary before this can happen.

Many of the women entered the program with significant levels of debt. With relatively low wages, they are often unable to get a handle on their debt. Coordinator Denise Needham recalls debt collectors and landlords calling the shop demanding money from the women. "I've had guys [debt collectors] come by and sit in their cars for hours waiting to see a particular woman and serve her with papers for the money she owed," explains Denise. One woman, who did cocaine and led a "fast life," had a debt load of more than $250,000 and was terrified that someone to whom she owed money would cause her physical harm. She recalls her enormous anxiety about her debt: "It was a lot of money. That is money that I didn't even know existed, and there I was sniffing it into my lungs and my head." She was relieved when she was able to reach a private agreement regarding her drug debt and to publicly declare bankruptcy. Now she and her partner no longer associate with "the fast crowd," and their wages are garnisheed to help reduce their debt. "After a long time I am no longer afraid for my safety. We are learning to save for the first time. Now things are really working out."[94]

A number of the women have student loans hanging over their heads. According to Denise, "The minute any of our women start working, start trying to change their lives, the student loan people are harassing them for money."[95] One woman spoke about how frustrating it was to have a debt that she could not erase. "You would like to pay it off quicker. I mean, instead of the $4,500 debt, [with interest] I will pay back something like $7,500. It is good that I don't have to pay it back tomorrow, but I mean, you can't help but think about what you could have done with an extra $3,000."[96]

The women who are scraping by find the seasonal nature of their retraining program difficult. Sheila, a single mother, said she was debt-free until the second winter in the program, when they were laid off because there was no work. "That is the baddest time I ever had because I had to spend whatever I had in my pocket on groceries and Christmas gifts and that's when the bills started."[97] Almost all of the women interviewed have debts. While these debts range from as high as $250,000 to as little as $1,700, the majority have debts hovering around $15,000. This produces a constant anxiety – one that they can do little to ameliorate on an income that is just slightly above minimum wage.

Daring to Dream

Given the many barriers these women face, it is no wonder that they doubt whether it is truly possible to become journeyed carpenters and to get out of poverty. Such a dream seems impossible, even illogical, given their previous history. During the first week of the program, the women were asked to write down their dreams. For many, this was very difficult and sometimes emotionally overwhelming. Denise says she learned a lot by watching the women struggle with this assignment:

> I'd always gone after what I wanted. But some of them had no vision ... These women have had such tough lives. They've had their dreams broken. They have dreamt and hoped and wished for things and it has never ever happened for them. So that is their pattern. And, I mean, we are asking them to hang on to a dream that just seems so unreal to them.[98]

Denise also believes that women who have spent the majority of their lives on welfare find it particularly difficult to have goals and realize them: "You're so used to having other people pulling your strings; why would you make a decision on your own? You can't, you don't have the room to do that."[99] Violence as well as poverty can inhibit goal-setting. Jenny Horsman explains that violence leaves women feeling as if they have no control, no ability to make decisions or to set goals for themselves.[100]

Now, because of this retraining program, a number of the women are beginning to believe that their dreams are achievable. Sheila explains: "Carpentry is something I never really thought of as I was getting older. And I never knew what I wanted to do with my life until I came here. And now I know that this is probably what I'm going to be doing for the rest of my life. And I really enjoy it."[101] The dream for some of the women is to run their own construction company.[102] Others want to continue working at the construction co-operative. "Maggie" wants to make furniture that incorporates fine wood with the stained glass that she makes in her spare time.[103] Some hope to buy houses, pay off their debts, and have lives that are not wracked with poverty. Others want to return to their reserve, to build homes of their own, and to become teachers in their Native communities. Pat says: "Since I first took shop I wanted to be a shop teacher, but I was so shy I didn't think I could do it. I didn't think I'd be able to get in front of people and teach them anything." But now, having been a shop assistant to teenage and adult women being introduced to carpentry, Pat believes she could teach after all. Her other dream is to help run a construction company with her brothers and sister.

"Judy" wants to be a role model for young Native children: "I'd like to be working as a carpenter but in the evenings I'll volunteer with children ... I want to have something strong, too, for myself so they can see it, you know.

Well, right now I do have something strong."[104] Jackie says: "I told my kids I'm going back on the reserve one day, but I don't want to go back without something to go back for. I want to work. Now I can do that."[105] Audrey wants to help build the Saskatchewan Indian Federation College. Zena also wants to work on this project: "There is going to be a teepee made with glass, and I want to be part of it. To make us all proud."[106]

Once they believe in their dreams, good things happen. Sharon, one of the forewomen, recalls how the women begin to do things they previously feared doing:

> Sheila looked at me with the shingles on my back going up the ladder to do the roofing and said, "If that little squirt can do that, I can too." She's terrified of heights, and I looked behind me and there she was carrying a bunch of shingles up the ladder. Those things are priceless. They really are, and I don't expect them to do anything that they find that they can't. But I do expect them to try. And if I hear the "I can't" before they try, I give them attitude because I don't like that word, I really don't like that word.[107]

Another woman who was terrified of heights now runs up and down the ladder. "Weren't you afraid of heights?" I ask. "Oh yeah," she says and laughs, "I almost forgot." She, along with many of the other women, were afraid to make a mistake when they started the program. "But now I know that I learn more when I make a mistake because I don't want to make the same one again," she explains.[108] One of the visible changes in the women is in their physiques. Their shoulders seem to broaden, their waists slim down, and their muscles develop. They appear proud and confident in these new bodies. "My boys always want to feel my muscles," laughs Sheila. "They can't believe how strong I am now."[109] In many ways, the women's newly strong bodies symbolize their journey towards their dreams. For women who have experienced violence, taking control of their bodies and making them fit and strong is a very empowering experience. It marks the beginning of assertiveness, the beginning of a new life.

Support for Their Dreams

Despite the many obstacles, these women defy the odds every single day they attend the Women's Work Training Program. Despite intense racial discrimination, mothering responsibilities, violence, little previous work experience, and grinding poverty, these women are at the shop by 8:00 a.m., ready to face the challenge of a new day in their chosen trade. As well as iron-steel determination, these women count on the support of family and/or one another to help them hold on to their dream.

The family support received by these women comes in three forms. First, families who have members who work in the trades enable the women to believe that carpentry is something they can do; second, families support the women financially, helping to buy them work clothes and tools; and third, families provide the women with childcare. All of these familial supports are vital to the women's ability to continue in this retraining program.

Studies have demonstrated that women with family members in the trades tend to be more willing than other women to enter this non-traditional work and to remain in it. Almost every woman interviewed either came from a family of tradespeople or had a partner in the trades. Jackie explains why joining this retraining program was a natural decision for her: "My husband's a roofer and my dad's a carpenter. I've been around carpentry all my life. My Dad always tells me I grew up with a hammer in my hand."[110] Evelyn comes from a similar family background: "My brothers all are carpenters, and my cousins are carpenters. I have one girl cousin ... and she's a carpenter, too."[111] Pat, whose father ran a construction company, says joining the retraining program was the most natural thing for her: "Carpentry was really second nature. All the wood smelled familiar and the tools looked familiar."[112] Michelle recalls helping her dad fix things around the house: "He taught my sister and me to use power tools. He made it seem normal for girls to do that."[113] Ginny recalls helping her father, who is a welder, with all kinds of projects: "We made a swing set. We made a tree house. We made a trailer so that we could haul the rest of the lumber away." Her brothers are mechanics. "They were razzing me before about starting carpentry ... but now, this weekend I'm going to go over and help my brother finish his go-cart ... And now my sister calls me to fix things around her house."[114] Some of the women have male partners who are in the trades. Rhonda M.'s partner is a mechanic, and she dreams of one day going into business with him. Rhonda H.'s partner is in construction, and she does the odd weekend job with him. And Shirley does roofing with her partner.

Some of the women's families show their support in all kinds of ways. Pat's older sister comes to the worksite on her days off: "We call her our construction groupie because she's been at every worksite. And then she brags about us to her friends."[115] Sherry's dad is a taxi driver: "He's got my business card in the taxi and he gives it out to anyone who needs carpentry work done. He had a younger guy in the taxi who said he was a first year carpenter apprentice, and my dad goes, 'Well, my daughter is third year.' He was as proud as anything and it burst the young guy's bubble."[116]

Some of the women have received financial support from their families. Emily says that, because she comes from a family of carpenters, they were willing to help her with expenses: "My Dad bought my work boots. My Mom sent me some money from Calgary to help pay for my tools."[117] One single woman lives in the basement of her parents' home while she takes the retraining program. She pays a small amount of rent, helps her parents out occasionally, and, in return, her mother makes her supper every night: "For me, right now, it's a very cozy thing ... Having supper made for you when you're absolutely exhausted from the mental and physical work is a big thing."[118] For Heather, it is her grandmother who has supported her new career:

> When I was sixteen, I told my grandmom that she was my best friend. She came over one day and told me she wanted to give me an inheritance. She would pay off my debts or she would buy me a truck. I chose the truck because of my career. It is my commitment to this [program]. I got a long-box, quarter-ton, teal green 1993 Mazda. She gave it to me on graduation day. I wrote the [carpentry], exam and my grandparents drove me after the exam to the Mazda lot. I went afterwards to school and showed the women.[119]

Heather is very proud of her truck. She often volunteers to transport women from one job site to another or to pick up supplies.

Family support also comes in the form of childcare. A number of the women rely upon sisters, brothers, or parents to take care of their children either full time or part time. Generally, these family members engage in short-term childcare (e.g., when a child is sick) or look after the children before or after school. Pat's sister-in-law, who lives down the street, often looks after the children before school begins. And Rhonda H's mother looks after her children when school is out: "I've been helping my mom do remodelling on her house – free labour because she does free babysitting."[120] For Shelley, her husband is the biggest support with the children. He became a house-husband when she began this retraining program: "I have the best of both worlds. I have a really good man. I tell him that every day ... He cooks, he cleans, he takes care of the kids, he looks after me, pays the bills. Oh yes, he does it. He's excellent."[121]

In three cases, the women have family support right in the retraining program. Pat and her sister Roxanne were the first sisters in the program. Pat said: "They [the founders] were afraid to take siblings. They thought that there might be some kind of sibling rivalry. After they tried it with us they took two other pairs of sisters [Milarin and Charlene, and Sheila and Karen]."[122] All three sets of sisters agreed that having a sister in the program gave them someone they could talk to about all the hard parts.

For most of the women, their greatest support is one another. Time after time, they said that it is the other women who keep them going. When times are tough these women phone and check up on each other, bring food, provide shelter when they are hiding from an abusive partner, or go and have a beer together and forget about their troubles for a while. These friendships cross race, age, and marital status. Diane, a Native mother of two, explains how her friendship with Michelle, a single white woman, is a tremendous support: "Michelle and I kind of made this pact in the beginning that we were going all the way, that we would kill for it or not, we were going to get our degree in this."[123] Heather also speaks emotionally about her connection to the other women in the program: "We are all family. I didn't have female friends before I came to the program. And now, when I come here, they say hello, and there is laughter in the shop. It makes me feel strong." Shirley, a mature Native mother, often has coffee before work at the home of Ginny, a young Native single mother.[124] Shelley takes a lot of strength from Diane:

> Our lives are like carbon copies of each other ... She grew up fast, had a hard life, found her love early in her life. So did I ... We both have two kids, we're both left handed, our birthdays are six days apart ... We think alike, we work together awesome, we're just close in every perspective.[125]

The women also help each other by going to parenting classes together, telling each other where the good sales are, and recommending childcare centres. "We bring clothes that we don't need any more and just leave them in one area, and everyone just goes there and helps themselves," explains Pat.[126] And the women also help defend each other from male harassment. During one period when the women were at the provincial technical institute, a man in the class caused constant disruption, talking all the time so the women could not hear the instructor. Michelle and Diane took the matter into their own hands. Michelle recalls the incident with a grin on her face: "He was bothering all the women who were sitting near him. We had asked him to stop talking but he didn't, so Diane and I just gave each other 'the look' and picked up his chair with him sitting in it and moved it across the room. He wasn't a problem after that."[127]

Pat, a Métis single mother, is considered the quiet leader of the group. Everyone calls on her for advice and support. She also appears to be the first to notice when someone is having a difficult time. Heather, a single young white woman, recalls when she asked Pat for advice about whether to leave the program for a few months and follow her dream of building straw houses in New Mexico: "She didn't even breathe – she just instantly supported me," remembers Heather. "She gave me the confidence to ask the Co-op for time off."[128] Although Pat is extremely modest, she is aware of her role within the retraining program: "I feel obligated to stay because I do know they come to me a lot and they depend on me and they ask me a lot of stuff and I help them make decisions. I just do it. I don't really think about why they are asking me. I just try to listen and relate."[129]

"Maggie," a white single woman, also watches over the others. She calls people at home when they've been away from work; she makes soup and takes it to those who are ill. She used to invite me over for supper when I was in town doing interviews. When Sharon, the woman hired to be the foreperson, was diagnosed with lupus, Maggie went into action: "I went to the library and I got books and I read up about it. I knew that maybe she'd never do carpentry again and I got really worried about her."[130] Sharon is managing to work and keep her lupus under control, and Maggie continues to be on hand to help anyone in need. She's a smoker and she's very quick to give cigarettes to anyone who doesn't have the money for them. She gives in a quiet way, well aware that, as a single white woman, she has more income at her disposal than do most of the other women. Yet she's surprised and touched when anyone returns the care: "Last week I was sick on Wednesday and so I was home half the day – just a half day and [Judy] calls me at home at 4:30 that afternoon and says, '[Maggie] you're sick. What's the matter with you? You never miss' ... It was really nice to have this person from work call me up just to see if I was OK."[131] Denise considers this incident and others like it to be important: "For an Aboriginal woman to call a white woman at home to see if she's OK – that's success. And for a white woman to ask an Aboriginal woman advice on her future – it brings tears to my eyes."[132]

The women help each other get through the most challenging parts of the retraining program. Those who are further along in the program often tutor the junior women in math skills, helping them with their assignments, encouraging them to study for the carpentry exams. Sheila explains that she had two different women help tutor her through Level 2: "While they were helpful, eventually I [realized] I had to learn it my own way, by myself. But they encouraged me all the way."[133]

The women also support each other through difficult periods in their personal lives. Diane explains how she counselled one of the women when her husband left: "I said, call that bank and get them to hold your payments – don't be letting him take all of your money. I told her to call now at work – that I would cover for her because she was so upset it was obvious she couldn't work."[134] Rhonda M. is proud to say that other women in the program lean on her: "Being able to support them makes me feel good ... Like when Shirley lost her brother, she phoned and left a message at school that she wanted to talk to me, she wanted me to go and see her."[135]

The women also protect one another from abusive situations. Being survivors of violence themselves, they are quick to notice when another woman is experiencing abuse in her home life. Reagan, a single mother, explains how she supported another woman because she knew instinctively that she was experiencing many problems at home:

> She is going through a lot more than she sure lets on, you know ... And she tries to act so strong and I'll just go up and give her a hug and say, "You know, I'm glad you're here today" ... One night several of us were going to

go karaokeing, and she's scared 'cause she says her husband will hit us if she goes out with us. I asked if her husband had hit her and she said no, but I didn't believe her. I talked to Denise [coordinator] and said I was worried about her. I always keep my eyes on her.[136]

Pat recalls hiding one of the women at her house for a week when they were worried that her male partner would hurt her.

There is a tremendous amount of solidarity among these women. Heather sums it up best when she says: "These women are remarkable, Margaret. And I get to learn from them and I get to work beside them. And I am from the same company that they are from ... It just feels so good."[137]

Heroes of Their Own Lives

Despite all the obstacles, with the support of their family, friends and co-workers, these women come to the shop each workday to learn more about carpentry. Given their difficult lives, it is sheer determination that keeps them in this long retraining program. As they negotiate with abusive partners, manage childcare arrangements, deal with angry bill collectors, and struggle with their history of drug and alcohol abuse, these women somehow still arrive at the shop ready to begin a new day of learning. During the three years that I followed these women through different stages of the program, I never stopped marvelling at their will to continue training despite everything. Every time I arrived on site I would look for particular women whose lives were extremely difficult, wondering if they would still be in the program. Sometimes they weren't. Sometimes they had taken a leave of absence or had left the program because they could not manage the rest of their very complicated lives. But more often than not I was astonished to find the women whom I knew lived one step from "the street," or the women who were quietly battling alcohol and drug issues, up on a roof hammering. We would share a warm welcome. I know that it was truly a testament to their determination that they remained in the program. I was a journalist for a number of years before I became an academic, and I have been extremely fortunate to meet some very talented and fascinating people in all walks of life. However, without a doubt, these women are the most heroic people I have ever met.

These women have looked deep into their souls and found an inner strength. Evelyn describes how this experience has empowered her: "I don't know how to say this but I feel so good about myself here [in the program]. I know that I can do things around my house and I don't have to depend on anybody ... I know now that I don't need alcohol to make my life better."[138] Heather explains that her confidence has come from the co-instructors and the other women: "I'm not used to people believing in me. It's the greatest gift I ever received ... I've always been a believer in myself but this program made it strong. This healed me. The program went way beyond giving me a career."[139]

Some of the women are tremendously proud of what they have accomplished, and so they should be. Zena recounts her pride at getting off welfare: "We were in a taxi and the driver said, 'Oh, everybody's got their welfare cheques. That's why you're all taking taxis.' And I said, 'No, we're not on welfare. We're regular people now. I got a job.' And he shut right up ... Now when I take a taxi or get on the bus I keep my head up because I have a job."[140] Sheila had a similar experience: "I feel like somebody now ... and I don't have to hang my head."[141] She is particularly proud of her dry-walling skills. Everyone acknowledges that she's the best dry waller in the Co-op. Sometimes she grumbles because she is given so much dry walling to do, but somehow she juggles her five children and other responsibilities and comes in on weekends to get the work done. Ginny explains how satisfying she finds carpentry: "Carpentry is like our signature. Like the other day we made those computer desks and afterwards I looked at them and said, 'I'm proud of that' and the other girls agreed ... We can bring our kids here and show them what we did. These desks are our signatures."[142]

The Women's Work Training Program has enabled some women to set necessary boundaries between themselves and others. Shirley explains that it has taught her how to say no: "My sisters and brothers used to ask me for money and I never had much to give. I quit giving money since I'm in the program. I learned how to say no. I realized that my boys, my family, are more important than my sisters and brothers."[143] While some have set boundaries with family members, others have learned to set limits with their children. One mother credits the program for giving her the confidence to move her eldest child to a group home for a period when he was being extremely difficult and would not obey her.[144]

One woman claims that her upcoming marriage is a result of the retraining program. She was single when she entered the program and expected she would remain so:

> I used to keep my feelings to myself, not talk about them. But through life skills and the confidence I've built from this program, I can now say how I feel ... If I am mad at him [her fiancé] or if I'm feeling upset, I now talk to him about it and we get it sorted out and it doesn't build up ... This program has given me the confidence [to] marry him and know that we will be able to work everything out in the future.[145]

Pat is surprised to find that she can speak in front of a crowd of people, and she attributes this ability to her experience in the program. "I now have confidence and self-esteem – it makes a big difference. Before I started this program there would be no way I would speak in front of two or three people, but now I've talked to fifty people or more. I've spoken at national conferences. I've been interviewed by the media," she laughs as she recalls these triumphs.[146]

Even the time spent at SIAST has given the women more confidence. As Pat explains, "For most apprentices they just watch a lot and do the 'joe-jobs.' But we get to do everything. That showed when we went to school ... We already had framed walls and we'd hung boards and we'd hung windows and doors. That's why we did so well at school – we'd already done those things."[147] Pat proudly displays her certificates for Level 2 and Level 3 on her wall in her dining room. "The final [journey] ticket is a bigger certificate," she says, eyeing a place reserved on the wall.[148]

As coordinators of the program, Denise and Valerie have watched the women's progress day by day. The victories may be slow but they are very sweet. Denise recalls many of them:

> One woman was completely petrified of any kind of power tool that made any kind of noise, and I stood beside her and literally held her hand while I showed her how to use the chop saw. And in the summer, I watched her show somebody else how to use that particular piece of equipment ... That sharing of knowledge – that is success to me. Then there's Sheila, who hadn't finished public school, and while doing this program and raising her kids she goes to night school and gets her Grade 10. She did it all on her own. She didn't even ask me for a phone number – that's success too ... And then Sherry wants to have a deck, and she asks me if I can help her build [it]. Things get busy and we never set a date, and then she comes in one Monday and just says, "Yep, I built the deck this weekend. Looks nice." It's all success ... We tend to measure success by money and jobs, but there are so many more ways to measure it that are absolutely important.[149]

Valerie says that the women are surprised to find both themselves and their children much happier:

> They didn't know that would happen. They thought their kids were going to suffer because they had to be away all the time. But when they are happier with what they are doing, this rubs off on the family ... If I can only teach everybody who goes through these doors that they can control their own lives, that is enough ... That was a turning point in my own life when I realized that ... What we're really teaching them is that they can control their own lives, and we are trying to give them the tools so they can do that. Learning carpentry is just a means to an end.[150]

It is so clear when you speak with the women, when you watch them at work, that there is much more at stake than learning carpentry skills. The Women's Work Training Program provides women with skills for life, not just for carpentry.

4

From Blueprint to Reality: Challenges at the Job Site

The blueprints have long ago been drawn. And now the hammers are loudly tapping, the drill is buzzing, and women are fully absorbed in the construction project at hand. But even with the best blueprint and most enthusiastic, dedicated workers, there are bound to be challenges at the job site. It is through these challenges that new lessons are learned, and these challenges are the focus of this chapter. Each of them is significant in its own right. An analysis of these challenges does not imply that the Women's Work Training Program was a failure; rather, it assesses where the difficulties lay within the everyday details of the program. It is through an examination of such challenges that new lessons can be learned and even better training programs can be established.

There are five significant challenges to the success of this program. Each of them is present week after week, month after month; none of them is easily resolved. But any retraining program designed for low-income, mixed-race women can learn from the experiences of the Women's Work Training Program's participants and their instructors. The five challenges are: racism, addiction, the Co-op's viability, staff, and funding.

Racism

It is impossible to overstate the important role that racism plays in the daily operation of this retraining program. The program, its instructors, and participants are a product of a profoundly racist society that has a murderous history with regard to its treatment of Aboriginal peoples. Colonization is not a thing of the past, preserved in memories, museums and textbooks; rather, there is active colonization occurring right now.[1] And because of the higher proportion of Natives in Canada's West, this colonization is particularly visible in Regina.

The everyday racism that Native peoples in Canada experience takes several forms. One is overt racism, which most of us can detect, and which has both an ideological and a material manifestation. Racism is the belief that other ethnic groups are inferior to one's own. Certainly, it is widely accepted in Canada that the white race is the superior race. This belief serves to legitimize overt racist practices and helps non-Natives to live comfortably in their homes even while they know that many Native men, women, and children do not have clean water, good food, adequate housing, or opportunities for secure, well-paid employment. We have watched and remained silent when our state's legal system has minimized the rapes and murders of Native peoples and has imprisoned Natives at one of the highest rates in the world.[2] We ignore the fact that the Native pockets in our inner cities are the most heavily policed neighbourhoods in the country. There is an embarrassing record of police abuse and brutality towards Native peoples. We have also condoned state policies that forced Native peoples off their land and imprisoned them in reserves, effectively establishing an apartheid system. Canada's current welfare, unemployment, and small business policies are, at best, insensitive to the needs of Native peoples.

As well as overt racism, Native men and women must confront the much more subtle, indirect forms of everyday racism. These can include the subtle assumption that white ways of knowing and being in the world are superior to theirs. If other ethnic minorities suggest different ways of knowing and being in the world, whites can choose whether or not to acknowledge this cultural difference. And even when white people acknowledge cultural differences, they can still assume cultural superiority. White people wear their whiteness as a cloak from within which they need only address discrimination should they choose to do so. This "normative whiteness" can take several forms. It can devalue Native experience; it can promote a deeply ingrained sense of white superiority; it can anthropologize Native culture by making it an exotic artifact that does not challenge white cultural attitudes in any profound way. It is the group nature of this type of racism that makes it so difficult to confront and challenge. The fact that most of the dominant racial group accepts white ways of being in the world as superior turns racist incidents, no matter how common, into a personal, individual problem. *You*, the person who has experienced racism, become the problem because you have created division where white people see none. Such subtle but overwhelmingly powerful racism can force Native men and women to assimilate in order to survive. Native peoples have learned that it is best to think, speak, and act "white" or risk being ignored, ridiculed, or degraded. This form of racism can render whites indifferent to the presence of discrimination. And when all else fails, and the issue of racism insists upon being acknowledged, whites can simply insist that others' experiences of racism are exaggerated or invented.[3]

This subtle racism is further disguised in a country such as Canada, where tolerance is one of our favourite national myths. When white Canadians believe there is no racism, it is extremely difficult for ethnic minorities and

Native peoples to assert otherwise. When tolerance is assumed to exist "it is much more difficult for minority groups to challenge remaining inequalities, to take unified action and to gain credibility and support amongst the white dominant group."[4] As a result, Native peoples can be accused of being oversensitive and exaggerating the situation when they attempt to address the racist nature of everyday Canadian society.

In Regina, both the overt and the more subtle forms of racism play themselves out daily. In many ways, Regina is the heartbeat of white-Native relations in Canada. Regina has the highest Native population of all Canadian cities, with Natives representing 8 percent of the 200,000 Reginites. Its Native population is also the youngest in all of Canada – 40 percent of its Native population are fifteen years old or younger.[5] Even the name of the city speaks to white-Native issues. The Cree name Oskuna-Kasus-Teki, or "Pile of Bones," was changed to Regina (after the Queen of England) in order to more firmly solidify Anglo-Saxon culture.[6]

Regina is the site of a coercive colonial project with a long, bloody history – one that continues to play itself out on the city's streets. By the second half of the nineteenth century, the Canadian government had confined the majority of Native peoples to reserves, establishing Regina as a primarily white city surrounded by reserves. This demarcation of racialized space was never secure and often required intense policing to shore it up at the borders. In the 1950s, Native peoples were forbidden to live in, or even pass through, western Canadian cities such as Regina without a "pass." The federal government had reduced its housing funding on reserves, and Native men and women migrated to western Canadian cities looking for shelter and jobs. The whites were disturbed by this trend, so the federal government established a system that made it illegal for Native peoples to leave the reserve without obtaining a pass from the (white) Indian agent or agricultural agent. Native women were particularly suspect and were assumed to be prostitutes if they were found in the cities. Such apartheid policies separated whites from Natives and guaranteed the former "safety" from the latter. This also helped to turn the city into a violently racist space where whites could feel free to abuse and assault Natives who were found treading on "sacred" white ground.[7]

Regina is still marked by its colonial heritage. A mere drive through the city will reveal quite starkly that Regina is a city of divisions – that the majority of the Native urban population live in the industrial and downtown core, while the middle-class whites generally live in the various tree-lined suburbs.[8] Native peoples who come to the city looking for work and housing often find themselves limited to residing and socializing in the downtown core and the industrial zone. "The Stroll," located in the heart of the downtown core, is a Native zone, where Native women sell their bodies and Native street people beg for food. It is a place that white women tend to avoid, and where white men come to buy sexual favours. It is a place where violence is routine – where white men have taunted, raped, and even murdered Native women. One thinks of the infamous murder of Pamela George, a Native prostitute who was killed by white middle-class teenage boys from the suburbs on Easter weekend 1995.[9]

Despite its dangerous, brutal nature, Native peoples continue to flock to Regina. Once in the city they are left in "jurisdictional limbo" between the city and the reserve. One study of Regina's Native peoples found that urban Natives are more marginalized than are reserve Natives because the former do not have access to the same social services and support networks as do the latter. The consequences are devastating: only 2.8 percent of Regina's workforce is Native. Poverty in Regina is higher than the national average, with 91 percent of Native households living in poverty.[10] In Canada, Native people are over-policed and are incarcerated at one of the highest rates in the world. Their suicide rate is also one of the highest in the world – four times higher than that of the non-Aboriginal population.[11]

This intense everyday colonizing is distinctly gendered. Native women, who represent the majority (58 percent) of Native migrants to Regina, face enormous discrimination and poverty. While 60 percent of urban Native households live below the poverty line, 80-90 percent of Native single mothers are impoverished.[12] Recently, Native women were being incarcerated at an even higher rate than were Native men. In Pinegrove, a correctional facility in Regina, 80 to 90 percent of the inmates are Native women. Between 1976 and 1992, the number of Native women admitted to correctional centres in Saskatchewan increased by 111 percent.[13]

Native women have a distinct place in Canada's colonial history. They were initially considered helpful to the white settler and there were many common-law arrangements between white men and Native women. As settlements prospered and white women immigrated to the West, Native women's role was devalued. This is when the image of the dirty and immoral "squaw" became prominent. This negative stereotype helped justify confining Native women to reserves and harassing, assaulting, and even murdering the women who came to the city. As Pamela George's murder makes abundantly clear, Native women are never safe in Regina: harassment and discrimination are a part of the air they breathe.

It is extremely difficult for Native women to raise issues of racism. Anti-racist scholar Philomena Essed has demonstrated that non-whites go to great lengths *not* to name racism. Given the great extent to which whites deny racism and even counter-attack those who relate racist experiences, it is hardly surprisingly that non-whites are so reticent to raise the issue.[14] This is often the case amongst the Native women in the program. The issue of racism came up during each of the four times I went to Regina to interview the women. And yet, the Native women are hesitant to say that they, personally, have experienced racism. Rather, they assert that other Native women have experienced racism, and that they have heard of racist incidents, although they have not witnessed any. Generally, the Native women believe that racism occurs on a regular basis in the program, but they are hesitant to name the particular incidents that would prove this.

There are three particular forms of racism that occur regularly in the Women's Work Training Program: intolerance of cultural differences, exclusion, and a lack of Native role models. On their own, many incidents of discrimination appear minor, and most of the forms this discrimination takes occur regularly in our workplaces. However, their common occurrence does not minimize their significance. As anti-racist scholars argue, the cumulative effect of facing this overt and subtle discrimination day after day deeply affects a person's ability to work with and trust those from the dominant race. And as if this were not enough, these same women must close the doors of the retraining shop at the end of the day only to step into a city steeped in a bloody colonial heritage.

Given the epidemic nature of racism in Canadian society generally and Regina specifically, it is hardly surprising that Native women experience discrimination in this retraining program. However, what has surprised the coordinators is the intensity of the problem. Part of this may be due to the fact that Native women are the overwhelming majority of program participants. Initially, the coordinators expected that the participants would be approximately two-thirds white and one-third Native, corresponding to the racial distribution of Regina's population. Instead, the reverse is true: approximately two-thirds of the participants are Native (status Indian and Métis). Where the first intake of women participants was approximately half white and half Native, the second intake was entirely Native and the third intake was more than half Native. This may be because the retraining program is located in the industrial core, where most of the Native population in Regina resides. But it is also due to word of mouth, with Native women encouraging their sisters, cousins, and friends to join the program.[15] Because the majority of participants are Native, the issues of racism are very visible.

Intolerance of Cultural Differences

A number of incidents that occurred during the Women Work Training Program indicated that participants and instructors have problems with cultural differences based on race. While there are misunderstandings between Status Indian and Métis women, the vast majority of the difficulties occur between Natives and whites. It is not uncommon for white people to want cultural differences confined to "ethnic" days so that their white-as-norm way of proceeding in the everyday world need not be interrupted. And yet, it is clear from the everyday events in this retraining program that there are cultural differences in modes of communication, family responsibilities, and leadership styles.

Cultural differences in modes of communication add to misunderstandings within the program. These differences are apparent in both life-skills sessions and worksite situations. Generally, life-skills education has been criticized for its generic approach to developing communication and problem-solving skills. As Shauna Butterwick, an expert in adult education, explains, "These skills and the individualistic orientation ... reflect a middle-class and Western orientation." This focus on individual needs and interests is, at times, in conflict with Native values, which hold that people should strive for harmony and balance within the family rather than for individual gains. There is also a confessional aspect of life skills, and this can be difficult for those who are marginalized. Women who have already been "othered" by society in general are asked to expose their private lives, making them increasingly aware of how they do not fit the middle-class Western model.[16] Certainly, the Native women in the program speak forcefully against the life-skills component. "I am not used to this life skills," one Native participant explains. "It makes me very uncomfortable to talk about my family life, my difficult past experiences, in front of all those eyes."[17] When a Native female staff member conducted the life-skills component of this retraining program, participants were more comfortable. The coordinators would have continued to hire Native women in this role had they been available. Despite the cultural differences, which were exaggerated in life-skills sessions, all of the Native women who expressed their dislike for these sessions also insisted that they were vital to the success of the program.[18]

The job site is another area in which misunderstanding can occur due to different cultural modes of communication. At the job site, white women speak of their frustration and ask questions if they are confused; Native women do not. Denise, one of the coordinators, explains: "You never know whether they [the Native women] understand what you are trying to teach them or not. They don't speak up when they do not understand."[19] The difficulty of Native women's silence is exaggerated by the nature of cooperative work. Implicit in the nature of group work is the understanding that women will speak up about their strengths and skills, and talk about any difficulties with the job at hand. This is extremely difficult for some of the Native women, and their reluctance to speak out in the group is often perceived by the white women as apathy rather than as cultural difference.

There is also the fact that white women do not understand the Native women's non-verbal form of communication. Often the Native women do not make eye contact when an instructor or foreperson is relaying information. Sometimes the white women misinterpret this as insolence, as a refusal to show respect to the white women in charge. However, Native women believe it is a sign of respect and deference to lower one's eyes when addressing a teacher or leader.

The coordinators of the Women's Work Training Program insist that women within the program take leadership roles, that they be role models to other women, and that they advocate publicly for the program. This is extremely difficult for many Native women and leads to frustration and misunderstanding. For instance, at one point, a Toronto television journalist came to interview the Native women in the program. "Denise tried to talk to us about a week ahead of time to say he was coming out, and we were kind of shy at the moment, saying, like, 'We won't talk to him' and all that. But when the time came, we were going to talk to him if he came out," explains Charlene, one of the Native women in the program. "Denise never brought him out [to the worksite]. We never got to do the interview." Charlene was clearly upset by this experience but she also understood that Denise was equally frustrated.[20] All in all, it was an example of white and Native women not understanding each other, of white women not giving the Native women enough time and support to do something that was culturally unfamiliar to them.

When there are cultural misunderstandings, it is not easy to resolve them. "You can't just shove issues or problems they are experiencing in their faces and expect them to talk about it. They [the Native women] would find that disrespectful and embarrassing," explains Sharon Murray, a white foreperson in the retraining program.[21] In some ways, exposing the problem can create further problems. White people can become defensive, hostile, or simply dismiss the issue. They can also construct the problem so that it appears as though the Native women are creating the difficulties.

Many women in the program believe the solution to any cultural differences is to treat everyone the same. One white woman explains her insensitivity to Native women's issues as follows:

Q: Do you think there are different things that could be done to support Aboriginal women differently through the program?
A: Not really, like, we're all treated the same.
Q: But maybe Aboriginal women coming in are coming in with more difficulties – more alcohol problems maybe, more abusive partner problems.
A: Yes, that's basically right. Like, I've never had that situation before myself, so I don't know how different it is.
...
Q: Well, do you have any ideas how the program could be more helpful around these issues?
A: I guess they just have to help themselves first or, you know, get that help they need in order to be here all the time.[22]

This participant clearly takes a liberal approach to cultural differences. She believes that everyone should be treated exactly the same (i.e., according to white customs and rules). She sees no need for supports within the program – supports that might help women from a different cultural background than her own. She refuses to see the colonial context from within which Native women must negotiate their lives. She is not willing to accommodate any difficulties that Native women might encounter. In other words, she sees racism and the legacy of colonialism as a personal problem of Native women – one with which they must struggle on their own.

Given these liberal attitudes it is sometimes difficult for the white women in the program to adequately comprehend cultural differences. When questioned, some participants seem unaware of the heavier family responsibilities that the Native women carry. In addition, a number of the white women appear frustrated when Native women are reluctant to take leadership roles. And, most important, the white women in the program seem to be oblivious to the everyday racism that the Native women experience. These attitudes are even prevalent in the minds of white women who have Native partners and Native children. This suggests that the cultural divide between white and Native women remains deep.

But there is one bond that has brought at least some of the women together. Both white and Métis women believed that poverty bound the women in the program together, regardless of their racial backgrounds. One Métis woman explained, "[During the first year of the program] I don't think anyone even noticed that we were different shades. Everyone got along ... We were all there, single moms who wanted to become carpenters and do something for themselves and their kids, and we all hung onto that, I guess, and supported each other."[23] Although it is true that both white and Native women participants have experienced considerable poverty, it is also true that white women tend to have greater access to resources from extended family members than do Native women. This makes for real differences, even when both groups are single mothers living on welfare.

Exclusion
Exclusion is a more overt form of racism than is insensitivity to cultural differences. Native participants in the Women Work Training Program believe that the coordinators show favouritism to white women participants. One Native woman said, "There's racists here. And the white women – they get the better jobs than the Natives. That's for sure."[24] One white woman disagrees with this assessment.

I don't understand where they are getting their information from because two of the people, I will be very derogatory when I speak, are the teacher's pets. One is Métis and one is full-blown Native ... Both of them are given

really awesome jobs all the time ... and both of them are given more le-
niency than others.[25]

This suggests that Native women and white women have different experiences of exclusion and inclusion.

Seniority compounds the issue of exclusion. In the first intake group, the
women who have remained in the program are all white except for one,
who is Métis. In the second and third intake groups, the women who have
remained are mainly Native. Because of seniority, it is the white women in
the first group who have better wages and jobs, and who have more responsible positions. They are the ones who are selected as forewomen at job
sites. It was Pat, the Métis woman from the first intake group, who pointed
out this problem to me: "I think Denise needs to stand back and look at this
issue. She probably doesn't mean it to look this way, but it's how it looks
from the outside. But I don't think that was her intention."[26] In this instance, Pat is aware of the subtle nature of racism – that regulations such as
seniority, which are not motivated by racist assumptions, can nevertheless
have racist implications.

There is a spatial dimension to racism. It was very apparent to me during
my initial interviews with the women that the white women and the Native women inhabit different spaces within the program. The Native women
tend to congregate outside of the shop building, where they share cigarettes
as they joke with one another. The white women tend to go inside the shop
and upstairs to the office, where Denise, the coordinator, can usually be
found. Consequently, the white women have more informal chats with
Denise than do the Native women and so tend to feel more at ease with her.
Also, the white women, by virtue of spending time in the office, are more
aware of what decisions are being made and what jobs are coming up. While
there is no policy about who can and who cannot spend time in the office,
it was clearly established early on in the program that this was a white
space. The Native women are very aware of this spatial difference. In fact,
one Native woman, known for being silent, speaks passionately about this
issue: "That bugs me that they're [the white women] upstairs and we're
down here. And Denise tells them everything upstairs and we don't know
anything down here."[27]

This spatial issue intensified when certain women were given keys to the
shop. The rule was that all women who owned vehicles were given keys
because they often chauffeured others to and from the shop. Because the
white women tended to have more economic resources and more familial
supports than did the Native women, it happened that only white women
had vehicles that regularly came to the shop. As a result, only white women
had keys to the shop. Many Native women complained about this issue and

Women **Do** Regret Abortion

Silent
NO MORE
A w a r e n e s s

The National
Silent
a m p a i g n

www.silentnomorea

Silent
NO MORE

The National Silent No More Awareness Campaign is an effort to make the public aware of the devastation abortion brings to women, men, and their families. The emotional and physical pain of abortion will no longer be shrouded in secrecy and silence, but rather exposed and healed. This effort is a key to making abor-tion unthinkable, and per-suading society that women deserve better than abortion.

The campaign has three main goals:

1. Make the public aware that abortion is harmful emotionally, physically and spiritually to women and others;

2. Reach out to women who are hurting from an abortion, let them know help is available;

3. Invite women to join us in speaking the truth about abor-tion's negative consequences.

The Campaign is a non-denom-inational Christian ffort and it has no political or al agenda.

lentnomoreawareness.org

House '76, Inc. no. 434 SN
?040 www.hh76.com

considered it a racist rule.[28] After weeks of hearing about Native women feeling excluded, I raised this issue with the coordinators. They were surprised to realize that their shop-key rule had racist implications and immediately created a rule that all members of the Co-op board of directors should have a key. This led to one Métis woman having a key. This incident exemplifies how easily unintended exclusions can build on a powerful colonial history of exclusion to create a racially charged environment.

Racist incidents are only exacerbated by the white women's need to defend themselves against charges of racism. During discussions about racism, they were often quick to defend their white peers and the white coordinators. As one white woman says,

> Denise and Val set up this program for minorities and you have ... got to have some wild huge heart in order to be able to do that ... And how fucking dare you do that to these two beautiful women who created this thing for people like us? I just get so mad. How dare you scream and point a finger racist – for the very person that gave you this opportunity?[29]

This is a very common reaction among whites generally. When faced with questions about racism, one of their first reactions is to deny it and then to defend others who are accused of it. In fact, this woman is launching a counter-attack, arguing that it is absolutely unacceptable for anyone to have any problems with either the coordinators of the program or the program itself. Both are blameless. One white woman's denial of racism is quite aptly stated in her comments: "I just don't get it and *I don't want to get it* [my emphasis]. I don't want to be a part of it and I just think the whole thing is ugly."[30] Racism, if faced, would disturb in-group solidarity. It would ruin the good atmosphere that white people experience.[31] It is far easier for whites, like this woman, to simply dismiss such charges rather than to acknowledge that both they and their friends are racist in their attitudes and behaviours.

Internalized racism also plays a role within the Women's Work Training Program. This can take many forms, from the subtlest misunderstanding of cultural differences to miscommunication and spiteful comments about Native cultural ways. These misunderstandings and frustrations occur between urban Native and reserve Native women, Métis and Status women, and Native women from similar cultural backgrounds.

Métis women often feel a tug between two worlds and a sense that they belong in neither. Although they have a strong and distinct cultural heritage in western Canada, they have also experienced subtle and overt exclusion from both white and Native society. The Métis women in the program appear to move more easily between white and Native worlds, tending to be well respected by both white and Native women. And yet the Métis women feel caught between two cultures. They worry about how much time they are seen socializing with the white women or the Native women in the group.[32]

Some Métis women attempt to distance themselves from the Native women during interviews about racism. For instance, one Métis woman explained her frustration with cultural differences as follows:

> My husband's Native but he's grown up kind of in a white society so he knows what the meaning of time is and, no offence to the Indian women, but it just drives me nuts because they don't have a sense of time ... They run on "Indian time" and that bugs me, and then they kind of crap on the person who's trying to keep everything intact ... I was brought up in a white world, where if you start work at 9:00, you be there at 9:00.[33]

This woman is clearly asserting her whiteness in relation to other Native women in the program. She is also aware that she is making a racist comment as she prefaces it by saying that she does not mean to offend Native women.

Urban Native women, along with white women, are not particularly tolerant of Native women who have spent the majority of their formative years on a reserve. It is the reserve Native women who have most difficulty adapting to the white ways of negotiating the world. Shelley, an urban Native woman, appears more comfortable with the Métis and even with the white women in the program than she does with the reserve Native women. Her two best buddies are Diane, a Métis woman, and Michelle, a white woman. She explains the cultural differences between urban and reserve Native women:

> I'm an 'apple,' really. I look Aboriginal [red] on the outside, but on the inside, I'm white. A lot of them [the Native women] were brought up on the reserve, and I was brought up in the city, more or less traditionally white. And yes I can fit into their [the Native women's] way of thinking, but I also have the skills to get along with the white people ... They [the Native women] are sort of intimidated by me because I can drop in to their group and then the next minute I can be off laughing with Diane and Michelle ... I can shift my gears.[34]

Some urban Native women expressed prejudice against reserve life. These women have a way of demeaning reserve Native women's experiences while at the same time presenting themselves as superior because of their ability to negotiate the white world. For instance, one status woman described her experience of reserve life as follows:

I never grew up on a reserve. I'm a city girl. I did try reserve life and ... it's boring. Go to a farm and I will give you $92 to live on every two weeks. Let someone on payday weekend come and destroy your house, shoot it up, rip your screens off, whatever. And you do that for years and years and see how well you do ... And everybody knows your business ... And it's a big orgy. Really, honest to God, I swear, these people might be married, you know, for however long, and one big party happens, they're not married any more, and so and so has a new wife. Next month, flavour of the month, he's got another new wife, she's got kids and it's a big orgy. And they lack education, too. How many Aboriginal women on the reserve graduated from Grade 10? No, they get to Grade 7 and then they can have babies.[35]

Implicit in this description of reserve life is the belief that urban Native women have a better life and are, in fact, better people than are reserve Native women. "I lived on the reserve for fifteen months and I'll never do it again while I'm young. I'll never raise my children there," this woman says adamantly. There is an insinuation that she "saw the light" and, after fifteen months, left the reserve for the city. She argues that she came from brutal, abusive poverty but that she has triumphed over it. "My mom and dad were alcoholics when we were growing up. Dad would be at the bar all Friday and mom would join him Friday night and we wouldn't see them 'til Sunday night. We'd stay at Grandma's or by ourselves," she recalls. "But I'm raising my kids differently. Alcohol is an individual problem. You just have to be determined to make change."[36] This same woman believes that there is nothing the Women's Work Training Program can do for women suffering alcohol and drug addictions. She endorses the pioneer myth that anyone can make it on their own, just like she has. Ironically, even though her history is similar to that of many of the Native women in the program, she has little compassion or tolerance for those who have not adopted white ways.

Intolerance comes not only from inside the program: customers also often display racist attitudes. There were two instances in which Native women were accused of stealing while on the worksite. In one case, a white couple hired the Co-op to build them a fence around their yard in a very white suburb of Regina. The crew for the job was composed entirely of Native women. A watch went missing, and it was assumed that one of the Native women had stolen it. In the end, the watch was discovered under a towel in the bathroom.[37] This quick assumption that a misplaced object had been stolen by one of the Native women speaks to the long colonial history of Regina. On another job site, the participants found a sign posted when they returned from lunch. It read: "Get out squaw." Denise was shocked by this incident. "The Native women shrugged their shoulders and said they have experiences like this all the time and said it was normal! In the meantime I was angry and wondered why they weren't angry. We could do nothing except keep on plugging away and not be scared off the site," recalls Denise.[38] Where possible, the retraining program attempts to avoid these problems by assessing the attitudes of the potential customer during the first meeting, a difficult challenge. If the customer displays racist attitudes, the job is turned down.[39]

Incidences of racism also occur while the women are off duty. Sharon Murray has witnessed one such incident.

> We went for a drink after work – my [all-Native] crew and I. Two of the women went to the corner store for some cigs. One came out and got me and said that the shop owner was accusing the other woman of stealing. I walked in and said, "Look, these women work for me and I can vouch for them." He [the shop owner] immediately apologized and said he'd made a mistake. But what if I hadn't have been there? I was the white boss and so the shop owner stopped harassing the women.

In this case, the woman who was accused of stealing was the most senior Native woman in the program, respected by everyone.[40]

Such incidents of exclusion and accusation are everyday experiences for Native women in racially charged Regina. It is perhaps not entirely surprising that they also occur within the retraining program. What is disturbing is the degree to which white women either play a role in this exclusion or are insensitive to the degree to which Native women are affected by it in all aspects of their lives, including the program. This speaks to the need for more anti-racist education. As Valerie reflects, "We've only done one racism workshop – for the most part we've concentrated on cultural awareness – on informing the women about cultural programs such as pow-wows, teepee raisings, and sweat lodges."[41] Clearly, the cultural education integrated into this retraining program does not get at the heart of anti-racist behaviour and attitudes.

Lack of Native Role Models

Another form of discrimination that visible minorities face involves the lack of role models, which sends a subtle message that visible minorities are only acceptable in subordinate roles. This issue is also a factor in the Women's Work Training Program. From the beginning of the program, the coordinators hoped to hire Native women in leadership roles. Because they could not find any Native women with journeyed carpentry papers, it was impossible to provide Native role models. They were delighted to hire one Native staff member to do life skills. Valerie described her as "a non-status Indian woman with cultural pride oozing from every pore of her body. No better role model could be found." But this was a part-time, short-term contract. After one term, this woman went on to seek full-time, secure employment – something that this program could not offer her. Still, even after her departure, she remained a supporter, friend, and occasional consultant to the program.[42]

The significance of the lack of Native staff became increasingly apparent later on in the program. As Native participants increasingly out-numbered white participants, the lack of Native role models became a growing problem. As Valerie states, "In retrospect, a perfect fit would have been to include an elder on staff or an Aboriginal life skills facilitator with a close connection to an elder."[43] Sharon, the only female foreperson for the program, is also aware that the leaders are all white: "This was my first time supervising and it was a real learning experience because I hadn't been around their lifestyles that close before and a lot of them had a lot of problems ... When they introduced me to their families they'd say 'This is our crew – we have six Native girls and a little redheaded white boss.' It was quite funny."[44] Sharon said that this program had opened her eyes to racism. "No matter how good we are as instructors – we are still white. We can listen, we can be understanding. But the fact is that we are not Native and so we just don't totally understand," explains Sharon.

> I got a picture of my grandbaby. I've never ever told anybody because I didn't think it was an issue that my daughter-in-law is Native, and I showed them a picture of my grandson and he's as Native as can be ... They looked at me and asked if my son is Native, and I said, "No, my daughter-in-law is Native." And it just kind of changed their whole attitude about things.[45]

Because of Sharon's attempts to bridge the cultural divide she has been invited to many of the Native women's homes and to powwows and sweat lodges.

Sharon says she has learned a lot about racist misunderstandings through this program.

> This was my first time as a boss and I had a whole Native crew. So when I first started working here they would come strolling in about 8:20, grab a cup of coffee, [and] sit in the smoke room. And work is supposed to start at 8:00 ... So after a week, I wait for everybody to crawl in and I said, "coffee's in the coffee room, grab your smokes, we're having a meeting." And I just let them have it – saying starting time is 8:00 and if they come late they must be prepared to stay late ... I said I am not here to make friends, I am here to be your boss. And I didn't realize how much that would hurt them ... Emily [one Native woman] took it to heart and said, "You just told us you

don't want to be our friend, that you're too good for us" ... And so I had to call another meeting, and I said, "What I'm trying to say here is we've got a job to do, and I'm sorry I phrased it like that."[46]

Sharon is very concerned about creating a safe place for the Native women. "We are different from one another and we need to have some understanding within our crew. The [Native] women need to feel safe. If they can't be safe here where else can they be safe?" she says. She is well aware of the racist attitudes of some of the white women in the program. There are some white women whom she will not pair up with Native women because she knows the former are intolerant of the latter.

Experts in non-traditional training for women have only begun to address the issue of race and how it affects retraining. Patti Schom-Moffatt and Marcia Braundy found in their national study of non-traditional training programs that Native women have extra barriers to their advancement in non-traditional training and employment. They discovered that many of the Native women participants had previously been on welfare or unemployed: "Native women ... made up the majority of the women [interviewed] in the category of not being able to find their way out of the pattern of pregnancy and childbirth." These two experts assert that there has not been enough attention to the particular Native issues that emerge in non-traditional retraining programs.[47]

As the Women's Work Training Program progressed, the Native women (both status Indian and Métis) became role models in their own right. By 1999, the majority of the board of directors, the most senior women in the Co-op, were Native women. Four of the six on the board of directors were Aboriginal (three status and one Métis).[48] At one point, the program participants helped to put together an educational package on Native issues for the Saskatchewan public school system, kindergarten to Grade 12, called "Choosing the Beat of Her Own Drum." While assembling the packages, the women discussed their content and how this could benefit young Native girls. To launch the curriculum packages, the program participants set up display tables. They worked in groups to study the content of the material and then developed the display that they presented to teachers, students, and school administrators. After this public showing, one Native woman in the program said, "I have never been proud to be an Indian before and now I'm so full. I will never be ashamed again."[49]

It is the hope of the coordinators that the training program will solve the problem of role models. As more and more Native women are trained and become qualified carpenters, there will be Native role models as forewomen, instructors, and even coordinators of this particular program. Eventually, the coordinators hope that it will be the women themselves, including many Native women, who will run the Co-op and the program.

Addiction

From the beginning of the program, addiction issues have clearly been a challenge. During their application interview, women are asked whether they are alcohol- or drug-dependent. "I ask them where they are on the clean-and-sober scale," explains Denise. "They seem shocked by my question, but I think it helps them answer honestly."[50] In fact, many of the women recalled this questioning quite vividly when I asked them about addiction issues in the program. Despite the screening, numerous problems with addiction surface. Some women do not show up for work and do not call in to report their absence when they are hungover from a drinking binge. Some women come to work with severe hangovers and have to be sent home. Others disrupt the work atmosphere by being belligerent, uncooperative, or extremely moody. And many experience pressure from family and friends to drink during weeknights. The majority of the women in the program have dealt with alcohol and/or drug addiction issues at some point in their lives.[51] They know they are vulnerable in this regard. And they also know that this will severely impair their ability to continue in the retraining program.

In an effort to deal with the looming cloud of drug and alcohol addiction, the coordinators initially established a fairly simple addiction policy: "Alcohol is an absolute 'No-No' on a job site. This includes the after-effects of its use." This initial policy indicates an awareness of how alcohol, street drugs, and prescription drugs can affect a worker's performance. Anyone taking prescription drugs must inform the coordinators. Everyone is told that they are responsible for the enforcement of the policy. What is interesting to note is that a person found with an addiction problem will not be automatically removed from the program. To begin with, this person will be referred to a rehabilitation agency, and she will generally be permitted back into the program once she has resolved her addiction problem (see Appendix E, "Women's Work Training Drug and Alcohol Use Policy"). This is a firm, yet supportive, method for dealing with addiction.

As women moved into the Co-op segment of the program and became members of their own construction company, it became clear that a new policy needed to be developed. In the fall of 1997, coordinators, staff, and Co-op members decided to collectively revise the addiction policy. The new policy is more developed and covers the responsibilities not only of the offending Co-op member but also of the other members. Co-op members have the right to refuse to work with someone whom they feel is under the influence of drugs and alcohol. If a woman is suspected of being under the influence, she will be asked to go home without pay for that day. The offender will be granted time off to resolve the problem. If a third incident occurs within six months, the Co-op business manager will request that the offender enrol in a rehabilitation program. Once the program is completed, the woman will be reinstated in the retraining program, and from there she can reapply for membership in the Co-op. Only if a participant refuses to cooperate will she be refused re-entry into the Co-op and dismissed from the program altogether (see Appendix E).[52] Denise claims that she has never had to fire a woman because of addiction problems: "When we put the situation to their face, we make them make a choice. They almost always own up to the problem."[53]

Because the retraining program includes the Regina Women's Construction Co-operative, the women who own the Co-op must police each other's addiction behaviour. In a few cases, Co-op women have had to confront a woman in the program and force her to acknowledge her addiction problem and its effect on the program. In more than one case, the Co-op has refused a woman's membership application because of an addiction problem. In each case, the woman has been asked to take at least six weeks off before reapplying to the Co-op for membership. The reapplication includes a letter of proof of rehabilitation and a re-evaluation of the woman's performance on the job.[54]

It is a challenge to determine how to deal with addiction problems. A carpentry retraining program in Victoria for homeless women with histories of substance abuse found this to be very difficult. It established a zero-tolerance policy, which meant that a woman would be banned from the program if she was found to have an addiction problem. One woman in the Victoria program had a drug addiction problem, and when she returned to drugs she did not tell the program coordinators because she loved the program and did not want to resign. She died of an overdose during the program, and the shelter that the women built – the Sandy Merriman House – was named in her memory.[55] Valerie and Denise, as coordinators of the Regina Women's Work Training Program, were well aware of the challenges associated with the Victoria program. Along with the participants, they carefully developed an addiction policy that acknowledged the need for safety on the job but which simultaneously attempted to meet the long-term needs of the women.

Some women have left the program because of their inability to manage their addictions. One woman was addicted to Tylenol and Codeine, and displayed volatile moods while on the job site. Denise recalls the incident:

> The women told me that they didn't want to work with her. She was very unpredictable. One moment she'd be sweet as pie and the next she would swear at the instructor ... And so we confronted her and she denied her addiction. We told her to take two days off work. She then returned and came up to the office and 'fessed up that she did have an addiction but she didn't think it was serious because it wasn't prescription drugs. She promised

she would get off of them and she also promised that she wouldn't use power tools for the rest of the course ... Then one day she didn't show up – not the next or the next. So I called her in and then myself and two Co-op board members read her the letter saying she had a drug problem and she needed to go for rehab ... And she walked out. She was a very, very, very angry woman but everyone else was relieved. So she is out in the world somewhere. She actually wrote us a letter and she said that we should have a drug testing because she thought that other women were doing the same thing. But in the end she thanked us and she felt that she learned a lot ... She is still very angry though.[56]

Another woman, who was very well liked in the Co-op, was found to have alcohol addiction problems. Her sister, a Co-op board member, found the situation very uncomfortable. She recalls this as a difficult time, but she believes the Co-op made the right decision in encouraging her sister to seek rehabilitation: "It was very difficult – to be one of the ones who had to say to my sister, 'You need some help; you need to leave [the Co-op for rehabilitation].'"[57] The woman with the alcohol addiction has never returned to the Co-op, although she is working in construction in another town. Her sister, who remains in the program, still hopes that they will work together in the Co-op again one day.

The Co-op's addiction policy has helped some women control their addiction. And some women say that the life skills workshops on addictions have helped them make positive changes in their personal lives. One woman was addicted to cocaine when she started the retraining program, and she did not tell anyone; instead, she quickly detoxed and did not do cocaine again.[58] Another woman says she was doing drugs and alcohol and smoking oil when she started the program:

I'd done it [drugs and alcohol] for years and it had really affected my memory ... I was determined to stay in the program so I decided to only do the drugs and alcohol on my own time when it wouldn't interfere. But the program really helped me to quit with the drugs. I'm still working on the alcohol, but it's better ... And now my memory is really improving. Like, the chainsaw test – I didn't even study for it and I got 100 percent.[59]

Having to be at work every weekday has helped some women reshape their leisure time so that alcohol and drugs are no longer central. At the same time, others struggle daily to gain control.

The Viability of the Regina Women's Construction Co-operative
While the Co-op offers the women a number of advantages, it has also raised many challenges. It was established in order to provide job security. Once

the women finish the first year of training, they can apply to join the Co-op and be part of a member-owned construction company. The Co-op permits them to have a women-only workspace on a long-term basis, and it also provides them with a guaranteed income and work.[60] While the members were initially very enthusiastic about the Co-op, challenges regarding self-confidence, leadership, commitment, and business viability have threatened its foundation. Each of these issues has resurfaced at various points throughout the retraining program.

The Co-op demands confidence, but many of the women in the program have never felt confident about any aspect of their lives. They are very nervous about boldly stepping out on their own and making decisions about a job site or creating new Co-op policy. Many of the women were anxious about embarking on the retraining program. A number of them had never worked before, and they were worried about leaving their children, and balancing work at home and in the program. Many had left the educational system many years before and had painful memories of failing at school. Most had not participated in a retraining program before, and they were worried about the intensity of the program: whether they could keep up, whether they would be able to remember the things they were taught, whether they could pass from one level of skill to the next. The fact that they were acquiring non-traditional skills only added to their anxiety, as many had been told as girls that carpentry was men's work and that women were not capable of achieving such skills. Added to this stress was the need to run a business. Most of the women's previous work experience had been disempowering. Many had worked at part-time jobs, while others had never engaged in paid work. And none of them had ever been in management positions.

Studies of women's non-traditional retraining programs repeatedly assert that confidence is an essential ingredient when beginning such a program.[61] Because this retraining is non-traditional, women are bound to experience challenges from family, friends, and even themselves regarding their ability to undertake the program. Some experts in the field suggest that women build their self-confidence *before* they enter such a program.[62] Some of the courage needed to enter a male-dominated retraining program is not necessary in this case because the women are able to work in a women-only environment – although they must attend SIAST for seven weeks every year, where they are confronted by a male-dominated learning environment. On the other hand, these women need more confidence than do other women in non-traditional jobs because they actually own and operate the Co-op. These women are not merely female workers in a male-dominated industry; they are the employers to their co-workers, the public relations officers to their customers, and the business managers of their own business. This requires both a multitude of skills and a good dose of confidence.

Developing leadership skills is essential to the Co-op's survival. These include taking initiative, developing good communication, and demonstrating a commitment to the Co-op. The ability to take the initiative is helpful for all women in a male-dominated industry, but it is even more critical when they are also running a construction co-op. These women are not working for a boss; they are in charge of a small business in a competitive environment. However, before their co-op experience, the majority of these women had never taken on a leadership role. "They [the women] are so hesitant," explains Denise. "Some of the women want to hold my hand with one hand and to hammer with the other hand." As business manager of the Co-op, Denise finds it very frustrating when women are afraid to take the initiative: "Sometimes these women will sit on a job site because something was missing. They don't call; they just wait until the supervisor shows up, which may take a couple of hours!"[63] At one point Valerie told the Co-op board of directors that there was money to buy everyone matching T-shirts with the company logo. She asked the board to choose the colour and style and to let her know. Weeks and weeks went by, and the board could not decide. They surveyed all the members to see what colour they wanted; they discussed style, number of T-shirts, and size of lettering. Valerie was exasperated, but she refused to intervene. "*They* needed to make the decision, but it just showed how hesitant they were to do that. They were afraid of getting it wrong when there *was* no wrong. It was just T-shirts," recalls Valerie.[64]

Good communication skills are also a critical component of leadership. However, the women in the Co-op are often hesitant to speak their minds and to clarify matters. Denise recalls the time the board made a new policy on giving advances but forgot to tell her, the business manager. "It was six months before I realized there was a new policy!" she says. She has also been frustrated by the lack of delegation.

> I looked at the board minutes and it said we decided this and we are going to do that but they didn't say who "we" was – so nothing was happening. I went through six months of board meeting minutes and wrote in the margins all my questions. I had sixteen of them and I gave them to the board and said, "You deal with it." I can't run the business if I don't know what they've decided and if decisions are not followed through.[65]

Denise refuses to attend board meetings because she thinks that the women will rely on her too much if she is present: "I stop them from being free thinkers if I'm there ... They need to figure out how to run an effective meeting themselves. I can guide them from the sidelines."[66]

In many ways, the cooperative element of the program is one of its greatest strengths as well as one of its greatest weaknesses. To some extent, the

Co-op shelters the participants from the competitive market, acknowledges their difficult personal lives, permits them some flexibility in work schedules, and provides them with an environment free from sexual harassment. On the other hand, the Co-op demands that these same women, who have demanding personal lives, take on leadership and decision-making roles beyond those that would be required of a junior apprentice in an average construction company. This contradiction is inherent in the very purpose of the Co-op, and it creates tensions and dilemmas that are not easily remedied.

The coordinators have tried a number of initiatives to foster leadership skills in the Co-op members. Heather, one of the Co-op members, was sent to a national cooperative conference, and on returning was encouraged to educate the other members about co-op structure. She is often frustrated that the women are not interested in learning co-op procedures. "This co-op sticks out like a sore thumb. It is run more by Val and Denise than by the members. The women are having trouble understanding what a co-op is. And I'm not sure that Val and Denise are ready to let it go," she explains.[67] Several women have been trained as speakers and role models so that they can appear at schools and career fairs. Some have been trained as assistant shop instructors for women in trades programs. Four women, including Heather, have flown to other provinces for professional development opportunities. Three women have become active board members for other organizations, including two other cooperatives and a women's organization. And one of the women who is a Co-op board member sits on the Saskatchewan Women in Trades and Technology (SaskWITT) board.[68]

In another attempt to empower the Co-op members, Valerie and Denise have organized a local advisory committee, consisting of eight women from the community with solid business backgrounds. This committee meets with Co-op members once a month to offer advice and support. Some of the committee members have been willing to mentor individual Co-op members. The goals of this committee are to reduce the Co-op members' reliance on Valerie and Denise and to help them have more confidence in their own abilities. It has yet to realize these goals fully. Part of the difficulty is scheduling the committee meetings. If they occur after work, many of the women complain that they have other responsibilities and cannot attend; if they occur during work time, the Co-op loses money for lost work time.

Peer evaluations were established to enhance Co-op members' business skills. Denise was tired of all the complaining in the Co-op about who was not pulling their weight and of the expectation that she was supposed to fix these internal problems. "I wanted them to take ownership – to be able to tell their peers when their work wasn't satisfactory – to be part of the solution rather than bitching about the problem," says Denise.[69] Peer evaluations establish the Co-op members as the evaluators of their peers' work performance. These evaluations determine promotions, wage increases, warnings, and dismissals.

Some leadership skills have developed as the Co-op has progressed. After two years, Denise found that the women were beginning to take some initiative in running the Co-op and that the peer evaluations had become effective tools. The board minutes are now understandable and tasks are delegated. And some of the women are enjoying their new roles as leaders. Pat explains how she became a leader in the Co-op. As a member of the board of directors and as someone who is well respected by both the white and Native women, she is a key player in this organization:

> I had to make a tough decision within the Co-op, where I had to put the business interests of the Co-op before family ties. After I did that I got quite a bit more respect from a lot of the women ... A lot of times I've noticed when we have discussions, that no one will say anything and they will all look at me. So a lot of times I start discussions ... And years ago it would have never been me who started a discussion.[70]

But all of the leadership issues have yet to be resolved. An exasperated Denise said, "Yesterday one of the board members called me, actually the president, and said, 'Are we having a board meeting today?' And I said, 'I don't know – look at the minutes. If it says you are going to have a meeting today then you are.'"[71]

Co-op members have been hesitant to take on the commitment that joining a co-op involves. "This," says Valerie, "is the single-most unexpected output ... the members' lack of desire to take over the cooperative operation."[72] Because the Co-op is relatively new, it requires the members' extra time, energy, and commitment. Co-op members need to be educated regarding cooperative structures and procedures and they need to take leadership roles in its everyday functioning. As mothers, most of the women are already juggling home and work and, after a full day's work, have neither the time nor the energy to begin working on Co-op activities. It became clear that the women were concentrating on developing their carpentry skills rather than their commitment to the Co-op. This has been a disappointment to Valerie, in particular, who is strongly committed to the collective principles that provide the foundation of co-ops. "What was surprising was that, after a huge investment of time and energy into developing a supportive, collaborative work environment that would sustain them into their futures, the women wanted to work in a 'status quo' construction setting," explains Valerie.[73] Valerie and Denise expected that some of the women who participated in the retraining program would find that carpentry was not for them, but that they might be interested in Co-op business (such as accounting, job estimating, or customer relations). Several women were interested in developing these Co-op business skills, but some of them left the program due to injuries and other personal difficulties, and the staff did not have the time to teach these skills to those who remained. As a result, the majority of the Co-op business continues to fall on the shoulders of already overworked staff. From time to time the staff attempt to enlist the help of Co-op members, but this remains a struggle.

Another struggle for the Co-op involves the tension between its attempt to balance its business needs with the women's personal needs. "Sometimes I think I'm running a business and am concerned about contracts and deadlines; and other times I'm running a social agency and am worried about the woman who came to work black and blue and the other woman who didn't show up at all," explains Denise.[74] As someone who has operated her own business, she finds it frustrating to juggle these conflicting needs of the Co-op. "It's really a complete contradiction to pay this much attention to individual personal problems and to try to make money at the same time," she says.[75] Ideally the program would benefit from a full-time life-skills instructor who would also have the time to counsel and support individual women. This would relieve the business manager of the non-business aspects of her current job.[76]

As a business manager, Denise finds it difficult to balance what she sees as a contradiction. "Some of the women don't appreciate that the Co-op needs to make money," she says, recalling an incident in which a woman showed up for work without her boots and so was unable to work.

> She came to work and she didn't have her boots on. I said, "I'll drive you home to get your boots," and then she said, oh, she'd lent out her boots. And I flipped. So I gave her this talk and I said, "Look, your boots are like your underwear. You don't lend your panties to someone else, right? So don't you lend your boots out. They're what makes you money."[77]

Denise also finds it difficult to straddle the role of business manager and social worker on the job site. Some of the Co-op women claim Denise is too critical at work. "I come on the job site – I'm only stopping by – and I see what's wrong and I name it. They see this as criticism; they want more positive feedback. So now I have a policy that when I come to a job site I only say good things to the workers and then I discuss any problems with the supervisor," explains Denise.[78]

Some of the Co-op women do not fully appreciate that, in the business world, time is money. Denise is often concerned that the work is accomplished too slowly. "There are several who are just so paralyzed about making a mistake that they work very, very slowly. I try to tell them, 'Make mistakes, that's how you learn' ... But they don't appreciate that if we go over ten hours on this job we lose money for the Co-op. It's that simple," she explains.[79]

During the early days of the Co-op, attendance was a problem. As business manager, Denise found this very challenging: "There were major efforts made to strike a balance between accepting work contracts and being able to provide sufficient reliable workers to get the job done and on time. We were advertising our company as a 'reliable,' one, and there were days when we were short of workers due to personal problems."[80] From time to time, the coordinators have found it challenging to balance the conflicting goals of reliability and flexibility. Despite ongoing financial difficulties, the coordinators have generally put the women first, supporting them through their personal difficulties. Valerie and Denise find "that the more time and money invested in our labour pool, the more productivity and money in the bank ... So much is related to self-esteem issues. Building a house is easy, skill-wise. Believing we can do it is another thing. It is a constant struggle."[81]

Because the Co-op attempts to balance the conflicting needs of a business with that of a social agency, wages suffer. Women, when they entered the Co-op, began at the provincial minimum wage ($5.60/hour), and it was hoped that these wages would increase by $2.00/hour annually as the members were promoted through peer evaluations. Within five years, as the Co-op became increasingly profitable, it was hoped that members would be making $13.60/hour, which would still be below industry standards.[82] However, in its first four years, the Co-op has not proved financially sound enough to meet these wage expectations. Co-op members do receive peer evaluations and promotions, yet, despite these benefits, their wages remain significantly below what they would receive if they worked in the outside construction industry. On the other hand, they receive leniencies, such as days off to care for their sick children or time out to recover from personal problems, which they would never receive in the outside construction industry. Still, given that these women continue to live below the poverty line and have many who depend upon them both economically and emotionally, these low wages are always a source of grievance.

Most of the Co-op members complain bitterly about their low wages. "The money sucks," says Diane. "I've got a sister with seven children. She lives on welfare and gets almost $2,000 a month. We don't make that in a month. In fact ... [one woman in the program] is actually $200 [a month] shy of what she used to make on welfare!"[83] At the time of the interview Diane was paid $6.00/hour and had a take-home pay of about $800 a month. It seems wrong to Diane that she should work so hard for so little. Sherry compares her wages to those being received by others in the industry: "Kevin's friend came over and he's in first year and he's making $11/hour. I make $7.50 and I'm in third year."[84] Sherry used to be on welfare, and she misses its medical benefits because her daughter is asthmatic and requires regular medication: "And we all need to go to the dentist, but we can't afford to. Kevin needs glasses and I've got to finance that." But she still prefers working at the Co-op to being on welfare: "You've got your own life when you're not on welfare. Welfare has rules about everything ... but I miss the benefits."[85] The top wages at the Co-op are $9.75 an hour for the most senior participants. Linda, single with grown children and grandchildren (all of whom live with her), supplements her Co-op wages by working two shifts a week at the local grocery store. She receives $12.50/hour at the Superstore, which is $2.00/hour more than she makes at her "real" job at the Co-op.[86]

Some women left the Co-op because of the low wages. For instance, Rhonda H. left and joined her fiancé on another construction crew and now earns significantly more money. Shelley left the Co-op because, as the single earner in her four-member family, she was falling further and further into debt and needed a solution. She got a job at a casino that pays double what she made at the Co-op.[87] Both of these women miss working at the Co-op with other women and remain friends with many of them. In fact, both remain in contact with me and went to great lengths to be included in interviews after they had left the Co-op. They are adamant that they would go back to the Co-op if the wages were to significantly improve. "If the Co-op paid me $10.65/hour like I make at the casino, I would be back in a flash," says Shelley.[88]

Despite the numerous complaints about low wages, most of the Co-op women remain there. "It's inspiring to be part of the Co-op," explains one member. "The Co-op allows you to see ... that there are jobs [in the field] for women. And you can see other women who have more skills than you at the workplace everyday."[89] Michelle, another Co-op member, says that the Co-op provides important support to women in non-traditional occupations. "I applaud those other girls [sic] who have left and found other jobs. But, you know, most of them got other jobs because they've known a family member or someone. I'm not ready to spread my wings yet. I kind of need the support of the rest of the girls here yet," she says.[90]

It is not surprising that the Co-op has a number of challenges. There was no blueprint to follow when Valerie and Denise designed it, and they have been learning and revising as they go.

Staff

A number of challenges regarding staff issues have emerged as the Women's Work Training Program progresses. As well as the two coordinators, there is a need to hire a life-skills coach and supervisors to oversee the various job sites. These hirings often address issues of sexism, racism, homophobia, and a lack of understanding of the program.

Initially, the coordinators hoped to hire only women in staff positions. They believe that a female staff provides important role models to the women in the program. Unfortunately, it has been difficult to find qualified and available female staff members. While all the life-skills coaches have been women, the majority of the supervisors have been men. When men are the sole supervisors, this gives the women participants the message that women do not advance to leadership roles within the construction industry. But there is a potential advantage to having male supervisors. The first one hired was a kind, patient man with whom the participants enjoyed working. Given that many of the women come from abusive relationships with men, a male supervisor can act as a model illustrating that good men do exist. However, this particular male supervisor decided to have a relationship with one of the female participants. Because he understood that this was against the regulations, he kept the relationship secret. In another incident, a staff member at one of the job sites began a relationship with one of the women apprentices.[91] Unfortunately, for many women, incidents of this nature perpetuate a history of sex that is associated with secrecy and power. Naturally, these relationships created a conflict of interest and caused enormous friction between the apprentices and the staff.

Not all the male supervisors fully appreciate the difficulties that women face in the construction field and their need for a supportive environment. In one case, a male supervisor was impatient and provided negative rather than positive feedback to the apprentices. This created an unsupportive environment for the women, and he was fired.

The other male supervisors hired were positive additions to the Co-op. One man, while white, had significant experience working on the reserves; he had tremendous patience and brought out the best in each apprentice. However, even the good male supervisors did not remain with the Co-op for more than six months. They left the program because their salaries were not competitive and because their families were moving out of province.[92]

Eventually the program was able to hire Sharon Murray, a white mother who had taken an introductory Women in Trades and Technology (WITT) course on carpentry with Denise and Valerie a few years before. She understands the goals of the program and also knows how difficult it is for a woman to break into the field of construction. She has achieved Level 4 carpentry and was preparing to write her interprovincial examinations when she joined the staff. She did not initially pass these examinations, and the women apprentices watched her struggle until she was successful. The apprentices befriended Sharon, who delicately juggles the role of boss and confidante. She acts as a role model in numerous ways: the women see her juggle her home and work responsibilities; they admire her dedication to each job; they empathize with her economic struggles. In so many ways,

Sharon exemplifies why a female supervisor is key to non-traditional re-training programs for low-income women.

The program suffers because there has been no full-time Native woman in a staff position. As mentioned earlier, one of the four life-skills instructors for the program was a non-status Aboriginal woman who had tremendous cultural knowledge and pride. The women enjoyed a wonderful rapport with her; but, unfortunately, she could not continue because she needed full-time work. After she left, she continued to support the program and functioned as an occasional consultant. In retrospect, Valerie wishes the program had been able to maintain a Native woman as a life-skills instructor. It would also have been helpful if the program had had a close connection with an elder.[93]

The issue of homophobia emerged because Denise, the business manager of the Co-op, is a lesbian. Valerie and Denise discussed how Denise should approach this with the women participants. During the application process for the retraining program, the women are asked how they feel about working with lesbians. Also, during the orientation, Denise and Valerie explain to them that they will be working with Native and white women, lesbians and heterosexual women. "I want this to be a safe place for every woman – Aboriginal, white, gay, straight," says Denise. In 1982, when Saskatchewan did not have protection for lesbians and gays in the workplace, Denise was fired from a job when it was discovered that she was a lesbian. Now she prefers to be "out" from the beginning. "I made a pact with myself that I would not be closeted any more," says Denise.[94] She determined that her sexual orientation would be addressed openly.

> I didn't intend for it to happen the first day of class, but that's when it did. I was telling them about my history and then I realized where I was going, that I was going to come out. I got to the part where I left my husband and my daughter, and then I broke down into tears because I left my daughter and that was a real hard thing for me. There were women in the room crying, listening to me.

Denise recalls that this "coming out" was a bonding experience for her and the women in the program. "It was very moving ... Some of the women don't live with their kids either. They know that pain, so we had that in common – Aboriginal and white women," remembers Denise.[95]

Most of the women have never knowingly worked with a lesbian, which has led to several incidences of homophobia. First, some women have experienced homophobic comments from their families and friends, who say that they will become lesbians because they work in an all-female Co-op. This, in itself, has made some of them anxious about their close relationships with other women in the Co-op. "It's really hard for women who have been abused to develop close friendships with women. Usually that door has been shut to them," explains Valerie.[96]

Second, there are also numerous complaints about Denise that have a homophobic edge to them. More than one woman does not like the way Denise interacts with the Co-op women. For instance, one states:

> Well, sure we know she's a lesbian but to us, she's still a woman and trying to act like a man ... Sometimes when we go places and she acts like that and sometimes she tries to massage us too much and it annoys some women. A lot of them want to say, "Hey, don't put your hand on my butt, or don't slap me in the ass," or something.[97]

Another woman states clearly that the same touching would be acceptable if Denise were not a lesbian. "There've been incidences that were inappropriate, and Denise probably didn't realize it. And if you didn't know she was a lesbian, it wouldn't bother you, but you kind of have that in the back of your head ... And Denise doesn't bring it up much at work, which is good on her part ... But they didn't like the touching, and they wanted her fired."[98] Eventually, after two months of talking about the issue, the women had a meeting with Valerie when Denise was out of town. They complained that Denise swears too much and that she touches them too much. When Denise returned she had a meeting with all of the women.

> So, at our meeting I apologized if I had crossed a line. I said it was hard not to touch their knee or give them a hug when they came to the office and told me some heart-wrenching stuff. I said that I had got the impression that this touch was welcomed. I told them it would be very hard for me to promise never to touch them again, but I would try if that's what they wanted. And I said many of you have been touched inappropriately in the past, and I said I don't want to aggravate that, I don't want to upset you any further or push any buttons ... I suggested that anyone who did not want to be touched should leave me a note and they all nodded their heads in agreement with this solution, but you know, I've never gotten one single note. I've done what I can, as far as I'm concerned.[99]

Since this meeting, Denise has been more cautious about touching. She usually asks permission before she gives a woman a hug. And she only massages the shoulders of the women who have told her they like it.

The amount of homophobia came as a surprise to both the coordinators. "That's been the biggest shock of the whole program for me," says Valerie. "I realized there would be racist issues and tried to deal with them, but I feel like we missed the boat on this one." Valerie vividly recalls the meeting regarding Denise when it threatened to turn ugly:

> They started to say that it was okay if I touched them but it wasn't okay when Denise did ... One woman tried to explain that it was an abuse thing. She said, "We don't like any men touching us except our partners. And Denise is like a man touching us 'cause she has sex with women" ... And then there was hatred in the air ... I mean, they started suggesting lesbian assault and it was rampant ... I stopped the discussion and told them they were going in a very dangerous direction.[100]

The coordinators have learned an important lesson through this experience. In the future, they will be alert to early signs of homophobia and ready to address them. While they have not organized an anti-homophobia workshop to date, the coordinators are considering this as an option.[101]

Given the sexist, racist, homophobic world in which we all live, it is not surprising that these issues would permeate the retraining program. The important role that staff members from marginalized groups can play in helping to address these societal inequities is not to be underestimated. The absence of such women sends a subtle message to marginalized participants about what they can expect to achieve, but their presence challenges the status quo and can evoke further discrimination. This suggests that those creating women's non-traditional training programs must be ever alert to these difficulties and must provide sustained education in order to fight these forms of discrimination.

A final staffing concern involves the difficulty of finding staff members who appreciate the goals of the program. At times, there were staff members who were very competent in the field of carpentry and yet did not appreciate the unique skills it takes to train low-income women with multiple barriers to learning. At other times, there were life-skills staff members who had tremendous experience working with marginalized groups but no understanding of the world of construction. An ideal retraining program would include staff members who fully integrate life skills with carpentry skills and who also fully appreciate the goals of the participants and the program.

Funding

Funding has always been a challenge for non-traditional retraining programs. This problem is exacerbated by the federal government's decision to withdraw from the training arena. As Chapter 1 illustrates, this has had a severe impact on retraining programs that are specifically designed for groups marginalized due to race, class, or gender. Given that the Women's Work Training Program targets all three of these marginalized groups, it had little chance of receiving strong, secure federal government funding. The long-term nature of the program also works against its acquiring government funds. Politicians and bureaucrats prefer short-term training programs that require limited funding for "maximum results." The federal government prefers to fund training programs that can prove that their participants are able to find employment as soon as they finish their training. As a result, training programs are "creaming" their applicants, eliminating those with multiple barriers to employment and keeping those who are most employable. In addition, the federal government is reluctant to finance more than one fiscal year at a time; rather, it prefers to fund short-term programs, catering to people who are readily employable. This gives them the results they need in an era that blames the marginalized for their lack of employment.[102]

This political climate has made the funding of a long-term retraining program for low-income white and Native women a real challenge. Valerie has spent the majority of her working hours fretting about funding, writing countless grant proposals, and meeting and cajoling potential funders. This is an unavoidable headache in an era in which "training" has become a dirty word. In fact, it is close to a miracle that the Women's Work Training Program has been able to find enough funders, through a variety of sources, to keep the shop up and running through its various phases.

In order to attempt to meet the short-term goals of politicians and bureaucrats, the training program was designed in six phases. Funders were encouraged to "buy in" to one phase of the program rather than to commit to a five-year project. The six-phase design maximized funding possibilities: the New Careers Corporation of the Saskatchewan Government endorsed and helped fund carpentry and life skills instruction, and the Women and Economic Development Consortium was interested in the business angle of the program and financed various Co-op needs. The six-phase approach also produced results at the end of each short stage, which further increased the funders' confidence in the program (see Table 2.1).

However, short-term funding of discrete phases can severely limit a long-term retraining program that promises to change the lives of its participants. These life changes are long-term goals, requiring sustained financing. Funders who only focus on one phase of the project can miss the "big picture." This became particularly evident at one point in the program when one funder accused the program of double-dipping. The first funder did not understand why a second funder had come on board in order to fund similar line items (such as rent and telephone). Because the first funder missed the big picture, it did not understand that there were three distinct intakes, all of which required space and services. Costs were designed to be shared according to the number of participants and activities in each phase. A strategy that maximized the economic aspects of the situation backfired because the funders had blinders on when it came to the concept of joint use of facilities and services. While this misunderstanding was sorted out, funds were withheld and the program was temporarily discontinued just as it was time for the second intake of participants. This was a severe blow to all the participants and the coordinators. During the four months it took to sort out this misunderstanding, the shop was lost, the training portion of the program was put on hold, and the Co-op operated at minimum capacity under Denise's supervision.

Luckily, the provincial government provided some emergency funding to keep the operation afloat: an interim loan that helped finance tools that were lost when the shop was closed, and work placement funding that permitted the women to do carpentry work for non-profit organizations. "This funding was a stopgap measure which kept the women in the industry and on standby for further training from us," recalls Valerie.[103] Eventually the dust settled, a new shop was up and running, and the participants returned to training under the guidance of Valerie and Denise. But this funding crisis had an impact on the women's sense of security in the program and their commitment to the Co-op. And it forged a new relationship with the funders.

It became clear that funders needed to commit to the big picture if the program were to continue. A steering committee was established, consisting of representatives from all the funding organizations. All meetings with the funders took place at the shop, and each meeting began with a visit to some of the participants. Sometimes the participants prepared presentations for the funders; other times they gave the visitors a tour through the shop and displayed some of their current projects. Through these meetings, each of the funders came to understand how each grant fit into the larger whole. Also, some of the funders formed personal relationships with some of the participants. It all helped to give the funders a sense that this was not merely a program to train low-income women in specific carpentry skills but also a program whose purpose was to change lives. By getting to know the women participants, the funders began to understand the large challenges involved in the program's long-term goal.

This long-term retraining program and its ambitious goals require a variety of funders because it is virtually impossible to convince one funder to completely finance such a complex and long-lasting program. The Women's Work Training Program has received financing from two sources within the federal government, five sources within the Saskatchewan government, and two joint federal-provincial initiatives. It has also received private funding from the Women and Economic Development Consortium (WEDC) (see Appendix A).[104] Some of these funders were exclusively interested in the training portion of the program, whereas others were interested in the business angle. This required Valerie's full attention; she had to stop training the participants in order to become a full-time grant application and report writer. As she states:

> With one exception, the funders did not fund time to do this mandatory work! Every funder required accountability that took an exceptional amount of time and effort. All funders had their own financial reporting structure, statistical data structure, and evaluation formats that included question-naires for participants and descriptive reports by us.[105]

This overwhelming responsibility robbed Valerie of time and attention she otherwise could have devoted to the program's participants.

It is difficult to find funders who will commit to a long-term training program. The WEDC is the only funding source to provide a long-term grant to the Co-op, and this grant diminishes with each year as the Co-op becomes more self-sufficient. Valerie emphasizes the importance of WEDC funding:

> WEDC was our lifeline; not because they gave us lots of money, but because there was flexibility – allowing us to change course if the need presented itself and to pay for line items that no one else would even consider. Not that we didn't have to be accountable – we did. But we didn't have to re-write applications every time we had a change ... We needed to write a justification for a change and wait a week or so. They were responsive and responsible.[106]

While most funders are resistant to covering administrative costs, the WEDC agreed to finance many of the administrative supports connected to the Co-op. This included a part-time consultant who writes proposals, composes financial and narrative reports, and generally does the administrative work necessary to keep the funders satisfied. The WEDC grant also showed tremendous flexibility in covering part of the costs of the participants' seven weeks of schooling (which they take each year of the program). While Employment Insurance pays 60 percent of the participants' wages, it does not cover other school-related costs. The WEDC agreed to provide a grant that permits the program to provide loans to the participants, half of which are forgiven upon completion of their schooling.

Shoring up this complex web of funding arrangements has required an enormous effort on the part of the coordinators. All of this speaks to the need for long-term, flexible funding that would permit the coordinators to spend more time on the needs of the participants and less time chasing and cajoling funders. With additional funding, the program could hire a full-time life skills counsellor who could provide more training in cooperative work skills and leadership skills, as well as anti-racist and anti-homophobic education, individual counselling, and individual support. Additional funding could also increase the wages of the participants, providing them with a strong financial base for supporting themselves and their families. More funding would also permit the hiring of more forepersons, who would be able to stay at one worksite all day and guide the participants through every aspect of the job at hand. And there are many more dreams that could be fulfilled with solid, long-term, flexible funding.

Conclusion

There are always challenges at the worksite, and certainly everyday life at the Women's Work Training Program and the Regina Women's Construction Co-operative attests to this. Because the program is unique, some of these problems could not have been anticipated. For instance, the difficulties of convincing the women to commit to, and become leaders of, the Co-op were more daunting than expected. And some of those obstacles that could be easily anticipated have not been so easily resolved. Certainly, issues of racism, homophobia, addiction, staffing, and funding fall into the latter category. The coordinators have experimented, trying to improve the situation. Racism, in particular, has a long colonial history and cannot be erased – even with the best anti-racist practices in place. But more acknowledgment of the overt and the subtle forms of racism from the very beginning of the program could have helped to alleviate some problems before they became huge obstacles to a contented workplace.

The Women's Work Training Program, by its very nature, is imbued with challenges. And it is through addressing these challenges that a blueprint may be perfected. As the coordinators are always telling the women apprentices, "You learn more from your mistakes [than you do from your successes]."

Heather, resting after a good day of mudding

Photography: Don Jedlic – Oktober Revolution

Heather – no time to be afraid of heights

Shelley – exchanged
her high heels for work
boots

Building a two-storey addition to a home in Regina

Shirley, working hard on a hot day

A proud participant

Pat, the quiet leader of the Co-op

Sharon, the supportive foreperson for the Co-op

Michelle and her trusty level

A smiling participant

The coordinators, Valerie Overend and Denise Needham, planning the next step

Shirley, proud of her work

The graduates from Level 4 Carpentry: Sherry, Linda, and Pat

5
Measuring Success

The shop doors are now closed on the Women's Work Training Program and the Regina Women's Construction Co-operative. After four and a half years of operation, it was time to reassess what had worked and what had not.[1] However, a true evaluation of the program must start with an understanding of its impact on the everyday lives of the participants. The purpose of this chapter is to assess just how effective this retraining program was for low-income Native and white women.

Every time I spoke about this retraining program to people in the labour movement, they would quickly ask for the success rate. Just how many women actually received their apprenticeship papers in carpentry? How many women were still in the carpentry business? These are valid questions, but I do not believe that they are the only, or even the most important, questions with regard to assessing the success of the program. We cannot treat these women the same way we treat middle-class women who enter retraining programs. The low-income women who entered the Women's Work Training Program do not share a level playing field with women who have financial and emotional supports.

Apart from the skills that the participants in the program have learned, they have found a new appreciation of their own abilities. They have gained a new perspective on who they are in the world. As Shelley explains, "I traded my skirts and my pumps for blue jeans and work boots." She says it changed her life to be out getting dirty every day while her husband stayed home, cooked, and cleaned. "It's changed what I look like and who I am," she adds.[2]

So let us first begin with an assessment of how the program has changed the participants' lives. Generally, the women have left the program with three new types of skills: carpentry skills, life skills, and cooperative business skills.

Carpentry Skills
Knowledge of carpentry skills obviously led to major changes in the par-

ticipants' lives. The first time I met the participants they were in their first week of the program, learning to build a toolbox. As I watched, I felt that my carpentry skills were on a par with theirs. A number of them confessed that they were scared of the skill saw, and others were afraid of heights. When I returned six months later, they were using the skill saw with ease and clambering up and down ladders with no problem. By the end of the program, many had developed areas of specialty. Sheila was known as the best dry waller; Diane was known for her overall efficiency; and "Maggie" clearly loved the finer woodworking jobs.

These carpentry skills were developed in a methodical, step-by-step fashion. During the first twenty weeks of the program, the students were tested on their carpentry skills through written tests and practical application. This was a crucial twenty weeks, and the coordinators, Valerie and Denise, used alternative teaching techniques to foster a supportive and comfortable learning environment for the participants. They quickly realized that many of the women in the program had tremendous anxiety about writing tests, and they worked with them to lower their anxiety levels. They also realized that one or two women had misled them about their reading and writing skills, and they encouraged these women to begin the necessary upgrading so that they could comprehend written tests. Tests were held frequently – at least two per week. A pass was 70 percent or better. Those who did not achieve this mark could rewrite the test without penalty; if a student still did not pass, then she would be tested orally. The test could be repeated until the student received a satisfactory mark, but this was rarely necessary. The key was to ensure that the women were learning the skills. Over time, all of the women became more comfortable with written tests. At the end of twenty weeks, all participants wrote a provincial Level 1 carpentry exam arranged by the provincial Apprenticeship and Trade Certification Branch. Unlike the other course tests, which were held in a classroom area in the shop, this test was held at an external location with other carpentry apprentices from around the province. It accounted for 50 percent of their Level 1 grade, while the other 50 percent was determined through course work. The participants needed a final grade of 60 percent or better to receive their Level 1 Carpentry Apprenticeship Certificate. At the end of Level 1, the participants had gained forty-five carpentry skills, including first-aid and safety procedures, care and use of hand tools and stationary equipment, proper handling and storage of materials, applied mathematics, and construction techniques for finishing, framing, and concrete formwork.[3]

Many of the women were unaware just how much they were learning on a daily basis. Most of them had not enjoyed school and did not believe that they could learn new, challenging skills. During my visits, I acted as a measuring stick with regard to how far they had come. I would stop them during their work on site and say, "Hey, remember six months ago when you told me that you would never feel confident with the skill saw – well, look at you now." They would laugh and be surprised to realize that they had been using the skill saw with ease for a long time. They had a tendency to think that anything they learned had to be easy, because they did not consider themselves to be very smart. As Shirley explained, "You don't even realize you didn't know this a year ago. Like, I watched some women using the [carpenter's] square for the first time and they did not know how to hold it. So I showed them how. But until that moment I hadn't realized that I learned that – that handling a square was just like breathing for me now."[4]

Of the sixty-four women who walked through the shop doors, forty-two women completed Level 1 carpentry and wrote the Level 1 provincial exam. Thirty-six passed, with five receiving provisional passes pending completion of one to three practical tasks in the shop, and one failed. Of the forty-two, twenty-eight were registered as apprentices and continued working and training as carpenters. By the end of the program, four women had completed their requirements for Level 4 and passed their final level exams. Another woman achieved her Level 4 after the program ended. Four took the interprovincial exam to achieve their Journeyperson Certificate of Qualification in the Carpenter Trade, failed, and were too afraid to try again.[5] The rest are at various stages in their carpentry careers: some choosing to continue with the theory as well as the practical work in Levels 2 and 3, and some opting to work only. All of them will be able to pick up their theoretical training where they left off now that they are registered with the provincial government.[6] These statistics speak to a high level of commitment on the part of many of the participants to pursue advanced carpentry training. The non-traditional, long-term, and intensive nature of this training, along with the difficult personal circumstances of the participants, only makes such a feat all the more remarkable.

Since receiving their Level 1 training, several women have worked on housing projects on their home reserves. One of these women jumped ahead of her peers when she returned to the Co-op, thanks to the skills she had learned on the reserve. A number of women left the Co-op for short periods to deal with personal challenges and later returned to continue their training. Because of their absence, they lost some seniority, but generally they were quick to develop the skills that their peers had learned while they were away. Of the twenty-four participants I was able to track following the end of the program, nineteen are currently employed, either part-time or full-time, and thirteen of the nineteen are currently working in the field of construction. Some of these women work for other construction companies and receive good wages from the Carpenter's Union. One works on props for photography studios, and another works in a sheet metal fabrication shop. Pat makes Red River carts and is a key figure in the Métis cultural revival movement; another is a band councillor and wants to set up a carpentry training program on her reserve. One has built her own home, while others have renovated theirs. Six of them have received further training, mainly in carpentry. Diane went back to carpentry training and passed her Level 4 provincial exam, which means five of the participants now have the highest level of carpentry and need only pass their interprovincial exam in order to achieve full accreditation. Meanwhile, Cheryl and Rhonda M. returned and passed their Level 2 carpentry.

There is considerable evidence that most of the women continue to use their carpentry skills, even if they are not officially employed in construction. All of them continue to do renovations and repairs or assist family members in their projects. The women are very proud of their new capabilities, and when I visited them at their residences, they were always quick to point out the work they were doing. More than one has completely renovated her home bathroom, several have built decks, and almost everyone has fixed broken fences and stairs. They are pleased that they are able to live better within limited budgets as a result of their carpentry skills.

As a result of their carpentry skills, several of the women have been able to finance purchases that were previously well beyond their means. Four own their own homes – a dream they never expected to realize. One of these women built her own house on her reserve. Another bought a house in a housing cooperative, and she and her husband are active members of their co-op community. These women are not only able to house themselves and their children, but some of them are also able to house their extended families. The sense of security and pride they have in home ownership is very noticeable. I have visited two of the women in their homes and they spoke at great length about how the program had permitted them to have a new sense of security in their lives. Never again would they be worried about insecure housing. In addition, four women have bought vehicles (three trucks and one station wagon). I have ridden in these vehicles and seen the enormous pride the women feel every time they get behind the wheel. The sense of independence and self-worth that these purchases have created in the lives of the participants in the Women's Work Training Program is inestimable.

Life Skills
During the interviews, it became abundantly clear that the women had not simply learned carpentry skills during the training program. Even more important than the carpentry skills were their dramatic changes in attitude, behaviour, modes of communication, assertiveness, and self-esteem as the participants progressed through the program. These life skills were the real heart of the program. Valerie was always very aware of the importance of developing these non-carpentry skills. "Carpentry is merely a means to

achieve the end," she explained. "The real goal is for these women to turn their lives around, to believe in themselves, to create supportive environments so they achieve whatever is their dream." As Valerie explained, it does not matter, at the end of the training program, whether these women become carpenters; but it *does* matter whether they have developed the life skills that will enable them to become economically self-sufficient.[7] Heather, who is working full-time in commercial construction, confirmed that the program provided more than carpentry skills. "This program healed me. It went way beyond giving me a career," she said.[8]

Life skills education was offered for two hours every morning during the first six months of the Women's Work Training Program. Although life skills was a difficult part of the program, many women felt it was so vital that it should be expanded to continue well beyond the first six months of the program. Shelley believes that it is so valuable that it should be taught in all high schools.[9] One particularly quiet woman, who was the least emotionally revealing of all the women during my three years of interviews, really disliked the life skills class:

> A: There was a lot of crying in every life skills class ... You always had to bring your Kleenex to life skills. I mean, someone told a story and made you cry every day. It's nothing offending you, but it's just stories that ... [touches] your hurt and just makes you cry.
> Q: So, if you were in charge, would you get rid of life skills?
> A: No, some people do get something out of it.
> Q: Would you make it optional?
> A: No, everyone has to take it.[10]

This was very typical of how many women felt about life skills.

The women learned four basic categories of life skills in this retraining program:

1 Communication skills: listening, identifying feelings, giving and receiving feedback. For example, many of the women in the program found it difficult to identify their feelings and to speak them aloud. The life-skills coach often began sessions by having each woman simply state how she was feeling that morning.
2 Self-esteem and building confidence: balancing work and home life; learning to be comfortable with taking risks; self-acceptance; and time management. Many of the women participants had never been successful in a school setting, and they were afraid that they would fail again. They were encouraged to talk about their fears and lack of self-confidence, and to receive support from one another.

3 Assertiveness skills: conflict resolution methods, problem-solving techniques, different behavioural styles. Many of the participants were not accustomed to asserting themselves. They were afraid of any conflict and would do anything to avoid it. They needed a supportive environment within which to learn that asserting their own needs and opinions could actually benefit the entire group. They learned that it was possible to disagree and to still move forward as an organization.
4 Work-related skills: understanding the role of unions, occupational health and safety legislation, and the construction industry culture, as well as dealing with harassment in the workplace. For most, it was the first time they had worked in the construction industry, and they had to learn about its culture, rules, and regulations.[11]

The women became aware that the life-skills class was helping to transform their personal lives in ways they could not have predicted. Some women left abusive partners because they had developed better self esteem; some curbed their alcohol and drug abuse; one woman in her forties decided to marry during the program, and she attributed this decision to life skills work. "Life skills taught me how to communicate, how to believe that we can have differences and yet through talking we can negotiate and come up with a solution," she explained.[12] Another woman implemented one of the life-skills methods of communication in her regular family life. "I decided that at home we would create a circle and everyone would get a chance to be heard uninterrupted. It worked miracles," she explained.[13] Another woman found that the life-skills class allowed her to express her needs and wants more directly: "Before life skills I put everyone else's needs first. Now I can speak my mind without feeling bad ... So now I'm less grouchy. In fact, I'm happy."[14] Many found that they were able to speak assertively because of this personal training. For instance, Rhonda H. recalled her experience speaking about the Women's Work Training Program at a national conference: "Before life skills I used to hang my head and stuff, and now I make an effort to look people in the eye. It's still hard, but now I try and do it."[15] Others became role models and mentors to other women as a result of their new-found self-esteem and communication abilities. "Now I stand up for myself. I don't take the kind of crap from people I used to," explains Rhonda H.[16]

Part of the goal of the life skills class was to develop Native pride and to counteract centuries of degradation created by ongoing colonialism. Because Native women experience a hostile environment each and every day of their lives, they required even more training in self-esteem and assertiveness than did the white women. In a number of ways, the program attempted to develop Native pride and to educate all the women about

Native cultures. For example, the women who participated in the program played a major role in promoting an innovative educational program about Native culture for students from Kindergarten through Grade 12 called "Choosing the Beat of Her Own Drum." The participants viewed the video-tape, read the lesson plans, and worked to assemble the kit that is now available in all schools across Saskatchewan. They also visited museum exhibitions devoted to Native culture and attended sweet grass ceremonies and sweat lodges. In addition, some of the Native women participants were instructors at a camp devoted to non-traditional careers designed for Native girls.

Life skills did not begin and end in the life-skills classroom; much of the training continued on the job and at Co-op meetings. At some worksites, the women agreed to have a life-skills "check-in" at the end of the day to assess what worked, what still needed to be done, who should do what, and, most important, how to deal with any conflicts that had occurred. At Co-op meetings, the women encouraged others to assert themselves and to speak out. And from time to time various women were asked to speak to the media, to represent the retraining program at national conferences, and to assist others attempting to learn carpentry skills. Every hour of the training program provided an opportunity for women to enhance their life skills.

Cooperative Business Skills

One of the unique features of Women's Work Training Program was that, while learning carpentry and life skills, the women also learned cooperative business skills. Once the Regina Women's Construction Co-operative was established in 1997, educational workshops were conducted from time to time in order to help the women develop skills in business as well as co-operative management. In some cases the women were able to choose which skills they wanted to learn; however, for the most part, all of them were exposed to a variety of business skills, which they slowly developed over time. As with any construction business, many of the women learned how to provide realistic estimates for potential customers. They learned that their care and efficiency affected the amount of profit the company would earn and that this, in turn, would affect their salaries. They realized how crucial it was to set an estimate that would guarantee a profit and still be competitive in the local construction market. Sherry took an interest in payroll, becoming adept at determining how much everyone should earn, based on their attendance and years of seniority in the Co-op. Others became forepersons and were in charge of certain jobs. This required an ability to communicate clearly with their co-workers and with the business manager, an ability to pay attention to details, and an ability to appreciate the overall development of the job.

The participants acquired an impressive array of business skills, which would permit them to work on their own in the industry or to, one day, form their own company. These include the following four categories:

1 Communication and presentation skills: learning to work with customers and suppliers, making presentations in the community, instructing others in basic skills, and conducting media interviews
2 Office and clerical skills: organizing payroll, preparing estimates, budgeting, setting up accounts with banks and suppliers, using basic computer skills, filing, and record keeping
3 Management skills: developing policies, setting agendas, chairing meetings, scheduling jobs and personnel, and conforming to legal requirements for meetings and minutes
4 Marketing and promotional skills: developing marketing plans, designing advertisements, and developing customer service plans.[17]

Thanks to their on-the-job training, the women learned how to deal with all kinds of challenging customers. For instance, Sherry will never forget the time a customer called her to complain that a man had died because of her shoddy work. The customer accused Sherry of leaving a screw sticking up in the doorway, with the result that this person's friend had tripped and killed himself. "I couldn't believe it. I almost started crying. I mean we had just made a nice job of installing two windows and putting weather stripping around three doors," explained Sherry. "How could we be so sloppy? And how could a man trip and die?" However, Sharon, the foreperson, thought there was something wrong with the story and went to investigate. She found the doorways perfectly even, but she also found witnesses who said that the couple had been drinking and that he had tripped on the sidewalk *outside* of the house. "It shook me up," said Sherry. "I don't want to do weather stripping around doors for a while."[18] Although this was an extreme case, this incident taught the participants how to handle difficult customers.

The Regina Women's Construction Co-operative specialized in accessible construction. This was an area of construction that was not being adequately met by the local market, and the coordinators determined that knowing how to address it would help to make their business profitable. As a result, the participants became sensitive to disability issues, aware of appropriate language, and expert in barrier-free design and construction. They made the shop, washrooms, classroom, lunchroom, and telephone accessible in their own workplace. They learned skills that are on the cutting-edge of accessible construction.[19] Some of the women intend to renovate accommodation for family members who have ability challenges.

As well as traditional business skills, these participants learned how a co-op functions. They learned how to elect a board of directors, conduct democratic meetings, discipline members, and ultimately follow the basic principles of co-operative management. Not one of them had ever been a board member before, and they were unfamiliar with such responsibilities. The basic rules for co-op meetings were also new. Initially, most of the members did not appreciate the need to take careful notes of the meeting's business. Nor did they appreciate the need to vote on major decisions. Most were very uncomfortable with the idea of assessing and disciplining their peers. Initially, they wanted to assess everyone as being effective members of the Co-op: later some members wanted to severely discipline certain other members. It took time to find a middle ground, where members were both assessed and disciplined in a manner that met the Co-op's objectives. All of this was a tremendous learning experience for the members.

Being a Co-op member led Heather to become an active member in the larger co-operative movement. "When I worked at Burger King you had to keep your opinions to yourself or you would get fired; but here, in the Co-op, everyone's opinion counted. Everyone could contribute to make a job work better," said Heather. "Here we learned that we, we women, could make important decisions about our company. By being members of the Co-op I knew that the instructors were telling us that we could do it – that we could run a company. They had confidence in me. I am so grateful for that," she added.[20] Heather became very interested in cooperative management, locally, nationally, and internationally. She represented the Co-op at a national co-operative conference in Moncton, New Brunswick, and she travelled to New Mexico to work on a straw house cooperative.

However, most of the women did not share Heather's enthusiasm for learning co-op management skills. First, there was not sufficient time during normal working hours for Co-op members to learn these skills; rather, the members were expected to attend workshops and learn management and co-op business skills after hours. Unlike Heather, most of the women had intensive familial responsibilities that interfered with their commitment to the Co-op. Many found they were too exhausted after a day of learning carpentry skills to then spend time in the evenings or on weekends learning co-op management skills. Second, very few of these women had ever taken on leadership roles. They were not comfortable with the idea of being the boss. They were afraid of making mistakes that would alienate their friends in the Co-op or that would cost the Co-op money. As a result, they shied away from taking on Co-op leadership roles and continued to look to the coordinators of the program for advice and leadership. They actively resisted many attempts by the coordinators to hand over the reins. Third, the coordinators themselves had very little time to train the women in co-op management skills. Although several women would have been excellent in positions involving estimating, customer relations, and bookkeeping, their education in these areas only took place on a piecemeal basis. There was little attempt to link these women to courses outside of the program that would provide them with the skills necessary to taking on these business roles within the Co-op.

As a result of these difficulties, the Co-op suspended operations for one year on 1 June 2000. The Co-op shares were frozen, the tools were stored, and accounts were put on hold until the women could decide if they wanted to re-open it when the time was right.[21] In October 2002, the Co-op held its final dissolution meeting, at which the members' shares were disbursed and the accounts closed. Valerie and Denise had devoted five years to the operation of this program, hoping that at the end of that time their jobs would become redundant and that the Co-op members would be ready and willing to take on the responsibilities of running the business.

Frankly, it is not surprising that the members lost energy after four and a half years of operation. This was a very intensive program. Many of the women I have met outside this program who work in the carpentry and construction trade have not done their training all at once; rather, because of family needs, finances, or other demands, they have had to take some time off from their retraining and to return when other facets of their lives permitted. In addition, many women who are employed in construction have never received all of their credentials. It is quite possible to make a wage well above the poverty line without having achieved all four levels of carpentry instruction. Many women in the field have learned their trade from putting in the hours at the construction site rather than from attending school and taking exams. Therefore, it is quite natural for many of the women in this program to have received some carpentry instruction without going on to earn all of the credentials. It is also natural for these women to want to see what it's like to work in the construction field outside the Co-op before pledging more time and energy to their own company. After three to four years of intensive training, both in the classroom and on the worksite, it was, perhaps, time for the Co-op members to take a step back from the day-to-day grind of the program and to re-energize before continuing to perfect their skills.

The Co-op members can be proud of the skills they have learned and the company they established. By the time its doors closed, the Co-op had met its objectives, which were:

1 to become a well-respected and self-sufficient co-op
2 to develop a good reputation for quality, hard work, and customer satisfaction
3 to empower women and to increase opportunities for women in trades
4 to value teamwork, cooperation, and individual initiatives and opinions

5 to create an atmosphere in the workplace that promotes both personal and professional development

6 to produce experts in the field of adaptable and barrier-free construction and renovation.[22]

All members of the Co-op can be proud of this legacy. Its good reputation will long be remembered throughout the Regina community. Initially, customers called the Co-op because they wanted women to do the work. But, over time, more and more customers were referred by other construction companies. This signalled the construction community's recognition that the Co-op did good work at a reasonable price. During my three years of interviews, I met many customers and found them to be unanimously satisfied with the work done by the Co-op. One customer named two rooms in a seniors' home after local Aboriginal tribes as a way of honouring the Co-op women who had renovated the site. Another decided to extend the renovation project because she was so pleased with the preliminary results. This was all a result of the determined effort of the Co-op women to make every job site count.

With regard to being recognized by the construction industry, the Co-op began receiving calls from partners of men working in the construction industry about the Women's Work Training Program. Contractors struck up conversations with Co-op members at order desks and congratulated them for running a good business. Other members of the construction industry stopped at Co-op worksites and praised the Co-op women's work. All of this demonstrated that the Co-op was an accepted member of the local construction industry.

Equity Issues

The Women's Work Training Program's very existence gave rise to a number of equity issues. First, it is unusual for white and Native women to work side by side. For many of the participants, this was the first time they had done so. When you entered the workshop you saw a number of posters pertaining to Aboriginal women's achievements and the achievements of women in the trades. There were also posters explaining sexual harassment, and numerous newspaper articles with photographs of the Co-op women undertaking projects. All of this created an environment that welcomed women – both white and Native. It is hoped that any future retraining of white and Native women will grant even more attention to the many difficulties Native women face on a daily basis.

While the retraining program attempted to incorporate some aspects of Native culture into the program, overall the program was dominated by white cultural values. When Native culture was addressed, it was as an addition to the everyday structure of the program. For example, the participants took a special trip to the local museum to learn more about Native history and culture; and the Native participants were encouraged to be part of the trades and technology program specifically designed for Native women. These events did not challenge the "whiteness" of the structure of the program. For instance, everyone in the program was expected to be punctual, to be assertive with their peers and customers, and to be direct in their communication. These values were perhaps foreign to some women raised in Native cultures who had little interaction with non-Native cultures. Many times, the Native women mentioned to me that they found it extremely difficult to "speak up" at the job site and meetings. "Denise gets frustrated 'cause we don't speak up when we don't understand, but that looks like you are challenging your elder and that's not OK," explained one Native woman. Some Native women confided that they found it excruciating to look people in the eyes and also felt overwhelmed when others did the same to them. "This is [a] very disrespectful [thing] to do ... in my culture," explained one Native woman. "I can't just unlearn it, and I don't want to."[23]

The goals of the Women's Work Training Program were dominated by white values. Although rarely stated, it was generally assumed that all of the women wanted full-time jobs in the construction sector, which would make them financially independent. These goals did not necessarily meet the needs of all the Native women in the program. Some of the Native women met resistance from their families and communities when they began to become financially independent. Some of them did not want to be independent of their families and communities; they appreciated the ties of interdependency. In fact, many of them wanted to be able to leave the program for long periods of time when extended family members were ill or otherwise required assistance. They saw the goal of independence as a white, feminist goal that did not mesh with their cultural desires.

While others have noticed that Native women do not always excel within feminist retraining programs, there has been little attempt to redress this issue. For instance, one study of women in a non-traditional training program noted that "of the five Native women in the retraining program, three of them were still in that learned helplessness position ... [They] were not able to find their way out of the pattern of pregnancy and child-rearing."[24] While it is true that many of the Native women in retraining programs remain caught in a web of cultural expectations regarding mothering and caregiving, the solution is not simply to deny these strong cultural pulls.

I would suggest that retraining programs need to be more aware of the distinctness of Native culture. More attempts must be made by white instructors and white participants to realize that the overall design of retraining programs assumes a white way of knowing and understanding the world. Just as feminists in the non-traditional training sector have argued that women have different ways of learning and negotiating the world than men, these same leaders must become more aware of the assumed whiteness of the retraining environment. This will require integrating Native instructors and counsellors into retraining programs so that they balance out the impact of the white instructors. It will also require that the very structure and content of feminist retraining programs be examined and altered to be more compatible with the cultural values of the participants.

The Women's Work Training Program attempted to address equity issues faced by low-income women. As a rule, low-income women have few opportunities to retrain in any meaningful way; rather, the retraining programs that are offered to them are short-term, preparing them for a part-time, low-paid, and very gendered workforce. These programs lead to very few financial improvements in these women's lives. The Women's Work Training Program was distinctive in that it offered low-income women and their families real opportunities to improve their lives. It offered carpentry and life skills that these women could take to any corner of the country. It offered them a chance to realize a better life. This is not to say that *all* the women realized their dreams, but the program did provide some financial security for several of its members – a feat that few retraining programs for low-income women manage.

The Women's Work Training Program helped to transform both construction training and everyday life in the trade. This was the first women's carpentry cooperative in Regina to compete against other construction companies. At times, the Co-op members worked alongside men at various job sites; the latter were always surprised at the skill and confidence that these women displayed. Through everyday construction work, the Co-op women taught the men of their trade to make their workplaces more welcoming to women: "girlie" posters came down, sexist language was checked, and the men learned to respect their female peers. All of this affected attitudes and behaviour in the Regina construction trade.

The program also significantly changed the nature of construction education in Regina. Previously, women who went to the Saskatchewan Institute for Applied Science and Technology to train in carpentry had to learn to adapt to a male environment. The program ensured that several women would be entering the college system at once. This influx of a group of women spurred SIAST to change its teaching environment to one that was more welcoming for women. Over time, the program coordinators developed a good rapport with carpentry instructors at SIAST. As a result of the presence of the Co-op women, SIAST instructors became increasingly interested in providing a learning environment that would accommodate a greater diversity of students. The coordinators worked with SIAST instructors to address different learning styles. When half of the classroom consisted of Co-op women, it was impossible not to notice that learning styles can differ according to gender. For instance, the women tended to ask more questions than did the men; this could be interpreted to mean that women know less, or it could be interpreted to mean that women like to acquire as much information as possible about what is expected of them. In addition, the women were often more intimidated than were the men about making mistakes. Already they were working in an environment that was foreign to them, and they were terribly afraid that they are going to demonstrate that women should not be in this environment. On the other hand, men, who are confident that this is a "natural" environment for them, do not feel that a mistake represents their inability to do the job. By the end of the program, both the instructors and the male students had learned a lot about how to make the carpentry classroom a welcoming place for women.

Finally, the Co-op helped to promote equity throughout the Saskatchewan construction industry. In 1996, the federal government passed a new federal contractor's bill, which exempted the construction sector from employment equity legislation. This meant that, for all the billions of dollars spent on federal infrastructure projects across the country, not one of these projects had to hire women or other equity groups. This was a significant setback in the struggle to foster more equitable hiring practices in the industry. However, in Saskatchewan there is a small ray of hope. "As the 1990s drew to a close ... equity became a new issue and the term began creeping into contracts where [Saskatchewan] provincial money was invested," recalls Valerie Overend. In 2000-2001, the Saskatchewan government established an equity clause that ensured the participation of women and other equity groups for all construction projects that they contract. Valerie, along with Saskatchewan Women in Trades and Technology, was a pivotal lobbyist in the cause; she believes that the good reputation of the Regina Women's Construction Co-operative within the construction industry helped to secure this equity victory.[25]

Where Are They Now?
Now that the shop doors are firmly closed, it is interesting to note the dramatic changes in the lives of the women who worked there. One of the most difficult issues in any attempt to follow low-income women's lives is to keep track of them. Some low-income women do not have telephones; others move frequently. Given the difficulties in my previous studies of low-income women, I was surprised to be able to find twenty-four of the thirty women I interviewed during the course of the Women's Work Training Program. Of the twenty-four, nineteen are currently employed either part-time or full-time. Thirteen of the twenty-four women are currently involved in carpentry work either part-time or full-time (see Table 5.1). Only four of them are full-time wives and mothers who are not involved in paid work.[26] It is hard for these numbers to capture the tremendous changes in

Table 5.1

Where are the participants now?

	No. of participants	
Full-time employment: construction	4	17%
Full-time employment: other	5	21%
Part-time employment	10	42%
Family responsibilities (babies)	2	8%
Not working	3	13%
Total	**24**	**100%**
Working with their carpentry skills	13	54%
Did more training, upgrading	6	25%

Source: These statistics are based on the combined knowledge of Valerie Overend, Denise Needham, and myself about the employment situation for 24 participants we were able to track in July 2003, two years after the training program closed. In particular, I am indebted to Valerie Overend for remaining in close contact with many of the participants in the program (correspondence with Valerie Overend and Denise Needham, July 2003).

some of these women's lives. It is important to recall that more than one-third of these women had been on welfare all their lives until they joined the Women's Work Training Program. The fact that the vast majority of the women are now working is a huge victory. This is not to say that all of the women have been successful since the program ended. While some have left abusive partners, at least four remain in homes filled with abuse and/or alcohol. Still, there is evidence that this retraining program has improved the lives of the majority of its participants. Given the tremendous barriers these women faced in their lives (see Chapter 3), this is a significant accomplishment.

It is important to note that many of the women did not complete the Women's Work Training Program. For many, life crises interrupted their ability to concentrate on themselves and their goals. Of the sixty-four women who entered the program, twenty-two left during its initial phase and therefore did not receive their Level 1 carpentry certificate. Many of these women left during the first few weeks of the program. Most had quickly discovered that they were not in a position to commit to such an intensive program. They had abusive partners who were threatened by the program; they had not been able to find reliable childcare; they had emotional and/or psychological challenges that did not give them the necessary self-confidence to persist with the program. In addition, of the forty-two who completed Level 1 carpentry, many took time off at some point during the four and one-half years to attend to their personal lives. While five now have Level 4 carpentry, none has passed the interprovincial carpentry exam that will grant them full journeyed carpenter status. Four have tried the exam and failed and are too afraid to try again. As a result, not one of the women has achieved the final rank of journeyed carpenter. Yet this is not to say that the program failed these women; rather, it is important to put their achievements in a context that fully appreciates the many barriers to their participation in an intensive retraining program.

The Women and Economic Development Corporation (WEDC) has studied women's experiences in sustainable development and appreciates that it is difficult to transform one's life, attitudes, and behaviour. In total, WEDC acknowledges five stages of personal transformation:

Stage One: Awareness and Commitment to Change is a launching point on the long journey towards personal change. This is a pre-employment period, when women must resolve their determination to change deeply held beliefs and attitudes about what is possible in their lives.

Stage Two: Foundation Building occurs when women build a foundation of self-knowledge, planning, and personal development. Here, women may renegotiate family relationships, plan their own needs and goals for the very first time, and develop a support group of people who will help them along the way. This requires new problem-solving skills and new abilities to transform relationships and health problems that have hindered self-growth in the past.

Stage Three: Transition occurs when women start to see the financial rewards of their involvement in this program. They start to earn wages and, consequently, achieve some economic independence. They become clearer about the long-term forces, behaviours, and relationships that are holding them back, and they are able to take a step-by-step approach to resolving these problems. According to the WEDC study, women often move back and forth between Stages 2 and 3 as various events happen in their lives. For instance, resolving negative relationships takes time and patience. This stage can feel quite scary to women who are teetering on the brink of a new future but worry that they could fall backwards if they are unable to break out of old patterns.

Stage Four: Consolidation addresses the period when women have resolved the difficulties of Stage 3 and are able to concentrate on the skills that will secure their new life of economic independence. In this stage women become increasingly optimistic and confident. They have stopped relying upon external financial help (be it welfare or loans) and have consolidated their business skills in order to become self-sufficient.

Stage Five: Financial Security is the last step towards long-term security and sustainability. According to WEDC research, the transition from Stage 4 to Stage 5 takes a long time. Most women in the WEDC case studies are still at Stage 3 after two to four years of training. Given that it generally takes five years to consolidate a mainstream business, it makes sense that it would take low-income women even longer to achieve the same goal.[27]

According to the WEDC studies, women do not progress through these stages in a linear fashion: they can go back and forth between one stage and another until something finally resolves for them. In addition, it is important for women to focus on learning numerous types of skills simultaneously. If a woman focuses on only one stage of development, such as carpentry skills, neglecting life skills and business skills, then she will find that family problems or substance abuse may hinder her ability to develop the carpentry skills she desperately desires to achieve.[28] WEDC research reveals the delicate transformation that can occur if women's learning is properly nurtured. These five stages demonstrate the need for long-term retraining programs that permit women to falter along the road as they attempt to negotiate and renegotiate new ways of being.

Certainly, the history of the participants in the Women's Work Training Program supports the WEDC theory that progress is non-linear. Often the women took two steps forward and one step back. It is interesting to note the reasons women gave for leaving the program. Of the 44 women who temporarily or permanently left the program, 23 percent did so because of alcohol and drug addictions. The second most common reason for leaving the program was behavioural (14 percent) and absenteeism (9 percent), while mental health problems, physical health problems, abuse, and children's needs each accounted for 7 percent of the women who left. Women also left due to pregnancy and the need to make more money. The two women who left for financial reasons continued to maintain close connections to the program and to me. Rhonda H. explained the dilemma: "I really miss all the girls I worked with. I keep in touch with some of them. But I like where I'm working now and the pay is much better"[29] (see Table 5.2). Clearly, these women have a number of everyday challenges that make it difficult for them to participate in an intense, ongoing retraining program.

While some of these women dropped out of the program for reasons beyond their control, it is interesting to note that the vast majority of them left due to personal problems. It can often be extremely disorienting to see oneself in a new role. Fear of new-found success, as well as fear of failing, can drop women back to a place where they are more comfortable, to a set of behaviours and attitudes with which they have lived all their lives. Some of the participants sabotaged themselves just when they were about to achieve a new level of success. For instance, some of them would go on a drinking binge the night before writing a provincial carpentry examination; others would not show up for work on the day they were going to learn a new skill. It all produced the same results: they did not allow themselves to succeed. "Some of the women don't expect that they can succeed. Whenever they start to succeed, their extended families put more demands on them. They're surrounded by needy people. And if the needy people don't drain them, then the women start self-sabotaging," explains Valerie.[30]

Table 5.2

Reasons for leaving the retraining program (both temporary and permanent leaves)

Reason		No. of participants	
Temporary leave	Alcohol and drug addiction	10	23%
	Behavioural problems	6	14%
	Absenteeism	4	9%
	Mental health	3	7%
	Physical health	3	7%
	Abuse	3	7%
	Children's needs	3	7%
	Financial reasons	2	5%
	Pregnancy	1	2%
Permanent leave	Spiritual retreat	1	2%
	Never came back after first day	1	2%
	No financial support	1	2%
	Ran away with EI cheque	1	2%
	Moved to reserve	1	2%
	No reason given	4	9%
Total		**44**	**100%**

Source: These statistics are based on the records kept by the retraining program and the form completed by all participants who left the program stating the reason for their departure. My thanks to Theresa O'Keefe for her tabulations and to Valerie Overend for her help with this assessment.

These self-sabotaging behaviours have been found in other adult learning programs. As Aboriginal adult educators Beverly Sabourin and Peter Globensky explain, participants feel "that they can't succeed anyway, so why bother trying. Old fears [about school] may be triggered ... and it is easier to move to anger or indifference than to look at and deal with the fear."[31] Some of the women participants never overcame these fears, while others struggled to overcome them.

Some experts in women's training believe it takes between five and ten years for low-income women to reach economic sustainability. The transformation of low-income women takes a great deal of time, energy, and resources.[32] Such intensive and personal training frequently causes staff burnout, which is an inevitable part of a job in which instructors may receive phone calls in the middle of the night and be required to counsel participants who are suicidal, in abusive relationships, struggling with alcohol and drug addiction, and dealing with the everyday burdens of extreme poverty.

Some who enter such a program find that the construction business is not for them. This does not mean that the retraining program recruited the wrong type of women or that the women failed because they did not pursue a future in the construction industry. As with all education, a number of students discover that their future does not lie in the particular field for which they have trained, but they will have learned many important skills that they will utilize throughout their lives.

Once the Regina Women's Construction Co-operative closed its doors, the opportunities for women in the construction industry significantly diminished. A 1980s cross-Canada study of 212 female graduates in trades and technology found that these women experienced severe discrimination when applying for jobs in the trades. Even when they graduated at the top of their class, they could not find jobs. The study showed that 66 percent of the women were employed in non-traditional fields, although not necessarily the ones in which they were trained. Another 33 percent were working in fields that were more traditional, but the study nonetheless found that the WITT program had helped them gain the confidence and focus they needed to direct their lives.[33]

Although the women are now no longer working for the Co-op, their employment records have dramatically improved because of their experience there. Now 80 percent, the vast majority of women, are employed, whereas before the program the majority were unemployed and more than one-third had been on welfare their entire lives. Thirty-eight percent have full-time employment, with 17 percent of them working in full-time jobs in some sector of the construction industry (see Table 5.1). This is a remarkable change in these women's lives. For those who have yet to find full-time employment, the training program has taught them what it is like to be economically self-sufficient. Even when they face future setbacks, they will remember the feeling of success, and this will help them structure their lives around healthy choices that lead to economic independence.

While four and one half years is a short time in which to dramatically change the students' lives, it is clear that the program has had a very positive influence. Valerie explains: "I know that as you gain competence in one part of your life it transfers to another part of your life. And you can see this in the women." Many of these women had never invested in themselves before, and they automatically assumed that doing so would have a negative impact on their families. Valerie sees that the opposite has happened – and sees that as one of the important victories of the program: "You hear them saying, 'I'm happier and so are my kids.' They didn't know that would happen. They thought their kids would suffer because their moms were away all day in the program. But instead, as these women became more confident and happy in their work, it translated into a happier home life."[34] Of course, Valerie wishes that the Co-op could continue indefinitely: "I want the Co-op to continue – well into the future. But regardless, I know that we had an impact on the women – a very positive impact."[35]

What is clear is that the Women's Work Training Program helped many of these women transform the way they experience life. Most of them came into the program believing that they had little or no control over their lives, that life just happened to them. Through the course of the program they began to actively change aspects of their lives that they had previously just accepted. While crises still befall them, many have begun to make active life choices over the parts of their lives they can control: they have conquered addiction problems, left abusive partners, resisted destructive family and friends, moved out of severe poverty, and bonded with other women who share the same goals of dramatically improving their life paths. While the program did not provide the solution to all of the challenges low-income women face on a daily basis, it did provide them with a real opportunity to envision a different future: a future free from abuse, alcohol and drug addiction, and the everyday grind of severe poverty. This window to a better life is something that many of the women will cherish as they continue to define their own paths.

6
"A Hand Up, Not a Hand Out": Let's Get Serious about Retraining

"Retraining" is a word that is rarely heard during the neoliberal era in which we live. Politicians win elections by promising "a hand up, not a hand out" to the poor. They claim the answer to poverty is jobs, and they slash welfare rates, intensify the policing of welfare recipients, and establish workfare programs that coerce people to work in order to receive a meagre welfare payment. But almost every workfare study shows that workfare does not lead to jobs, it merely reintroduces slavery. Coercing the poor into minimum-wage, part-time employment only moves them from welfare poverty to job poverty.[1]

The neoliberal agenda is also gender-blind in its promise of paid work. For most of the twentieth century, provincial welfare policies stipulated that low-income single mothers should not be involved in full-time paid work.[2] Their first priority should be the care of their children, and no paid work should interfere with this. The neoliberal propaganda has dramatically altered how we see low-income single mothers: no longer is it acceptable for single mothers to stay at home and raise their children. Today, in half of the provinces, welfare legislation stipulates that single mothers should be participating in paid work well before their children are of school age. Based on interviews conducted with provincial and territorial welfare departments, single parents are required to work or retrain when their youngest child is a specific age: six months old in Alberta; one year old in Nova Scotia; two years old in Saskatchewan, Quebec, Newfoundland and Labrador; three years old in British Columbia and the Northwest Territories; and six years old in Manitoba, Ontario, Nunavut, and the Yukon. Only New Brunswick and Prince Edward Island have no age criteria established.[3] These policies of forced employment and retraining remain gender-blind with regard to the conflicting responsibilities of low-income single mothers. Although provincial governments force such mothers to participate in the workforce, they do not provide the accessible, quality childcare that would make paid work a viable option. As a result, low-income single mothers are coerced into the low-paid, insecure workforce and forced to involve their children in inadequate childcare arrangements. This is no solution for either the mothers or the children; rather, it is a punishment inflicted upon them by neoliberal politics, which cares little about women or the future generation of citizens.

Workfare studies have demonstrated that forced participation in the workforce has not led to long-term employment. In fact, evidence shows that workfare has hindered people from finding employment because welfare recipients cannot be actively looking for work when they are engaged in workfare placements during normal office hours. Moreover, some workfare placements force people to conduct dangerous work with little physical or legislative protection. Still other workfare requirements have merely kept low-income people busy, without providing them with the skills to improve their future prospects for employment.[4]

Upon closer examination, it becomes clear that workfare is part of a larger neoliberal agenda that punishes and demeans the poor. Welfare rate cuts, increased surveillance of welfare recipients, more punitive welfare fraud measures, along with forced employment and inadequate retraining encourage a climate that degrades those who are poor. This neoliberal agenda encourages all of us, in our comfortable armchairs, to blame the poor for their economic circumstances and to forget that not everyone has the advantages of birth, education, and family support that many of us take for granted. There is also an important moral agenda attached to most workfare policies. Forced employment and retraining are required, according to the rhetoric, because the poor are lazy and do not want to work. Yet welfare studies, including my previous research and the data from the participants in this retraining program, clearly demonstrate that many low-income Canadians are both prepared and eager to work, even when it will not significantly improve their financial circumstances.[5]

This does not mean that we should dismiss the neoliberal agenda as being without relevance. Indeed, there was something wrong with a history of welfare that provided little chance for single mothers to move beyond the welfare rolls simply because they were supposed to be at home caring for their children. The neoliberal doctrine is correct to suggest that we should offer single mothers the possibility of joining the paid workforce. But what needs to be understood is that all mothers in society should be able to choose when they want to participate in paid work. A mother knows best when her children need her at home and when she is ready to participate in a new learning environment. Middle-class mothers exercise their right to make this difficult choice all the time. To a much greater extent than working-class and poor mothers, resource-rich middle-class mothers have some flexibility to choose when and under what circumstances they will participate in the paid workforce. Low-income single mothers should have the same ability to choose their employment conditions.[6]

In order for all mothers to be able to choose their employment trajectory, we, as a society, need to provide quality childcare and paid employment that promises a financially secure future. Quality retraining can help low-income women find well-paid, secure employment. The lessons learned from the Women's Work Training Program provide an excellent foundation from which we can begin to build retraining programs that *really* work for low-income women. Many of the features of this retraining program must be maintained in any successful future program. These include:

1   *Choice:* No one should be forced to participate in a retraining program. Retraining programs are intense and require concentration and commitment. They will not be effective unless participants choose to be there.
2   *Flexibility:* The WWTP permitted women to leave their training program for both short and long-term periods as they dealt with family demands and personal crises. As such, it focused on the needs and interests of the participants.
3   *Holistic, Learner-Centred Learning:* The WWTP understood the importance of appreciating all of the circumstances of the participants' lives.
4   *Long-Term Program:* It takes three or four years to gain skills that enable one to be competitive in the non-traditional job market. But it takes many years to rewire learned attitudes and behaviours that have made it impossible for low-income women to compete successfully.
5   *The Co-operative:* The Co-op permits women to learn from and teach one another, thus increasing their confidence in their own abilities. It also allows women to learn and develop non-traditional skills in an all-female environment, free from sexual harassment.
6   *A Warm, Non-Hierarchical Learning Environment:* For women who have had bad experiences in the school setting it was imperative that the WWTP be run in a more personal and collective manner.
7   *Instructors as Role Models:* The instructors must be women who have struggled with poverty and family needs while learning their non-traditional skills. This enables them to serve as an everyday reminder that it is possible both to achieve financial independence and to raise healthy, happy children.[7]
8   *Retraining That Leads to Secure Employment:* Too many retraining programs for low-income women train them for employment that is insecure, part-time, and low-paid. This simply moves women from welfare poverty to working poverty. Instead, we need programs that lift women out of poverty and create more secure lives for their children.

These eight features of the Women's Work Training Program constituted its core philosophy and explain why so many of the participants were both challenged and enriched as a result of their experiences in the program.

As Chapter 4 clearly illustrates, the Women's Work Training Program encountered many challenges. There is more that could be done to make a retraining program work effectively for low-income women. An ideal retraining program would include six other important features:

1 *Native Understanding:* Any retraining program that includes Native women must incorporate Native understanding into every part of its structure. This means that some of the instructors, forepersons, and life-skills staff must be Native. This also means that both staff and participants will be educated in the many insidious ways in which whiteness is assumed in everyday interactions. Attempts must be made to reach a compromise between white and Native ways of being in the world.[8]

2 *On-site Childcare:* Childcare issues were a constant background noise for many of the participants, who often worried about the care their children were receiving while they were taking the program. When asked about her dream retraining program, Denise promptly answered that it would include an on-site daycare: "It would be great if the women could bring their kids to the daycare at work – then they could visit their kids during their breaks. They wouldn't be so worried about the retraining program taking time away from their kids. They would see that everyone was benefitting."[9]

3 *Living Wages:* A few of the women left the program because they needed to earn higher wages than the program allowed. Higher wages would ensure that low-income women are lifted out of poverty and are able to concentrate on the program without any additional financial stress.

4 *More Staff:* An ideal program would have more staff to instruct the women in carpentry skills, to provide full-time life skills throughout the entire program, to help train participants in co-op management, and to act as forepeople at the various worksites. "We've always been stretched when it came to staff. There just wasn't enough of us to be everywhere, all the time," explains Denise.[10] Often Denise, the business manager, was forced to remain on the job site as foreperson, and all staff members acted as life-skills counsellors whenever they could squeeze in the time or whenever a crisis made it vital to intervene. With a full-time life skills counsellor, Denise believes the women could really work on their issues in a consistent fashion: "I want a life-skills counsellor to come in here and do personal training with each of the women so that they set up their lives from now until they get their [carpenter's] licence. And there would be milestones along the way to meet – about themselves, about their

children, about their relationships."[11] More staff would also provide the Co-op participants with more time to gradually develop leadership skills. More staff with various types of expertise, from construction skills to co-op management skills, would provide more possibilities for guidance and free the coordinators to do the necessary administrative jobs. These extra staff members could also be trained in how to gradually relinquish their responsibilities to the Co-op members and to carefully monitor this transfer of power.

5 *More Flexibility:* Because of the intense family demands that many of the women experience, Valerie would like to see even more flexibility in the program. She wants to set up a pool of carpenters who would work as work was available. "I believe this would work well for those women who simply can't commit to five full days a week but would like to gain some work experience and hours in carpentry," she explains.[12]

6 *Stable and Secure Long-Term Funding:* Above all, the ideal retraining program for low-income women requires stable and secure long-term funding that provides numerous financial resources and supports for the participants and the coordinators. Much of Valerie's work time was spent on locating funding sources and writing applications. With these in place, Valerie could concentrate more fully on the other pressing needs of the program. Adequate and predictable long-term funding would permit the coordinators to make concrete, realizable plans for the future of the program. With more resources, it would be possible to give the participants a living wage that would raise them well above the poverty line. Some of the women who loved the program had to leave because their wages were not high enough to meet the needs of their families. If the wages were higher, the participants would not have such a financial struggle. With additional resources, the coordinators would propose a number of extras for the program. Denise would organize weekend retreats for the women and their children. "Their lives are constantly coping with one crisis after another. I'd like to give them a little time out when they could be with their kids and just take it easy," she explained. "It would also be great to pack everyone up and go off to a reserve and build a house from start to finish." She would also love to have enough money to finance driver's education and driver's licences for all the women. "It would be so much easier if we had more drivers and more women with trucks," Denise suggests, "and a walkie-talkie communications system so we could talk easily to the women on the various job sites."[13] More resources would also permit the women to learn some of the co-op management skills on the job, rather than after work when they have familial responsibilities. In so many ways, stable and secure funding would reduce the stress levels of both the participants and the coordinators, and it would permit all of them to concentrate on the job at hand.

All of these features would make a retraining program that would adequately meet the needs of low-income participants. If only neoliberal politicians would understand that the required funding would be money well spent, such a program would reduce the welfare rolls and the line-ups at the food banks and shelters. But it would do so much more than that. It would also produce a new generation of low-income women who were financially independent and free to choose their own futures. If you had spent any time with the women in this retraining program, then you, too, would know that all this is possible. It just takes a good blueprint, strong financial backing, inspired leadership, and committed workers. With political will, all is possible. If we really do believe in a "hand up," then it is time we demand that our federal and provincial governments commit to the retraining of low-income women.

Appendices

Funding summary for Women's Work Training Program (includes Regina Women's Construction Co-operative funding)

Phase	Funder	Amount ($)	Dates	Resources (program inputs) purchased
Development	Prov. of Sask. Future Skills	6,000	May/ Jun. 95	Development of original concept proposal.
Development	Sask. New Careers Corp	600	Dec. 95	Advertising and recruitment.
Development	Sask. New Careers Corp	19,702	Dec. 95	Purchase of tools for Phase 1 (tools turned over to permanent possession if 12 women continue in Phase 2 – they do).
Development	CMHC	5,000	Nov. 96	"Loan" to investigate and develop a non-assisted cooperative housing project (used as basis of business land for Co-op).
		500	Dec. 96	Seed money for resource centre for barrier-free/ universal housing and needs-assessment tools.
1	Prov. of Sask. Future Skills	106,000	Jan.- May 96	Carpentry instruction; life-skills instruction; overhead for shop, classroom, office; training allowance for some participants (others on UI or independently funded).
		103,453	Feb.- Jun. 97	

▶

◄ *Appendix A*

Phase	Funder	Amount ($)	Dates	Resources (program inputs) purchased
1	Sask. New Careers Corp	28,674	May-Sep. 98	Partial carpentry instruction; life skills instruction; overhead for shop, classroom, office; evaluation.
1	Gov't of Canada HRDC	17,224	May-Sep. 98	Not a grant to program but was given to 4 women who then turned it over to purchase Level 1 apprenticeship program.
1	Prov of Sask.: Apprenticeship Branch	23,000	May-Sep. 98	Partial carpentry instruction; life skills instruction; overhead for shop, classroom, office; evaluation.
2	Sask. New Careers Corp	86,587	May 96-Jan. 97	Partial supervision of workplace training; shop overhead.
		32,500	Nov. 97-Feb. 98	
2	Prov of Sask.: Future Skills	15,495	Aug.-Dec. 96	Partial supervision of workplace training; shop overhead.
2	Prov. of Sask.: Community Works	79,968	Sep. 98-Mar. 99	Partial supervision of workplace training; shop overhead.
2	Prov. of Sask.: Apprenticeship Branch	7,861	Feb.-Mar. 98	Training support for apprentices attending SIAST.
3-4	Prov. of Sask.: Strategic Initiatives	105,920	Apr. 97-Dec. 98	Journeyed site supervisor for Co-op; partial book-keeping, communications, rent; some professional development for apprentices; i.e., basic business skills, performing needs assessments for accessible housing.
3-5	Women and Economic Development Consortium	166,000	Jun. 97-May 02	Descending funds each year. Job-sharing wage replacement for business manager and organizational consultant; legal fees.
		1,909	Nov. 98	Expenses to send two Co-op members to National Co-operatives Conference.
		4,091	May 99	Training for new Co-op members and employees in accessible-housing construction and audit procedures.

►

◄ *Appendix A*

Phase	Funder	Amount ($)	Dates	Resources (program inputs) purchased
3-5	Women and Economic Development Consortium	17,000	Aug. 99-Jun. 00	Enhancement grant for development of business venture: show-home project.
		6,000	Sep. 99-Apr. 00	Training support for apprentices attending Level 2, 3, and 4 at SIAST.
3	Government of Canada HRDC	45,000	Jan.-Dec. 97	Wage subsidies for up to $3,000 per new apprentice upon employment with Co-op.
		25,000	Jun. 97-Mar. 98	
		25,000	Feb. 98-Feb. 99	Due to attrition, not all funds used.
3	Can.-Sask. Career and Employment	42,000	Mar. 99-Mar. 00	Wage subsidies for up to $3,000 per new apprentice upon employment with the Co-op. Additional $1,000 per apprentice for overhead for journeyed supervisor shop tools, equipment, and two vehicles for Co-op use.
5-6	Provincial Apprenticeship Commission	7,700	Oct. 99-Jun. 00	Training support for apprentices attending Levels 2, 3, and 4 at SIAST.
5-6	Prov. of Sask.: Economic & Co-op Dev't	10,000	Apr. 99-Mar. 00	Cooperative development including: board training, policy development, strategic planning, and implementation.
Subtotal – Grants		**$1,092,831**		
3-6	Customer Accounts	360,669	Aug. 97-May 01	Wages for Co-op employees. Increasing overhead costs each year as Co-op gains fiscal responsibility.
TOTAL REVENUE		**$1,483,500**		

Source: I am grateful to Valerie for providing this funding summary. Valerie Overend, *Foundation for Success: The Story of the Women's Work Training Program in Saskatchewan* (Regina: SaskWITT, 2001), 54-55.

Appendix B

Student guidelines for the Women's Work Training Project

1. CLASS SCHEDULE

8:00 – 8:30	Get coffee, exercise, get ready for the day
8:30 – 10:15	Life Skills Class
10:15 – 10:30	Break
10:30 – 12:00	Theory
12:00 – 12:30	Lunch
12:30 – 1:00	Math
1:00 – 2:15	Shop
2:15 – 2:30	Break
2:30 – 3:45	Shop
3:45 – 4:00	Clean-up

Staff meetings are on Fridays from 12:30 to 2:00.

Punctuality: Attendance and Life Skills start at 8:30 a.m. It is disruptive when people are late, so it is important to be punctual for starting classes, at breaks and at lunch.

2. ATTENDANCE

Full attendance is important. Any absenteeism, for whatever reason will be noted. Continued absenteeism will indicate disinterest in the program and discontinuance will be in order. Unexcused absences will result in a verbal warning for the first time, followed by a written warning for the second occasion, and finally a dismissal. Unexcused absences of four days will be considered abandonment of the program and you will be automatically discontinued.

Types of Leave: (a) Sickness
(b) Excused absence, i.e., funeral, illness in the immediate family, court
(c) Unexcused absence (no phone call)

Attendance will be taken morning and afternoon. If you are sick or absent, phone 565-3030 between 8:00 and 8:30 a.m., and leave a message if no one answers. If you are sick or absent for more than one day, please call daily to let us know your status.

Call in if you are going to be late. Unexcused lateness is considered an unexcused absence. Have a backup plan for babysitters and other personal matters to help avoid attendance problems.

Attend training in good shape: No hangovers, no booze, no drugs. If we suspect you are under the influence, we will ask you to leave for the day.

Please schedule doctor and other appointments after 4:00 p.m. Advise us, in advance, by writing of any appointments that conflict with class/shop time.

3. PROBATIONARY PERIOD

The first two weeks will be considered a trial period for both you and the program. During this time, you will be expected to establish stability in your life so you can attend each day of the program with enthusiasm and vitality!

Make sure all your child-care arrangements are in place and establish at least two backup plans.

Check bus schedules and arrange alternate transportation to class. At the end of the first two weeks, you will be asked to re-evaluate your intentions in regards to this program and to recommit to completing the program.

4. VICES

- Smoking is permitted outside ONLY during breaks and lunch.
- Please use a can to extinguish cigarettes, not the ground.
- No liquor or drugs on the premises.
- Clean up after yourself during lunch and breaks.

5. TELEPHONE CALLS

Messages will be taken during mornings and posted. Emergency messages will be passed to you immediately.

Outgoing calls can be made on the shop phone at noon and breaks. No long distance calls. That phone belongs to the Cooperative and is a business phone.

Please only use it for emergencies and keep your calls short. Please discourage people from calling here for personal reasons. Business and urgent family matters only, please. Afternoon messages can be retrieved during the break.

6. SHOP RULES

(1) Clean up daily.
(2) Thorough cleaning every Friday.
(3) Keep extra coats and books out of the shop.
(4) Tools must be put away every night.
(5) If you use a tool from the crib, put it back where you found it.
(6) Suitable clothing and footwear must be worn.
(7) No food or drinks in shop.

7. TRAINING SUPPLIES YOU NEED

(1) Pen and pencil
(2) Calculator
(3) Safety glasses and steel-toed work boots

8. TRAINING TOOLS AND MATERIALS SUPPLIED FOR STUDENTS

(1) Tape measure
(2) Hammer

(3) Tool belt

(4) Knife

No tools leave this shop unless an instructor goes with them. These items belong to the project.

9. FIRE REGULATIONS

- No smoking in the building.
- Memorize locations of fire extinguishers.
- Note where the exit doors are.
- Meet in the parking lot of Arrow Plumbing if there is a fire.

10. COUNSELLING

Donna, Denise, and Sharon are available for consultations. We are not social workers or psychologists, but we can listen and guide you to professional services.

11. BOOKS

Texts and materials will be provided to you. The text will be given to you IF you complete the program. You are responsible for their care and presence daily.

A resource library will be set up. Please keep all books here and in the classroom until we set up a borrowing system.

12. FIRST AID KIT

- Familiarize yourself with the kit and its location.
- Clean scratches and cuts immediately and bandage appropriately.
- Report any and all injuries to staff immediately.
- You will take a St. John's Ambulance First Aid course and CPR training during week 3 or week 4 of the program. If you already have this training, this will be a good refresher.

13. MARKS

- Transcripts go to the student and the Apprenticeship Branch.
- 70 percent is the mark needed to pass your final exam.
- Quizzes and practical tests count 50 percent towards your final mark. The other 50 percent will come from the final provincial apprenticeship exam.
- You must have an overall average on your quizzes of 70 percent, with no mark being lower than 60 percent. You will have opportunities to re-test any time you are having problems.
- You will be given quizzes upon completion of each module and several in between. You will have ample warning. They are short and multiple-choice.

- Practical tests will be in the shop and instructors will test skills individually. As you achieve a competency, we will check off that competency. Completion of competency will award you with 100 percent for the practical mark.
- Shop projects will be awarded according to completion of the projects. Final mark will be based on percentage of total projects completed.

14. MATH

- Will be practised daily.
- Both Imperial and Metric will be taught, with an emphasis on Metric.
- We will make it relevant to what we are doing in the shop when we can.

15. AVAILABLE CERTIFICATES

- Apprenticeship Level One Carpentry.
- Certificate of Completion from this program.
- St. John's Ambulance First Aid and CPR.
- Hilti Ltd. power actuated tools certificate.

16. FINAL EXAM

The final exam will take place on the morning of September 18, 1998.

17. CLOTHING

After the two-week trial period and your re-commitment to the program, you will be expected to acquire CSA-approved steel-toed work boots with a green tag. Locate a pair that fit you properly and get a price, with taxes included, in writing, and present it to your case worker. At this time, discuss any other essential clothing needs you may require (i.e., work gloves).

Our understanding is that you will receive a cheque for the exact amount of the agreed-upon purchase and you will be expected to wear your boots daily from Week 4 to the end of the program if you are on assistance.

Women on EI will receive an allowance from HRDC.

Appendix C

Regina Women's Construction Co-operative Mission Statement and Objectives

MISSION STATEMENT

Our mission is to provide high quality carpentry contracting that satisfies the consumers' needs at a competitive price.

OBJECTIVES

1 To become a well-respected and self-sufficient co-operative.
2 To develop a good reputation for quality, hard work, and customer satisfaction.
3 To empower women and increase the opportunities for women in trades.
4 To value teamwork, cooperation, and individual initiatives and opinions.
5 To create an atmosphere in the workplace that promotes both personal and professional development.
6 To become experts in the field of adaptable and barrier-free construction and renovations.

Appendix D

Survey of the Women's Work Training Program (July 1999)

This is a completely *anonymous* survey. Many women have been in abusive relationships. I know these are personal questions, but I am asking them because it is important to understand more about this kind of abuse. I am interested in your entire history of abuse, i.e., any experiences with your current partners/spouse and any experiences with previous partners/ spouses or other people.

You will help other women by telling me about your personal experiences of abuse. Thank you so much for your time and your honesty.

[Total who responded to the survey: 14]

Sections A and B are about your entire history of abuse.
Check Yes or No to the following questions:

A. GENERAL HISTORY OF ABUSE WITH ANY PARTNER	*Yes*	*No*
1. Have you ever felt worried that a partner might hurt you?	8	4
2. Has a partner ever destroyed or taken any of your possessions?	8	6
3. Has a partner ever tried to keep you from seeing your friends or family?	8	6
4. Has a partner ever put you down verbally? For example, told you that you were worthless?	10	4
5. Have you ever been hit, slapped, or kicked by a partner?	10	4
6. Have you ever been thrown or shoved by a partner?	10	4
7. Has a partner ever cut, bruised, choked, or seriously injured you?	8	6
8. Have you ever been hurt badly enough by a partner that you went to a doctor?	3	11
9. Has a partner ever used a gun, knife, or sharp object to threaten you?	5	9
10. Has a partner ever forced you to have sex?	6	8

B. YOUR EXPERIENCE OF CHILDHOOD ABUSE	*Yes*	*No*
1. When you were a child, were you ever made to feel uncomfortable by an adult?	8	6
2. When you were a child, were you ever slapped, kicked, or shoved by an adult so that you were left with bruises?	2	12
3. When you were a child, were you ever hit badly enough by an adult that you had to go to a doctor?	1	13
4. When you were a child, were you ever fondled or touched in a sexual way by an adult?	6	8
5. When you were a child, were you ever forced to have sex with someone?	2	12

The rest of this survey is about your experiences since you began this retraining program.

C. ABUSE DURING THIS RETRAINING PROGRAM	Yes	No
1. How many years have you been in this program? ___ years		
2. Have you felt worried that a partner might hurt you?	4	10
3. Has a partner destroyed or taken any of your possessions?	2	12
4. Has a partner tried to keep you from seeing your friends or family?	4	10
5. Has a partner put you down verbally? For example, told you that you were worthless?	6	8
6. Have you been hit, slapped, or kicked by a partner?	3	11
7. Have you been thrown or shoved by a partner?	1	13
8. Has a partner cut, bruised, choked, or seriously injured you?	3	11
9. Have you been hurt badly enough by a partner that you went to a doctor?	0	14
10. Has a partner used a gun, knife or sharp object to threaten you?	0	14
11. Has a partner forced you to have sex?	0	14
12. Has this abuse impacted on your ability to participate in the training program?	0	13
13. Has a partner told you that working women are bad mothers?	0	14
14. Has a partner told you that you must keep up with the housework while you are doing this retraining program?	0	14
15. Has a partner threatened to leave or withhold affection if you continued this program?	0	14
16. Has a partner threatened or harassed you at work?	2	12
17. Has a partner been jealous you might meet someone new at work?	3	11
18. Has a partner worried you would become a lesbian because you work with women?	2	12

D. WAYS YOU HAVE COPED WITH ABUSE DURING THIS RETRAINING PROGRAM	Yes	No
1. Have you been to a counsellor or therapist to talk about the abuse in your life (this includes a staff person in the program)?	4	9
2. Have you talked to other women in this retraining program about your abuse and asked for advice or help?	4	10
3. Have you gone to court because of an abusive partner?	3	11
4. Have you avoided going to places where you knew an abusive partner might be?	5	9

E.   STRESS YOU HAVE EXPERIENCED DURING THIS RETRAINING PROGRAM

Circle the answer that best explains your experience:

1. How often do you have trouble concentrating at work because of stress in your home?

never	once a month	once a week	almost every day	other
5	4	1	1	3

2. How often do you have intrusive memories of abuse while you are at work?

never	once a month	once a week	almost every day	other
9	4	0	0	1

3. How often do you feel depressed?

never	once a month	once a week	almost every day	other
3	4	1	2	4

4. How often do you feel you have no energy?

never	once a month	once a week	almost every day	other
4	3	4	1	2

5. How often do you feel angry?

never	once a month	once a week	almost every day	other
3	4	2	1	3

6. How often are you easily startled?

never	once a month	once a week	almost every day	other
8	0	4	1	2

Appendix E

Regina Women's Construction Co-operative Drug and Alcohol Use Policy

WOMEN'S WORK TRAINING DRUG AND ALCOHOL USE POLICY

Safety is #1 on this training site and it will be on every construction site that you work on in the future.

Taking ANY drugs – prescription or non prescription drugs – for anything such as a headache can affect your work performance. Antihistamines often cause drowziness. Tylenol or 222's with codeine alter one's consciousness in ways that can seriously affect decisions on a job site. Drugs stay in your system often for more than 24 hours. Taking pills in the evening can still affect you the next day.

Alcohol is an absolute NO-NO on a job site. This includes the aftereffects of its use, i.e., hangovers. When you feel like shit, you cannot possibly make intelligent and safe decisions. If you are an alcohol user, it will affect your work at some time or another. You need to decide what is more important.

Trust is extremely important on a job site. You need to depend on your co-workers to make decisions that do not jeopardize your safety along with theirs.

It is everyone's responsibility, from the workers to the supervisors, to be aware and informed of anyone not working at 100% full capacity, totally un-affected by any drugs or alcohol. You have a right as a worker to speak up to confront someone that you see using drugs, to check it out to see how those drugs affect job performance.

We expect anyone who is taking any drugs – prescription or non prescription – to inform us about the situation, and this includes providing us with a description of the drug from a pharmacy, stating the side effects of the drug.

While you are experiencing these drugs, you will not be allowed to use power tools. This is for your safety and the safety of your co-workers.

If you deem it necessary to take drugs, we encourage you to inform us and to continue coming to the program. Refrain from power-tool use and any other activity that could put you or others at risk. If drug use is habitual we encourage you to look further and explore the possibility of addictions. We can refer you to agencies that can help.

As supervisors we will continue to approach you when we notice you are behaving tired or you appear to not be your "self." We would rather be safe than sorry.

When you joined this program you were made aware of our policies. This bulletin expands on the statement that says, "The use of drugs and alcohol or their aftereffects will not be tolerated."

APPENDIX TO THE DRUG AND ALCOHOL POLICY

Procedures to deal with the use of drugs/alcohol on the job:

1 Everyone must read, understand, and agree to the drug and alcohol policy as stated. This is part of the employment contract.

2 Drug/alcohol use on the job is a safety issue. Any employee has the right to refuse to work with an employee who is under the influence of drugs/alcohol.

3 If any woman smells alcohol or suspects drug use from a worker on the job, then she has the right to question and check out her suspicion with that person. The worker who suspects that person must report the incident to her supervisor or operations/business manager. The supervisor will report this to the operations/business manager.

4 The offending worker will be asked to go home without pay for that day. If there is no operations/business manager or supervisor available at the time of the incident, then the employee must ask the offending worker to leave for the day.

5 The operations/business manager will talk to the offending worker and fill out an incident report. There is a maximum of two written incidents (warnings). The operations/business manager will offer time off to the offending worker to resolve any personal issues.

6 If a third incident occurs within six months or less, the operations manager will recommend enrolment in a drug and alcohol rehabilitation program. Upon confirmation and completion of the program, the worker will be reinstated for employment.

7 There will be a six-month probation period upon return to work with no alcohol/drug related incidents allowed.

8 If an offending worker refuses to cooperate with the recommended disciplinary measures, she will be dismissed.

DRUG/ALCOHOL INCIDENT REPORT

Date _____

Worker being reported _____

Report of the incident _____

_____

_____

_____

Signature of the offending worker _____

Additional comments: _____

_____

Signature of the reporting supervisor
or business/operations manager _____

P.O. Box 33084 Regina, SK S4T 7X2
Phone (306) 565-0556 Fax: (306) 565-3484

Notes

Chapter 1: Introduction

1   I call this a "retraining" rather than a "training" program for political reasons. Government policy has generally delineated between those on welfare who required "training" and those on Employment Insurance who were believed to have skills and required "re-training" or re-skilling. However, I do not accept this distinction. Through my research with low-income people, I have found that they have a number of skills I have yet to acquire regarding how to survive on very limited incomes without the luxuries of transportation, in-house laundry, or family support. To me, all low-income women who have raised children or cared for other family members have skills already. When they enter this particular program they are learning new skills – not merely carpentry and construction skills but new ways of asserting themselves in the world around them.

2   Please note that I generally refer to status and mixed-race women as "Native" because that is the term they themselves most commonly use. I use "Aboriginal" occasionally to avoid constant repetition. When appropriate I specify "Status" or "Métis" to differentiate between these two groups. I am grateful for discussions with Bonita Lawrence and for her research on mixed-race Aboriginal men and women. See Bonita Lawrence, *"Real" Indians and Others: Mixed-Blood Urban Native Peoples and Indigenous Nationhood* (Lincoln: University of Nebraska Press, 2004); Bonita Lawrence, "Mixed-Race Urban Native Identity: Surviving a Legacy of Genocide," *Kinesis* (Native Women's Issue: December 1999/January 2000) 15: 18.

3   It is important to note that four of the five have tried their interprovincial exam and failed. The pass rate was less than 50 percent.

4   According to the most recent Ontario government welfare fraud report, there were 201,717 welfare cases and 418,436 beneficiaries as of March 2002. Between 1 April 2001 and 31 March 2002 there were 393 welfare fraud convictions. Therefore, 0.01 percent of Ontario welfare recipients were convicted of welfare fraud. See Ontario Government, "Welfare Fraud Control Report 2001-2002," online at <http://www.cfcs.gov.on.ca/CFCS/en/programs/IES/Ontario Works/Publications/fraudReport0102.htm> (accessed 25 September 2004).

5   A comprehensive study prior to the implementation of workfare in Ontario revealed that 26.3 percent of sole-support parents were already employed: 11.7 percent on a full-time basis and 14.6 percent on a part-time basis. In addition, 7.7 percent of single parents were pursuing training or attending school full-time, while 42 percent indicated that they were looking for employment; 15 percent of single parents also reported that they did regular volunteer work in their communities. See Michael Ornstein, "A Profile of Social Assistance Recipients in Ontario," paper prepared for the Institute for Social Research, York University, Toronto, June 1995.

6   For example, Ontario Premier Mike Harris announced the withdrawal of supplementary benefits to pregnant single mothers on welfare, arguing that "what we are making sure is that those dollars don't go to beer, don't go to something else." This quote was carried by Southam newspapers across the country on 17 April 1998. For more discussion of the

discursive attack on poor single mothers, see David Zucchino's Pulitzer Prize-winning portrait of low-income women's survival strategies, *Myth of the Welfare Queen* (New York: Simon and Schuster, 1997).

7 Patricia Evans and Karen Swift conducted an important study of Canadian newspapers from 1982 to 1984 and from 1994 to 1996. They found compelling evidence that the discourse about single mothers had significantly shifted during this time. Previously, single mothers were viewed as stressed and over-burdened, but today they are increasingly condemned as "bad" mothers and as a frightening moral problem. See Patricia Evans and Karen Swift, "Single Mothers and the Press: Rising Tides, Moral Panic, and Restructuring Discourses," in *Restructuring Caring Labour: Discourse, State Practice, and Everyday Life*, ed. Sheila M. Neysmith, 93-116 (Toronto: Oxford University Press, 2000), 93-116.

8 For an important discursive analysis of the term "dependency," see Nancy Fraser and Linda Gordon, "'Dependency' Demystified: Inscriptions of Power in a Keyword of the Welfare State," *Social Politics* 1, 1 (1994): 4-31. For a critique of this neoliberal welfare agenda, see Sylvia Bashevkin, *Welfare Hot Buttons: Women, Work, and Social Policy Reform* (Toronto: University of Toronto Press, 2002), esp. Introduction.

9 Jennifer Stewart and Martin D. Dooley, "The Duration of Spells on Welfare and Off-Welfare among Lone Mothers in Ontario," paper prepared for the Canadian International Labour Network, McMaster University, 1998, 21.

10 Nearly half of all single-parent families on welfare in March 1997 had only one child, and another 31 percent had only two children. See National Council on Welfare, "Profiles of Welfare: Myths and Realities" (Ottawa: National Council on Welfare, Spring 1998).

11 For a discussion of the many good qualities of single-parent families, see Nancy E. Dowd, *In Defence of Single-Parent Families* (New York: New York University Press, 1997), esp. 4-7 and 109.

12 According to the National Council of Welfare's study, there were 1,842,600 people on welfare in Canada in March 2002. Out of a total Canadian population of 31,902,268, this represents 6 percent of the entire population. In 1993 the national case load was 2,975,000; in 1994 it was 3,103,300; in 1995 it was 3,070,900; and in 1996 it fell to 2,937,100. See National Council on Welfare, "Fact Sheet: Welfare Recipients," March 2003.

13 According to the most recent Statistics Canada information, which ranks families into ten deciles according to net worth, the "median wealth fell in the bottom three deciles of the wealth distribution but rose 27 percent or more in the top three deciles. Furthermore, only families in the 10th decile (and in some samples in the ninth decile as well) have increased their share of total net worth" between 1984 and 1999. See Rene Morissette, Xuelin Zhang, Marie Drolet, *The Evolution of Wealth Inequality in Canada, 1984-1999* (Ottawa: Statistics Canada, 22 February 2002), 7.

14 For a discussion of provincial welfare rate cuts, see Jane Jenson, "Redesigning the 'Welfare Mix': Policy Challenges," Canadian Policy Research Networks, February 2003; and National Council on Welfare, "Welfare Incomes 2000 and 2001," Ottawa.

15 For a discussion of the gendered impact of welfare reform, see Ontario Social Safety NetWork, "Welfare Reform and Single Mothers," *Backgrounder*, Toronto, 1998; and Sylvia Bashevkin, *Welfare Hot Buttons: Women, Work, and Social Policy Reform* (Toronto: University of Toronto Press, 2002).

16 In 1995, the Ontario government prohibited single mothers from living with men and receiving welfare as a single mother. As a result, 10,000 recipients, 89 percent of whom were women, were deemed ineligible and cut off welfare. For more details see Margaret Little and Ian Morrison, «'The Pecker Detectors Are Back': Changes to the Spousal Definition in Ontario Welfare Policy,» *Journal of Canadian Studies* 34, 2 (1999): 110-36.

17 See Chapter 6 for further details regarding provincial and territorial workfare and employment regulations for mothers with young children.

18 Of the 39 percent of mothers in 2001 who did not receive birth-related benefits, 23 percent were not in the labour force, 12 percent were paid workers who were ineligible or did not apply for benefits, and 5 percent were self-employed. Statistics Canada, "Benefiting from Extended Parental Leave," *The Daily* (press release bulletin), 21 March 2003, online at <http://www.statcan.ca/Daily/English/030321/d030321b.htm> (accessed 24 September 2004).

19 For a detailed study of how the federal government viewed women's employability from the Depression to the post-Second World War era, see Jennifer A. Stephen, "Employing Discourses of Employability and Domesticity: Women's Employment and Training Policies and the Formation of the Canadian Welfare State, 1935-1947" (PhD diss., University of Toronto, 2000).

20 *Report of the Royal Commission on the Status of Women in Canada* (Ottawa: Supply and Services Canada, 1970), 406.

21 These statistics are for 1993-94. See Ursule Chritoph, "Who Wins, Who Loses: The Real Story of the Transfer of Training to the Provinces and Its Impact on Women," in Marjorie Griffin Cohen, ed., *Training the Excluded for Work: Access and Equity for Women, Immigrants, First Nations, Youth, and People with Low Income* (Vancouver: UBC Press, 2003).

22 For a more detailed discussion of women's training policy history, see Karen Lior and Susan Wismer, "Still Shopping for Training: Women, Training, and Livelihoods," in Cohen, *Training the Excluded for Work*, 214-29, esp. 215-16.

23 For a gender breakdown of federal retraining programs, see Joan McFarland, "Public Policy and Women's Access to Training in New Brunswick," in Cohen, *Training the Excluded for Work*, 193-13.

24 WITT held its founding conference in 1992 to establish a national network of women in trades, technology, operations, and blue-collar work. See Women in Trades, Technology, Operations and Blue-Collar Work, *An Invitation to Membership: WITT National Network* (London, ON: WITT Publications, n.d.).

25 Bridging programs are training programs that focus on overcoming or compensating for barriers to women's labour force participation. See Marcy Cohen, *Report to the Second Annual Consultation for the Women's Reference Group on Labour Market Issues* (Ottawa: National Women's Reference Group, 1993); Lior and Wismer, "Still Shopping for Training," 214-29, and Ursule Chritoph, "Who Wins, Who Loses: The Real Story of the Transfer of Training to the Provinces and Its Impact on Women," in Cohen, *Training the Excluded for Work*, 14-33.

26 Chritoph, "Who Wins, Who Loses," 18-19.

27 For more analysis of these agreements, see Lior and Wismer, "Still Shopping for Training," 218.

28 Chritoph, "Who Wins, Who Loses," 19.

29 Women are overrepresented in part-time and temporary jobs, and this makes them less eligible for EI. Currently, 31 percent of unemployed women and 39 percent of unemployed men are eligible for EI. See Lior and Wismer, "Still Shopping for Training," 218.

30 This process of selecting the easy-to-serve clients for retraining is called "creaming." See Ursule Chritoph, *Women's Access to Training and Employment Programs in the Post-Labour Market Development Agreement Era* (Edmonton: Ursule Chritoph Consulting, August 2002), 18; Chritoph, "Who Wins, Who Loses," 24.

31 Jennifer Stephen, *Access Diminished: A Report on Women's Training and Employment Services in Ontario* (Toronto: Advocates for Community-based Training and Education for Women, June 2000).

32 For further analysis of the impact of EI changes, see Women's Employment and Training Coalition, *Participating for Change* (Toronto: Drishti Consulting Service, April 2000), 1-44; Mary Ferguson and Janet Murray, *Voices From the Field: Impacts of the Changing Federal Funding Context on Women's Access to Training* (Toronto: National Women's Reference Group on Labour Market Issues, 1998), 5-31; and Lior and Wismer, "Still Shopping for Training," 224.

33 There is some discussion of the definition of "non-traditional" versus "traditional" employment for women. In fact, some skilled tradeswomen oppose the term "non-traditional," arguing that it continues to segregate rather than to encourage women to seek many diverse types of occupations. I utilize the definition endorsed by WITT. See Women in Trades, Technology, Operations and Blue-Collar Work, *An Invitation to Membership: WITT National Network* (London, ON: WITT Publications, n.d.).

34 Abt Associates of Canada, for the Program Evaluation Branch, Employment and Immigration Canada, *Evaluation of the Job Entry Program: Final Report* (July 1989), 100 and 123; Patti Schom-Moffatt and Marcia Braundy, *National Survey of Women in Trades and Technology Orientation Courses,* report prepared for Employment and Immigration Canada, April 1989, 20.

35   For discussion of bridging programs, see New Brunswick Advisory Council on the Status of Women, *Training for Results: A Study of Women and Employment Training in New Brunswick* (Fredericton, December 1994); and Mary Carlisle, *A Guide to Adult Basic Education in Women's Bridge Programs* (Ottawa: Ministry of Education, Skills, and Training, 1996), esp. 1-14.

36   Mothers' allowances were established in Manitoba in 1916, in Saskatchewan in 1917, in Alberta in 1919, and in Ontario and British Columbia in 1920. The policy was established in Nova Scotia in 1930, in Quebec in 1937, in New Brunswick in 1943, and in Prince Edward Island and Newfoundland in 1949. See Dennis Guest, *The Emergence of Social Security in Canada* (Vancouver: UBC Press, 1985), 63.

37   For a discussion of the type of employment that welfare administrators encouraged single mothers to undertake, see M. Little, *No Car, No Radio, No Liquor Permit: The Moral Regulation of Single Mothers in Ontario, 1920-1997* (Toronto: Oxford University Press, 1998), 51-6, 89-96, 126-8, 168-72.

38   For a detailed discussion of NB Works, see Joan McFarland and Bob Mullaly, "NB Works: Image vs. Reality," in *Remaking Social Policy: Social Security in the Late 1990s*, ed. Jane Pulkingham and Gordon Ternowetsky, 202-19 (Halifax: Fernwood, 1996).

39   A follow-up study of the Self-Sufficiency Projects reveals that the greatest difference between participants and non-participants' full-time employment status occurred three years after the program ended; it waned but remained statistically significant six years after the program. This suggests that supplements to low wages do help low-income single mothers remain in the labour force and do reduce their dependence on welfare. But it also suggests that there are other factors to consider. One difficulty not addressed by the program is the problem of how to find full-time employment in the first place. I met low-income single mothers in British Columbia who were desperate to find any full-time job in order to qualify for the program, but they were having great difficulty doing so in a resource-based local economy. And while the participants' lives did financially improve, they were not lifted out of low-wage employment. Six years after the program, very few participants owned homes or had access to other middle-class luxuries. For a fuller analysis of the follow-up study, see Reuben Ford, David Gyarmati, Kelly Foly, and Doug Tattrie, with Liza Jimenez, *Can Work Incentives Pay for Themselves?* (Ottawa: Social Research and Demonstration Corporation, October 2003), esp. Chapters 2 and 4. Interviews with Self-Sufficiency Project participants in British Columbia, Vancouver, March 1993.

      There has been less detailed study of NB Works. A year following the end of NB Works I interviewed a dozen women who were NB Works participants, along with their advocates. All of them were disillusioned with the program. Most of them had received some community college education through NB Works but were not able to finish it when the program ended. None of them had secure, full-time employment at the time of the interviews. This is also based on informal discussions with Self-Sufficiency Project participants in British Columbia and their social workers during the project's tenure. For more discussion about NB Works and Self-Sufficiency Projects, see Joan McFarland, "Public Policy and Women's Access to Training in New Brunswick," in Cohen, *Training the Excluded for Work*, 201. Interviews with NB Works participants, Fredericton, July 1997.

40   Jennifer Stephen, "Access Diminished," 17; Ursule Chritoph, "Who Wins, Who Loses," 24.

41   According to interviews with provincial government officials only Prince Edward Island considers student loans exempt from any calculation of income. All other provinces consider student loans as income and deduct it from an applicant's welfare cheque. My thanks to Theresa O'Keefe for her careful research on this question. In Ontario, Kimberly Rogers, a woman who was eight months pregnant, died during her house arrest when she was convicted of welfare fraud because she simultaneously received money from the Ontario Student Assistance Plan and welfare. See discussion in Margaret Little, "A Litmus Test for Democracy: The Impact of Ontario Welfare Changes on Single Mothers," *Studies in Political Economy* 66 (Autumn 2001): 9-36.

42   Chritoph, "Who Wins, Who Loses," 15-16.

43   Ross Finnie and Gaetan Garneau, "Student Loans in Canada: A Cross-Cohort Micro Analysis of Student Borrowing for Post-Secondary Education," Research Paper R-96-16E (Ottawa: Applied Research Branch, Strategic Policy, Human Resources Development Canada, 1996).

44 Women represent approximately 70 percent of the part-time labour force in Canada. See Maureen Baker and David Tippin, *Poverty, Social Assistance, and the Employability of Mothers: Restructuring Welfare States* (Toronto: University of Toronto Press, 1999), 28.

45 Ursule Chritoph, "Who Wins, Who Loses," 15; Canadian Labour Force Development Board, *Putting the Pieces Together: Toward a Coherent Transition System for Canada's Labour Force* (Ottawa, 1994), 16; and Kathryn Running, "A Focus on Retention of Women in Trades, Technology, Operations and Blue Collar Work" (paper prepared for WITT National Network, July 1997), 12.

46 For a discussion of why open-ended interviews are essential when interviewing Aboriginal women, see Sheri Streisel and Tracy Myers, *Career Information Resources for Aboriginal People* (Saskatoon: Aboriginal Human Resource Development Council of Canada, 2000), 11.

47 "Heroes of their own lives" is part of the title of Linda Gordon's important book on women and violence. It also aptly describes the women in *If I Had a Hammer*. See Linda Gordon, *Heroes of Their Own Lives: The Politics and History of Family Violence* (New York: Penguin Books, 1989).

Chapter 2: Laying the Foundation

1   Interview with Denise Needham, Regina Beach, 19 July 1999.

2   Interview with Valerie Overend, Regina, July 1999.

3   Valerie Overend, *Foundation for Success: The Story of the Women's Work Training Program in Saskatchewan* (Regina: SaskWITT, 2001), 20.

4   Valerie Overend, "Trades Are the Ticket: Women and Carpentry Training," *Kinesis*, October 1998, 15-16.

5   For a discussion of the problem with retention for women in non-traditional trades, see Kathryn Running, "A Focus on Retention of Women in Trades, Technology, Operations and Blue Collar Work," WITT National Network, paper no. 1, 1997; Mary Ferguson, Janet Murray, and K. Running, *Organizational Culture: Leading the Way to Understanding WITT National Network's Employment Retention Consulting Service* (WITT National Network, 1999); Clare McClean-Wilson, M. Ferguson, J. Murray, and K. Running, *A Sampling of Key Points and Best Practices to Accompany the WITT NN Retention Model* (WITT National Network, 1999); M. Ferguson, J. Murray, and K. Running, *Understanding the Causes of Turnover: A Clue to Understanding How to Promote Retention – A WITT NN Approach* (WITT National Network, 1999); Marcia Braundy and Patti Schom-Moffatt, "What Happened to the WITT Grads?" *Women's Education des femmes* 7, 3 (1990): 10-14.

6   Interview with Denise Needham, Regina Beach, July 1999.

7   Overend, "Trades Are the Ticket: Women and Carpentry Training," *Kinesis*, October 1998, 15-16.

8   Overend, *Foundation for Success: The Story of the Women's Work Training Program in Saskatchewan* (Regina: SaskWITT, 2001), 28.

9   I define a "single mother" as anyone who was a single parent during at least one year in which she participated in the retraining program.

10 Overend, "Trades Are the Ticket," 15-16.

11 One of the sisters-in-law is white, and she is related through her Aboriginal male partner. The other familial ties in the program are all Aboriginal.

12 E-mail correspondence with Valerie Overend, August 2003.

13 Overend, *Foundation for Success*, 26.

14 Comments on the anonymous evaluations completed by thirteen of the twenty participants following Phase 1 of the program. See SaskWITT-Regina, "Women's Work Training Program 1997," paper presented to Future Skills Bridging Program, 15 November 1996, 5.

15 Interview with Denise Needham, Regina Beach, May 1998.

16 Overend, *Foundation for Success*, 66-8.

17 Adult literacy programs have been at the forefront of holistic learning. For a discussion of the importance of holistic learning, see Beverly Anne Sabourin and Peter Andre Globensky, *The Language of Literacy: A National Resource Directory of Aboriginal Literacy Programs* (Winnipeg: Beverly Ann Sabourin Associates, 1998), 248.

18 Overend, *Foundation for Success*, 68-9.
19 Interview with Zena, October 1998.
20 Interview with "Maggie," Anonymous Participant no. 1, October 1998.
21 Overend, *Foundation for Success*, 71.
22 Marcia Braundy, *Orientation to Trades and Technology: A Curriculum Guide and Resource Book with Special Emphasis on the Needs of Women* (Burnaby: BC Ministry of Advanced Education, Training, and Technology, 1997), 7.
23 Sherry Lynn Owens, Bobbie C. Smothers, Fannye E. Love, "Are Girls Victims of Gender Bias in Our Nation's Schools? *Journal of Instructional Psychology* 30, 2 (2003): 131; Ellen P. Cook, Mary J. Heppner, Karen M. O'Brien, "Career Development of Women of Color and White Women: Assumptions, Conceptualization, and Interventions from an Ecological Perspective," *Career Development Quarterly* 50, 4 (2002): 291.
24 Susan Booth and Carol Brooks, "Relational Learning Styles," in *Surviving and Thriving: Women in Trades and Technology and Employment Equity*, ed. Marcia Braundy (Winlaw, BC: Women in Trades and Technology, 1989), 95.
25 For a more detailed discussion of how to adapt relational learning to non-traditional retraining programs for women, see: Elizabeth Bohnen, Susan Booth, and Judy Klie, *Bridges to Equity Program Manual and Trainer's Guide* (Toronto: Management Services Department, 1991), 252-68.
26 E-mail correspondence with Valerie Overend, August 2003.
27 Valerie Overend, "Regina Women's Construction Co-operative Ltd.," *SaskWITT Newsletter* 5, 1 (1998): 14.
28 Valerie Overend and Denise Needham, "Women's Work Training Program, Feb. 1996 - Dec. 2000: Five-Year Funding Proposal," proposal submitted on behalf of SASK-WITT-Regina, October 1995, 3. (Person quoted is Valerie Overend.)
29 Overend and Needham, "Women's Work Training Program," 14.
30 Running, "A Focus on Retention"; Ferguson, Murray, and Running, *Organizational Culture*; McClean-Wilson, Ferguson, Murray, and Running, *A Sampling of Key Points*; Ferguson, Murray, and Running, *Understanding the Causes of Turnover*; Braundy and Schom-Moffatt, "What Happened to the WITT Grads?"
31 E-mail correspondence with Valerie Overend, August 2003.
32 Ibid., February 2004.
33 Ibid., August 2003.
34 Interview with Denise Needham, Regina Beach, May 1998.
35 Overend and Needham, "Women's Work Training Program," 12-13.
36 E-mail correspondence with Valerie Overend, August 2003.
37 Valerie Overend and Denise Needham, "Women's Work Training Program 1998, Phase 2," funding proposal to New Careers Employment Program, Community Works Work Placement, Regina, April 1998, 3.
38 Valerie Overend and Denise Needham, "Women's Work Training Program, Phase 1," funding Proposal to New Careers Employment Program (Bridge, Apprenticeship, and Trade Certification Branch), Regina, April 1998, 4.
39 Valerie Overend, "Proposal for the Women and Economic Development Consortium," on behalf of SaskWITT, Regina, 1997, 9.
40 E-mail correspondence with Valerie Overend, August 2003.
41 Running, "A Focus on Retention"; Ferguson, Murray, and Running, *Organizational Culture*; Ferguson, Murray, and Running, *Understanding the Causes of Turnover*; Braundy and Schom-Moffatt, "What Happened to the WITT Grads?"
42 Valerie Overend and Denise Needham, "Concept Proposal: Women's Independent Work Project," Regina, Saskatchewan, 3 May 1995, 1.
43 Interview with Valerie Overend, May 1998. With only two exceptions, Valerie has lived by this philosophy. Since this statement, Valerie has told a couple of participants that they must leave because they were a danger to themselves or others. E-mail correspondence with Valerie Overend, August 2003.
44 Email correspondence with Valerie Overend, August 2003.

Chapter 3: The Everyday Lives of Our Heroes

1 It was impossible to interview all the women in the program each time I visited. Some would be away at a remote job site, others would be at the community college in Moose Jaw, and still others would be away from work for personal reasons. Of the thirteen participants I interviewed more than once, six were interviewed twice, three were interviewed three times, and three were interviewed four times. I interviewed the coordinators and other available staff on each visit.

2 One woman's partner opened the transcript I sent in the mail and was quite upset by the amount of personal detail he found in the interview. Given that some of the women were in abusive relationships, I determined it was unsafe to send the transcripts in the mail.

3 For a number of personal reasons, only fourteen women were available for the fourth interview about violence. All of them were interviewed one-on-one, and all chose to respond to the anonymous survey. Because it was my last visit, those interviewed did not have the opportunity to edit the transcripts. They did, however, sign a consent form, and, at the end of each interview, we did discuss whether or not they wanted any details to be removed.

4 This was a difficult decision to make without discussing it with them, but I did so mainly because I felt the details around some of their experiences of violence were just too painful and personal.

5 For a more detailed assessment of the impact of residential schools, see J.R. Miller, *Shingwauk's Vision: A History of Native Residential Schools* (Toronto: University of Toronto Press, 1997); and Assembly of First Nations, *Breaking the Silence: An Interpretive Study of Residential School Impact and Healing as Illustrated by the Stories of First Nations Individuals* (Ottawa: Assembly of First Nations, 1994).

6 Interview with Anonymous Participant no. 2, July 1999.

7 Interview with Emily, October 1998.

8 Interview with "Judy," Anonymous Participant no. 3, October 1998.

9 Interview with Jackie, May 1998.

10 Interview with Rhonda M., May 1998.

11 E-mail correspondence with Valerie Overend, August 2003.

12 For a more detailed discussion of this baby-snatching phenomenon and its impact on Native identity, see Bonita Lawrence, "'Real' Indians and Others: Mixed-Race Urban Native People, the Indian Act, and the Rebuilding of Indigenous Nations" (PhD diss., Ontario Institute for Studies in Education, 1999), esp. 178; Bonita Lawrence, *"Real" Indians and Others: Mixed-Blood Urban Native Peoples and Indigenous Nationhood* (Lincoln: University of Nebraska Press, 2004).

13 Interview with Shirley, December 1999.

14 Lawrence's exploration of mixed-race identities is extremely helpful. See Lawrence, "'Real' Indians and Others."

15 Interview with Ginny, July 1999.

16 Interview with Anonymous Participant no. 2, July 1999.

17 Kim Anderson, *A Recognition of Being: Reconstructing Native Womanhood* (Toronto: Second Story Press, 2000), 86.

18 Interview with Pat, July 1999.

19 Anderson, *A Recognition of Being*, 87.

20 Interview with Cheryl, October 1998.

21 Interview with Rhonda M., May 1998.

22 Interview with Rhonda M., October 1998.

23 Interview with Valerie Overend, July 1999.

24 Interview with Tanya, May 1998.

25 Interview with Rhonda H., October 1998.

26 Interview with Jackie, May 1998.

27 Interview with Lorie, October 1998.

28 Interview with Shelley, October 1998.

29 Interview with Pat, July 1999.

30   Ibid.
31   Ibid.
32   Interview with Lorie, October 1998.
33   Interview with Rhonda, October 1998.
34   Interview with Shelley, October 1998.
35   Interview with Evelyn, July 1999.
36   Interview with Shelley, October 1998.
37   Ibid., July 1999.
38   Interview with Diane, May 1998.
39   Ibid., October 1998.
40   Interview with Pat, December 1999.
41   Interview with "Judy," Anonymous Participant no. 3, October 1998.
42   "Women with a household income of $15,000 and over reported 12-month rates of wife assault consistent with the national average, while women with household incomes under $15,000 indicated rates twice the national average." See Karen Rodgers, *Wife Assault: The Findings of a National Survey* (Ottawa: Statistics Canada, 1994), 6.
43   The rate of spousal homicide among Aboriginal women was 47.2 per million, whereas the rate for non-Aboriginal women was 5.8 per million. See Catherine Trainor and Karen Mihorea, *Family Violence in Canada: A Statistical Profile* (Statistics Canada, CCJS Profile Series, Catalogue no. 85-224-XIE, 2001), 29-31.
44   I want to be clear that I am not suggesting that, by nature, Aboriginal men are more violent than non-Aboriginal men; rather, I am arguing that colonialism has created a culture of violence that results in domestic violence, high rates of suicide, and addiction problems. Aboriginal men and Aboriginal women are products of this violent history, although they may manifest it in different ways.
45   Recently, community representatives and academics have been engaged in research about the relationship between welfare and abuse. See the Ontario Association of Interval and Transition Houses, *Some Impacts of the Ontario Works Act on Survivors of Violence against Women: A Brief to the Standing Committee on Social Development* (Toronto: Ontario Association of Interval and Transition Houses, 1997); and Janet Mosher, Patricia Evans, Margaret Little, Eileen Morrow, Jo-Anne Boulding, and Nancy VanderPlaats, *"Walking on Eggshells: Abused Women's Experiences of Ontario's Welfare System," Final Report of Research Findings from the Woman and Abuse Welfare Research Project* (Toronto: York University, April 2004). I am grateful to this latter project for stimulating my interest in violence and poverty issues for women.
46   Eleanor Lyon, "Poverty, Welfare and Battered Women: What Does the Research Tell Us?" a paper distributed through the Welfare and Domestic Violence Technical Assistance Initiative, Minnesota Center against Violence and Abuse, 1998, 1. Online at <http://www.vaw.umn.edu/vawnet/welfare.htm> (accessed 25 September 2004).
47   Anderson, *A Recognition of Being*, 97-8.
48   For a more detailed discussion of how young Native females are overtly sexualized in, for example, Walt Disney's *Pocahontas*, see Emma LaRoque, "The Colonization of a Native Scholar," in *Women of the First Nations: Power, Wisdom, and Strength*, ed. Patricia Chuchryk and Christine Miller, 11-18 (Winnipeg: University of Manitoba Press, 1996); Rosemary Weatherson, "When Sleeping Dictionaries Awaken: The Re/turn of the Native Woman Informant," *Post Identity* 1, 1 (1997): 113-44, esp. 114; and Rayna Green, "The Pocahontas Perplex: The Image of Indian Women in Popular Culture," *Massachusetts Review* 16 (1975): 698-714.
49   Sherene Razack, *Looking White People in the Eye: Gender, Race and Culture in Courtrooms and Classrooms* (Toronto: University of Toronto Press, 1998), 69.
50   Lee Maracle, *I Am Woman* (Vancouver: Press Gang, 1996), 56.
51   Interview with Emily, October 1998.
52   Interview with Anonymous Participant no. 4, October 1998.
53   Interview with Anonymous Participant no. 5, July 1999.
54   Interview with Sharon Murray, July 1999.
55   Ibid.

56 Interview with Anonymous Participant no. 5, July 1999.
57 Lyon, "Poverty, Welfare and Battered Women," 4.
58 Ibid.
59 Jody Raphael, "Domestic Violence and Welfare Receipt: The Unexplored Barrier to Employment," *Georgetown Journal of Fighting Poverty* 3, 1 (1995): 31.
60 Lyon, "Poverty, Welfare and Battered Women," 5.
61 Horsman provides a detailed assessment of how violence affects women's abilities to learn literacy skills, but these issues can be applied to many learning situations. See Jenny Horsman, *Too Scared to Learn: Women, Violence and Education* (Toronto: McGilligan Books, 1999), esp. 106-8, regarding trust and betrayal; 141-3, regarding assertiveness; 143-5, regarding communication skills; and 164-8, regarding goal setting.
62 Interview with Anonymous Participant 6, July 1999.
63 Interview with Anonymous Participant 7, May 1998.
64 Interview with Donna Thomson, October 1998.
65 Interview with Anonymous Participant no. 8, October 1998.
66 Jenny Horsman, *Too Scared to Learn*, 133-6.
67 Valerie Overend, *Foundation for Success: The Story of the Women's Work Training Program in Saskatchewan* (Regina: SaskWITT, 2001), 30.
68 Ibid., 31.
69 This is what one woman told Reagan. Interview with Reagan, July 1999.
70 Interview with Anonymous Participant no. 9, December 1999.
71 Interview with Denise Needham, Regina Beach, December 1999.
72 Interview with Anonymous Participant no. 10, July 1999.
73 The coordinators of the program were not fully aware of the extent to which the women protected one another from further abuse. This was clearly an example of the women learning about abuse in the program, re-examining their own lives, and attempting to make healthy changes to reduce the violence and domestic conflict in their lives.
74 Interview with Anonymous Participant no. 6, May 1998.
75 A study of 923 Canadian women in training for employment in non-traditional trades revealed that more than 65 percent had family employed in the trades. See Frances Cherry, Nancy McIntyre, and Deborah Jaggernathsingh, "The Experiences of Canadian Women in Trades and Technology," *Women's Studies International Forum* 14, 1 and 2 (1991): 17-18. Other reports support this finding. See Nancy L. Marshall, "Women in the Trades: Final Report of a Survey of Massachusetts Tradeswomen," Working Paper No. 195, Wellesley College, Centre for Research on Women, 1989, 2-3; Ken K. Ramdeen, "Perceived Barriers to the Entry of College Women into Non-Traditional Technical and Blue Collar Training: Implications for Career and Program Planning" (PhD diss., University of Toronto, 1987); Robert Sweet and Paul Gallagher, *Women and Apprenticeships: An Analysis of the 1994 National Apprentice Trades Survey* (Ottawa: Human Resources Development Canada, 1997), 18-19.
76 For further discussion of Aboriginal fear of education and the impact this has on further learning, see Beverly Anne Sabourin and Peter Andre Globensky, *The Language of Literacy: A National Resource Directory of Aboriginal Literacy Programs* (Winnipeg, Beverly Anne Sabouring Associates, 1998), 235-6.
77 Interview with Anonymous Participant no. 11, May 1998.
78 Interview with "Maggie," Anonymous Participant no. 1, May 1998.
79 Interview with Michelle, May 1998.
80 Interview with Rhonda H., October 1998.
81 Interview with Delphine, May 1998.
82 Interview with Lorie, October 1998.
83 Interview with Suzette, May 1998.
84 Interview with Audrey, October 1998.
85 Interview Diane, May 1998.
86 Interview with Anonymous Participant no. 4, October 1998.
87 Interview with Sharon Murray, July 1999.
88 Kevin K. Lee, *Urban Poverty in Canada: A Statistical Profile* (Ottawa: Canadian Council on Social Development, April 2000), 38.

89   Interview with Evelyn, July 1999.
90   Interview with Anonymous Participant no. 4, October 1998.
91   Interview with Anonymous Participant no. 7, May 1998.
92   Interview with Anonymous Participant no. 5, October 1998.
93   For a discussion about escalating poverty rates and poverty lines see, David P. Ross, Katherine J. Scott, Peter J. Smith, *The Canadian Fact Book on Poverty* (Ottawa: Canadian Council on Social Development, 2000), chaps. 3 and 4.
94   Interview with Anonymous Participant no. 6, July 1999.
95   Interview with Denise Needham, December 1999.
96   Interview with Anonymous Participant no. 12, December 1999.
97   Interview with Sheila, July 1999.
98   Interview with Denise Needham, December 1999.
99   Ibid., October 1998.
100 Horsman, *Too Scared to Learn*, 164-8.
101 Interview with Sheila, October 1998.
102 Interview with Pat, May 1998; Interview with Sherry, May 1998.
103 Interview with "Maggie," Anonymous Participant no. 1, May 1998.
104 Interview with "Judy," Anonymous Participant no. 3, October 1998.
105 Interview with Jackie, May 1998.
106 Interview with Zena, October 1998.
107 Interview with Sharon Murray, July 1999.
108 Interview with "Maggie," Anonymous Participant no. 1, July 1999.
109 Interview with Sheila, July 1999.
110 Interview with Jackie, May 1998.
111 Interview with Evelyn, July 1999.
112 Interview with Pat, July 1999.
113 Interview with Michelle, May 1998.
114 Interview with Ginny, October 1998.
115 Interview with Pat, July 1999.
116 Interview with Sherry, July 1999.
117 Interview with Emily, October 1998.
118 Interview with "Maggie," Anonymous Participant no. 1, May 1998.
119 Interview with Heather, October 1998.
120 Interview with Rhonda H., October 1998.
121 Interview with Shelley, October 1998.
122 Interview with Pat, July 1999.
123 Interview with Diane, October 1998.
124 Interview with Ginny, July 1999.
125 Interview with Shelley, July 1999.
126 Interview with Pat, July 1999.
127 Interview with Michelle, December 1999.
128 Interview with Heather, July 1999.
129 Interview with Pat, December 1999.
130 Interview with "Maggie," Anonymous Participant no. 1, July 1999.
131 Ibid.
132 Interview with Denise Needham, July 1999.
133 Interview with Sheila, October 1998.
134 Interview with Diane, December 1999.
135 Interview with Rhonda M., October 1998.
136 Interview with Reagan, July 1999.
137 Interview with Heather, July 1999.
138 Interview with Evelyn, July 1999.
139 Interview with Heather, October 1998.
140 Interview with Zena, October 1998.
141 Interview with Sheila, October 1998.

142 Interview with Ginny, October 1998.
143 Interview with Shirley, December 1999.
144 Interview with Anonymous Participant no. 10, July 1999.
145 Interview with "Maggie," Anonymous Participant no., 1, December 1999.
146 Interview with Pat, July 1999.
147 Ibid.
148 Interview with Pat, December, 1999.
149 Interview with Denise Needham, July 1999.
150 Interview with Valerie Overend, December 1999.

Chapter 4: From Blueprint to Reality

1 My thanks to Bonita Lawrence for making me more aware of the many manifestations of active colonization in everyday Canadian life.
2 Approximately 3 percent of the national population is Aboriginal, yet Aboriginal people represent 12 percent of the federal inmate population. The highest percentage of Aboriginals incarcerated is in the Prairies, where 64 percent of the total federal Aboriginal offender population is either incarcerated or on some form of conditional release. See Canadian Criminal Justice Association, "Aboriginal Peoples and the Criminal Justice System," *Bulletin* (special issue), 15 May 2000, 3. Today Aboriginal women make up 25 percent of the federal prison system. See Royal Commission on Aboriginal Peoples, *Gathering Strength,* vol. 3 (Ottawa: Supply and Services Canada, 1996), chap. 2.
3 My thanks to Sherene Razack for her detailed list of types of subtle racism. See Sherene Razack, "Racism in Quotation Marks: A Review of Philomena Essed's Work," *Resources for Feminist Research* 20, 3-4 (1991): 148-51.
4 For a discussion of the many subtle forms of racism and the many ways that the dominant racial group denies this racism, see: Teun A. van Dijk, "Discourses and the Denial of Racism," *Discourse and Society* 3, 1 (1992): 87-118 (quote taken from p. 96).
5 Del Abaquod and Vikas Khaladkar, "Case Study: The First Nations Economy in the City of Regina," in *For Seven Generations: An Information Legacy of the Royal Commission on Aboriginal Peoples* (Ottawa: Research Studies Database, Libraxus, 1997), 6, cited in Sherene Razack, "Gendered Racial Violence and Spatialized Justice: The Murder of Pamela George," in *Race, Space, and the Law: Unmapping a White Settler Society*, ed. S. Razack (Toronto: Between the Lines, 2002), 130n12.
6 In fact, it was Princess Louise, wife of the Governor General of Canada and daughter of the Queen of England, who proposed to rename the settlement "Regina," meaning "Queen." See W.A. Riddell, *Regina: From Pile o' Bones to Queen City of the Plains* (Regina: Windsor Publications, 1981), 9 and 20.
7 Sarah Carter, "Categories and Terrains of Exclusion: Constructing the 'Indian Woman' in the Early Settlement Era in Western Canada," in *Gender and History in Canada*, ed. Joy Parr and Mark Rosenfeld, 30-49 (Toronto: Copp Clark, 1996), esp. 40-1.
8 Today the racial divisions of the city are not quite as stark as they were in the recent past. Now a small but emerging Aboriginal middle class lives in some of the suburbs, and some white middle-class people with a propensity for social-justice work live in the downtown area. But to date, in both cases, this accounts, for just a small group of citizens.
9 For a compelling analysis of this tragic event, see Razack, "Gendered Racial Violence."
10 Royal Commission on Aboriginal Peoples, *Looking Forward, Looking Back*, vol. 4, *Perspectives and Realities* (Ottawa: Supply and Services Canada, 1996), 518, cited in Razack, "Gendered Racial Violence," 133n26.
11 Royal Commission on Agoriginal Peoples, *Choosing Life: Special Report on Suicide among Aboriginal People*, vol. 3 (Ottawa: Supply and Services Canada, 1995), x, chap. 3, sec. 1.3.
12 Jim Harding, "Presentation to the Royal Commission on Aboriginal Peoples," p. 323, cited in S. Razack, "Gendered Racial Violence," 134n30.
13 Royal Commission on Aboriginal Peoples, *Bridging the Cultural Divide: A Report on Aboriginal People and Criminal Justice in Canada*, vol. 3 (Ottawa: Supply and Services Canada, 1996), 31-2, cited in Razack, "Gendered Racial Violence," 134n30.

14 Philomena Essed, *Understanding Everyday Racism* (London: Sage, 1991).
15 Valerie Overend, *Foundation for Success: The Story of the Women's Work Training Program in Saskatchewan* (Regina: SaskWITT, 2001), 30.
16 Shauna Butterwick, "Life Skills Training: 'Open for Discussion,'" in *Training the Excluded for Work: Access and Equity for Women, Immigrants, First Nations, Youth, and People with Low Income*, ed. Marjorie Griffin Cohen (Vancouver: UBC Press, 2003), 161-77, esp. 163 and 172-3.
17 Interview with Anonymous Participant no. 10, October 1998.
18 There was a clear cultural difference between Native and white women participants' reactions to life skills. Where a few white women did not wholly appreciate this component of the program, almost every Native woman expressed her strong discomfort. Because of this I was quite surprised that all of the Native participants interviewed believed it was an essential component of the program. When asked what they would do if they were in charge of the program, all of them included a life-skills component.
19 Interview with Denise Needham, Regina Beach, July 1999.
20 Interview with Charlene, October 1998.
21 Interview with Sharon Murray, July 1999.
22 Interview with Anonymous Participant no. 13, July 1999.
23 Interview with Pat, July 1999.
24 Interview with Anonymous Participant no. 14, October 1998.
25 Interview with Anonymous Participant no. 6, July 1999.
26 Interview with Pat, July 1999.
27 Interview with Anonymous Participant 15, October 1998.
28 Interview with Anonymous Participant 16, October 1998.
29 Interview with Anonymous Participant 6, July 1999.
30 Ibid.
31 For further exploration of the in-group solidarity that occurs when racist charges are raised, see Dijk, "Discourse and the Denial of Racism," 90.
32 Interview with Anonymous Participant no. 17, October 1998.
33 Interview with Anonymous Participant no. 17, October 1998 and July 1999.
34 Interview with Shelley, October 1998.
35 Interview with Anonymous Participant no. 2, July 1999.
36 Ibid.
37 E-mail correspondence with Denise Needham, August 2003.
38 Ibid.
39 Overend, *Foundation for Success*, 79.
40 Interview with Sharon Murray, July 1999.
41 Interview with Valerie Overend, July 1999.
42 Overend, *Foundation for Success*, 40.
43 Ibid.
44 Interview with Sharon Murray, July 1999.
45 Ibid.
46 Ibid.
47 This was a national survey of 212 WITT graduates conducted between 1982 and 1987. See Patti Schom-Moffatt and Marcia Braundy, "What Really Happened to the WITT grads?" in *Surviving and Thriving: Women in Trades and Technology and Employment Equity*, ed. Marcia Braundy (Winlaw, BC: Kootenay WITT, 1989), 108.
48 Interview with Valerie Overend, July 1999.
49 This package was developed by an Aboriginal committee in partnership with Saskatchewan Women in Trades and Technology. Quote cited in Overend, *Foundation for Success*, 95.
50 Interview with Denise Needham, Regina Beach, October 1998.
51 The belief that the majority of the women have dealt with addiction problems is based upon my interviews and discussions with Denise Needham.
52 Women's Work Training Program, *Drug and Alcohol Use Policy* (Regina: Women's Work Training Program, n.d.).

53 Interview with Denise Needham, Regina Beach, October 1998.
54 "Letter to an Applicant," from the Regina Women's Construction Co-operative Ltd., 25 February 1998.
55 E-ail correspondence with Valerie Overend, August 2003.
56 Interview with Denise Needham, Regina Beach, May 1998.
57 Interview with Anonymous Participant no. 10, October 1998.
58 Interview with Anonymous Participant no. 6, October 1998.
59 Interview with "Judy," Anonymous Participant no. 3, October 1998.
60 Like other construction companies, the Co-op lays off some members during the winter months if there is not enough work.
61 See, for example, K. Deaux and J.C. Ullman, "Hard-Hatted Women: Reflections on Blue-Collar Employment," in *Women in the Work Force*, ed. H.J. Bernardin (New York: Praeger Publishers, 1982); and M. Walshok, *Blue Collar Women: Pioneers on the Male Frontier* (Garden City, NY: Anchor Press, 1981).
62 Barbara Carroll and Frances Cherry, "Some Advice for Overcoming Barriers to Women's Achievement in Non-Traditional Occupations," *Feminist Perspectives* 13 (1988): 4.
63 Interview with Denise Needham, Regina Beach, May 1998.
64 Interview with Valerie Overend, July 1999.
65 Interview with Denise Needham, Regina Beach, December 1999.
66 One of the Co-op members confirms that "everybody is too scared [to make decisions] in front of Denise." Interview with Denise Needham, Regina Beach, December 1999; Interview with Anonymous Participant no. 15, October 1998.
67 Interview with Heather, July 1999.
68 Overend, *Foundation for Success*, 94.
69 Interview with Denise Needham, Regina Beach, May 1998.
70 Interview with Pat, July 1999.
71 Interview with Denise Needham, Regina Beach, July 1999.
72 Overend, *Foundation for Success*, 100.
73 Ibid., 101.
74 Interview with Denise Needham, Regina Beach, May 1998.
75 Ibid.
76 Valerie makes this recommendation, but is well aware that this would require additional funding. See Overend, *Foundation for Success*, 42.
77 Interview with Denise Needham, Regina Beach, May 1998.
78 Ibid.
79 Ibid., December 1999.
80 Denise Needham and Valerie Overend, *Annual Report to the Canadian Women's Foundation* (Regina, 12 March 1998), 2.
81 Ibid.
82 Women's Work Training Project, *Proposal for Women and Economic Development Consortium* (Regina, 1997), 6.
83 Interview with Diane, July 1999.
84 Interview with Sherry, July 1999.
85 Ibid., December 1999.
86 Interview with Linda, July 1999 and December 1999. E-mail correspondence with Valerie Overend, August 2003.
87 At the time of the interview, Shelley estimated that she was $20,000 in debt and was quite distressed about this. She made $10.65 per hour at the casino. She claims that, because the Co-op occasionally did not have full-time work for her in the winter months, at the casino she was making almost double her Co-op average monthly wage. Interview with Shelley, July 1999 and December 1999.
88 After they left the Co-op, during each of my visits, both of these women would make great efforts to come to the shop to be interviewed. They have a strong commitment to the Co-op. Interview with Shelley, December 1999.
89 Interview with "Maggie," Anonymous Participant no. 1, October 1998.

90   Interview with Michelle, July 1999.
91   Details regarding the second relationship were discussed during an interview with Denise Needham, May 1998.
92   For more detailed discussion and assessment of each staff hiring, see Overend, *Foundation for Success*, 32-8.
93   Overend, *Foundation for Success*, 40.
94   Interview with Denise Needham, Regina Beach, May 1998.
95   Ibid.
96   Interview with Valerie Overend, July 1999.
97   Interview with Anonymous Participant no. 16, October 1998.
98   Interview with Anonymous Participant no. 18, July 1999.
99   Interview with Denise Needham, Regina Beach, July 1999.
100 Interview with Valerie Overend, July 1999.
101 Interview with Denise Needham, December 1999.
102 This policy ignores the long-term costs of a funding scheme that focuses on short-term training for the most employable. In the long run, this creates a large number of unemployed citizens who have multiple barriers to employment and no prospects. This increases the welfare rolls and the amount of public money needed to sustain those who are refused training. For thoughtful discussions about this trend in government funding, see Ursule Critoph, "Who Wins, Who Loses: The Real Story of the Transfer of Training to the Provinces and Its Impact on Women," in *Training the Excluded for Work: Access and Equity for Women, Immigrants, First Nations, Youth, and People with Low Income*, ed. Marjorie Cohen, 14-33 (Vancouver: UBC Press 2003); Karen Lior and Susan Wismer, "Still Shopping for Training: Women, Training and Livelihoods," in *Training the Excluded for Work: Access and Equity for Women, Immigrants, First Nations, Youth, and People with Low Income*, ed. Marjorie Cohen, 214-29 (Vancouver: UBC Press, 2003).
103 E-mail correspondence with Valerie Overend, August 2003.
104 The federal funding was from Human Resources and Development Canada and the Canada Mortgage and Housing Corporation. The provincial funding was from: the Post Secondary Education and Skills Training Department, including the Career and Employment Services Division, the JobStart/Future Skills Program, and the Apprenticeship Branch New Careers Corporation's Community Works Employment Program. The Department of Economic Development and Co-operatives provided some funding to the Co-op; and joint federal-provincial funding was provided by the Strategic Initiatives Work/Study Program and the Career and Employment Services Work Placement Program. E-mail correspondence with Valerie Overend, August 2003.
105 E-mail correspondence with Valerie Overend, August 2003.
106 Ibid.

Chapter 5: Measuring Success
1   Denise and Valerie began planning the retraining program in 1995; the first intake was in January 1996; and the Co-op was established in January 1997. The training program and the Co-op suspended operation in June 2000, when the accounts were frozen. In October 2002 the Co-op held its final dissolution meeting, at which time members' shares were reimbursed. E-mail correspondence with Valerie Overend, August 2003.
2   Interview with Shelley, October 1998.
3   For a complete list of the forty-five new skills, see Valerie Overend, *Foundation for Success: The Story of the Women's Work Training Program in Saskatchewan* (Regina: SaskWITT, 2001), 93.
4   The square is an essential carpenter's tool used for measurements. Interview with Shirley, December 1999.
5   It is important to note that the pass rate was less than 50 percent. E mail correspondence with Valerie Overend, August 2003.
6   Overend, *Foundation for Success*, 91-2.
7   Interview with Valerie Overend, October 1998.

8 Interview with Heather, October 1998.
9 Interview with Shelley, October 1998.
10 Interview with Anonymous Participant no. 13, July 1999.
11 The thirty-five life skills the women learned are detailed in Overend, *Foundation for Success*, 96.
12 Interview with "Maggie," Anonymous Participant no. 1, October 1998.
13 Interview with Zena, October 1998.
14 Interview with Shelley, October 1998.
15 Interview with Rhonda H., July 1999.
16 Ibid.
17 For a complete list of the forty business skills learned, see Overend, *Foundation for Success*, 99.
18 Interview with Sherry, July 1999.
19 For a more detailed discussion of these particular skills, see Overend, *Foundation for Success*, 97.
20 Interview with Heather, October 1998.
21 Seven women froze their co-op shares, while others withdrew theirs. All of them would be eligible to vote to determine the Co-op's future at a later date.
22 Overend, *Foundation for Success*, 103.
23 Interview with Anonymous Participant no. 10, Regina, July 1999.
24 Marcia Braundy and Patti Schom-Moffatt, "What Really Happened to the WITT grads?" in *Surviving and Thriving: Women in Trades and Technology and Employment Equity* (Winlaw, BC: Kootenay WITT, 1989), 108.
25 Overend, *Foundation for Success*, 108.
26 I am indebted to Valerie Overend for her assistance in tracking these women. Valerie has remained in close contact with many of the participants in the program, which again speaks to her commitment and the sense of family that was established by the program. Correspondence with Valerie Overend, July 2003.
27 For a more detailed discussion of these five stages of personal transformation, see Janet Murray and Mary Ferguson, *Women in Transition out of Poverty* (Toronto: Women and Economic Development Consortium, January 2002), 23-60.
28 Murray and Ferguson, *Women in Transition*, 17.
29 Interview with Rhonda H., Regina, July 1999.
30 Interview with Valerie Overend, July 1999.
31 Beverly Anne Sabourin and Peter Andre Globensky, *The Language of Literacy: A National Resource Directory of Aboriginal Literacy Programs* (Winnipeg: Beverly Anne Sabourin Associates, 1998), 247.
32 Murray and Ferguson, *Women in Transition*, 15.
33 Braundy and Schom-Moffat, "What Really Happened to the WITT Grads?" 106.
34 Interview with Valerie Overend, December 1999.
35 Ibid.

Chapter 6: A Hand Up, Not a Hand Out

1 There has yet to be an extensive study of the impact of workfare on low-income women in Canada. Initial studies in the United States confirm that workfare does not pull low-income women out of poverty. See Lynnell Hancock, *Hands to Work: Three Women Navigate the New World of Welfare Deadlines and Work Rules* (New York: Harper Collins, 2002); Nancy E. Rose, *Workfare or Fair Work: Women, Welfare, and Government Work Programs* (New Brunswick, NJ: Rutgers University Press, 1995); Frances Fox Piven, Joan Acker, Margaret Hallock, and Sandra Morgen, eds., *Work, Welfare and Politics: Confronting Poverty in the Wake of Welfare Reform* (Eugene: University of Oregon Press, 2002). Preliminary Canadian studies include: Patricia Evans, "Single Mothers and Ontario's Welfare Policy: Restructuring the Debate," in Janine Brodie, *Women and Canadian Public Policy*, ed. Janine Brodie, 151-72 (Toronto: Harcourt Brace, 1996); Patricia Evans, "Targeting Single Mothers for Employment: Comparisons from the United States, Britain and Canada," *Social Services Review* 66

(1992): 378-98; Melodie Mayson, "Ontario Works and Single Mothers: Redefining 'Deservedness and the Social Contract.'" *Journal of Canadian Studies* 34, 2 (1999): 89-109; Workfare Watch, "Women and Workfare." 1, 6 (1997).

2 See Margaret Hillyard Little, *No Car, No Radio, No Liquor Permit: The Moral Regulation of Single Mothers in Ontario, 1920-1997* (Toronto: Oxford University Press, 1998); Patricia Evans, "Single Mothers and Ontario's Welfare Policy: Restructuring the Debate," in *Women and Canadian Public Policy,* ed. Janine Brodie, 151-72 (Toronto: Harcourt Brace); James Struthers, *The Limits of Affluence: Welfare in Ontario, 1920-1970* (Toronto: University of Toronto Press, 1994); Veronica Strong-Boag, "Wages for Housework: Mothers' Allowances and the Beginnings of Social Security in Canada," *Canadian Journal of Canadian Studies* 1 (1979): 24-34.

3 These numbers are to some extent artificial. In Ontario, a single mother is eligible to participate in workfare once her child is of school age. If there is a public school, such as junior kindergarten, available for children aged three years old, then a mother may be expected to participate in workfare. As with most welfare regulations, there is considerable discretion left in the hands of individual welfare workers to determine precisely what rules to enforce and under what conditions. My sincere thanks to Theresa O'Keefe and Sarah Miller for this detailed and timely research.

4 For a careful study of the impact of workfare policies upon low-income Canadians, see Jamie Peck, *Workfare State* (New York: Guilford Press, 2001), chap. 6; Sylvia Bashevkin, *Welfare Hot Buttons: Women, Work, and Social Policy Reform* (Toronto: University of Toronto Press, 2002); Eric Shragge, ed., *Workfare: Ideology for a New Underclass* (Toronto: Garamond Press, 1997); Dean Herd and Andy Mitchell, *Discouraged, Diverted and Disentitled: Ontario Works New Service Delivery Model* (Toronto: Community Social Planning Council of Toronto, 2002); Lightman, Mitchell, and Herd, "Struggling to Survive."

5 Ernie Lightman, Andy Mitchell, and Dean Herd, "Struggling to Survive: Ontario Works Recipients Talk about Life On Welfare," Working Report No. 1, Social Assistance in the New Economy (SANE), Faculty of Social Work, University of Toronto, 2003; Margaret Little, "A Litmus Test for Democracy: The Impact of Ontario Welfare Changes on Single Mothers," *Studies in Political Economy* 66 (2001): 9-36.

6 In this era, it is very controversial to argue that mothers should be allowed to stay home full time with their children, yet Lynne Marks argues that this must be part of the contemporary feminist agenda. See Lynne Marks and Elizabeth Vibert's introduction to "Community Voices: Voices of Motherhood," *Atlantis* 25, 2 (2001): 73-4; Lynne Marks, "Feminism and Motherhood: Some Questions about Class, Race and History," *Atlantis*, forthcoming.

7 In the Women's Work Training Program, both of the founders came from middle-class backgrounds but had some experience of living below the poverty line. One left her child in order to join her lesbian partner and trained as a carpenter in order to support herself financially. The other was a single mother who left an abusive relationship and became a carpenter in order to provide a better life for her two sons. The foreperson in the program was also a single mother who saw carpentry as a way to better provide for her son.

8 One retraining program that effectively integrates Native understanding is the Urban Circle Training Centre in Winnipeg, Manitoba. This program includes educational upgrading, life skills, and job-readiness training. The staff and all participants are Aboriginal, and all aspects of the program include the medicine wheel and education about colonization and its long-term impact. See Jim Silver with Darlene Klyne and Freeman Simard, *Aboriginal Learners in Selected Adult Learning Centres in Manitoba* (Winnipeg: Canadian Centre for Policy Alternatives, June 2003), 33-43.

9 Interview with Denise Needham, Regina Beach, May 1998.

10 Ibid.

11 Ibid.

12 Interview with Valerie Overend, Regina, July 1999.

13 Interview with Denise Needham, Regina Beach, May 1998.

Selected Bibliography

Aaronson, Stephanie, and Heidi Hartmann. "Reform, Not Rhetoric: A Critique of Welfare Policy and Charting of New Directions." *American Journal of Orthopsychiatry* 66, 4 (1996): 583-98.

Abt Associates of Canada, for the Program Evaluation Branch, Employment and Immigration Canada. *Evaluation of the Job Entry Program: Final Report*. Ottawa: Employment and Immigration Canada, July 1989.

Anderson, Kim. *A Recognition of Being: Reconstructing Native Womanhood*. Toronto: Second Story Press, 2000. Bailey, Miriam. "Industrial Technology Training Programs for Women: Gender Issues and Program Success Factors." In *Training in Industrial Technology: A Collection of Essays*, ed. Michael Hatton, 27-49. Ottawa: Association of Canadian Community Colleges, 1995.

Baker, Maureen, and David Tippin. *Poverty, Social Assistance, and the Employability of Mothers: Restructuring Welfare States*. Toronto: University of Toronto Press, 1999.

Bashevkin, Sylvia. *Welfare Hot Buttons: Women, Work, and Social Policy Reform*. Toronto: University of Toronto Press, 2002.

Bohnen, Elizabeth, Susan Booth, and Judy Klie. *Bridges to Equity Program Manual and Trainer's Guide*. Toronto: Management Services Department, 1991.

Bohnen, Elizabeth, and Judy Klie, *Retention: Support Strategies for Women in Trades, Technology and Operations Work*. Toronto: Management Services Department, 1991.

Booth, Susan. *Bridges to Equity: Participant's Workbook*. Toronto: Management Services Department, 1991.

Braid, Kate. *Covering Rough Ground*. Vancouver: Polestar, 1991.

Braundy, Marcia. *Orientation to Trades and Technology: A Curriculum Guide and Resource Book with Special Emphasis on the Needs of Women*. Burnaby: BC Ministry of Advanced Education, Training, and Technology, 1997.

Braundy, Marcia, ed. *Surviving and Thriving: Women in Trades and Technology and Employment Equity*. Winlaw, BC: Women in Trades and Technology, 1989.

Braundy, Marcia, and Patti Schom-Moffatt. "What Happened to the WITT Grads?" *Women's Education des femmes* 7, 3 (1990): 10-14.

Canadian Criminal Justice Association. *Aboriginal Peoples and the Criminal Justice System. Bulletin* (special issue). Ottawa: Canadian Criminal Justice Association, 15 May 2000.

Canadian Labour Force Development Board. *Putting the Pieces Together: Toward a Coherent Transition System for Canada's Labour Force*. Ottawa: Canadian Labour Force Development Board, 1994.

Canadian Woman Studies: Women and Poverty. Special issue. 12, 4 (1992).

Carlisle, Mary. *A Guide to Adult Basic Education in Women's Bridging Programs*. Ottawa: Ministry of Education, Skills, and Training, 1996.

Carroll, Barbara, and Frances Cherry. "Some Advice for Overcoming Barriers to Women's Achievement in Non-Traditional Occupations." *Feminist Perspectives* 13 (1988).

Carter, Sarah. "Categories and Terrains of Exclusion: Constructing the 'Indian Woman' in the Early Settlement Era in Western Canada." In *Gender and History in Canada*, ed. Joy Parr and Mark Rosenfeld, 30-49, Toronto: Copp Clark, 1996.

Cherry, Frances, Nancy McIntyre, and Deborah Jaggernathsingh. "The Experiences of Canadian Women in Trades and Technology." *Women's Studies International Forum* 14, 1 and 2 (1991): 15-26.

Cohen, Majorie Griffin, ed. *Training the Excluded for Work: Access and Equity for Women, Immigrants. First Nations, Youth, and People with Low Income*. Vancouver: UBC Press, 2003.

Cohen, Marcy. *Report to the Second Annual Consultation for the Women's Reference Group on Labour Market Issues*. Ottawa: National Women's Reference Group, 1993.

Cohen, Marjorie, and Kate Braid. *Training and Equity Initiatives on the British Columbia Island Highway Project: A Model for Large-Scale Construction Projects*. Downsview, ON: Centre for Research on Work and Society, 1999.

Cook, Ellen P., Mary J. Heppner, and Karen M. O'Brien. "Career Development of Women of Color and White Women: Assumptions, Conceptualization, and Interventions from an Ecological Perspective." *Career Development Quarterly* 50, 4 (2002): 291-305.

Critoph, Ursule. *Women's Access to Training and Employment Programs in the Post-Labour Market Development Agreement Era: Phase One Report*. Prepared for the National Women's Reference Group on Labour Market Issues. Ottawa: National Women's Reference Group on Labour Market Issues, January 2002.

Deaux, Kay, and Joseph Ullman. "Hard-Hatted Women: Reflections on Blue-Collar Employment." In *Women in the Work Force*, ed. H.J. Bernardin. New York: Praeger Publishers, 1982.

Dowd, Nancy E. *In Defence of Single-Parent Families*. New York: New York University Press, 1997.

Essed, Philomena. *Understanding Everyday Racism*. London: Sage, London, 1991.

Evans, Patricia, and Karen Swift. "Single Mothers and the Press: Rising Tides, Moral Panic, and Restructuring Discourses." In *Restructuring Caring Labour: Discourse, State Practice, and Everyday Life*, ed. Sheila M. Neysmith, 93-116. Toronto: Oxford University Press, 2000.

Evans, Patricia. "Targeting Single Mothers for Employment: Comparisons from the United States, Britain and Canada." *Social Services Review* 66 (1992): 378-98.

–. "Single Mothers and Ontario's Welfare Policy: Restructuring the Debate." In *Women and Canadian Public Policy*, ed. Janine Brodie, 151-72. Toronto: Harcourt Brace, 1996.

Ferguson, Mary. "Welcoming Women into Trades, Technology, Operations and Blue-Collar Work." London, ON: WITT National Network, 1995.

Ferguson, Mary, and Janet Murray. *Voices from the Field: Impacts of the Changing Federal Funding Context on Women's Access to Training*. Toronto: National Women's Reference Group on Labour Market Issues, 1998.

Ferguson, M., J. Murray, and K. Running. "Understanding the Causes of Turnover: A Clue to Understanding How to Promote Retention – A WITT NN Approach." London, ON: WITT National Network, 1999.

–. "Organizational Culture: Leading the Way to Understanding WITT National Network's Employment Retention Consulting Service." London, ON: WITT National Network, 1999.

Finnie, Ross, and Gaétan Garneau. *Student Loans in Canada: A Cross-Cohort Micro Analysis of Student Borrowing for Post-Secondary Education*. Research Paper R-96-16E. Ottawa: Applied Research Branch, Strategic Policy, Human Resources Development Canada, 1996.

Ford, Reuben, David Gyarmati, Kelly Foley, and Doug Tattrie, with Liza Jimenez. "Can Work Incentives Pay for Themselves?" Ottawa: Social Research and Demonstration Corporation, October 2003.

Fox Piven, Frances, Joan Acker, Margaret Hallock, and Sandra Morgen, eds. *Work, Welfare and Politics: Confronting Poverty in the Wake of Welfare Reform*. Eugene: University of Oregon Press, 2002.

Fragniere, Gabriel. "Equal Opportunities and Vocational Training: In-Company Training Proposals for Future Action." Berlin: European Centre for the Development of Vocational Training, 1984.

Fraser, Nancy, and Linda Gordon. "'Dependency' Demystified: Inscriptions of Power in a Keyword of the Welfare State." *Social Politics* 1, 1 (1994): 4-31.

Freiler, Christa, and Judy Cerny. *Benefiting Canada's Children: Perspectives on Gender and Social Responsibility*. Ottawa: Status of Women Canada, March 1998.

Gaskell, Jane. "The Politics of Methodological Decisions: How Social Policy and Feminism Affect the Study of Careers." In *Methodological Approaches to the Study of Career*, ed. Richard A. Young and William A. Borgen, 221-33. New York: Praeger, 1990.

–. "What Counts as Skill? Reflections on Pay Equity." In *Just Wages: A Feminist Assessment of Pay Equity*, ed. Judy Fudge and Patricia McDermott, 141-59. Toronto: University of Toronto Press, 1991.

–. *Gender Matters from School to Work*. London, UK: Open University Press, 1992.

–. "Making It Work: Gender and Vocational Education." In *Gender In/forms Curriculum: From Enrichment to Transformation*, ed. J. Gaskell and J. Wilinsky, 59-76. New York: Teachers College Press, 1995.

Gordon, Linda. *Heroes of Their Own Lives: The Politics and History of Family Violence*. New York: Penguin Books, 1989.

Green, Rayna. "The Pocahontas Perplex: The Image of Indian Women in Popular Culture." *Massachusetts Review* 16 (1975): 698-714.

Grzetic, Brenda, and Jo-Anne Stead. "Employer's Handbook: The Integration of Women on Large Scale Projects." London, ON: WITT National Network, 1999.

Grzetic, Brenda, Mark Shrimpton, and Sue Skipton. *Women, Employment Equity and the Hibernia Construction Project: A Study of Women's Experiences on the Hibernia Construction Project*. St. John's, NF: WITT, June 1996.

Guest, Dennis. *The Emergence of Social Security in Canada*. Vancouver: UBC Press, 1985.

Hancock, LynNell. *Hands to Work: Three Women Navigate the New World of Welfare Deadlines and Work Rules*. New York: Harper Collins, 2002.

Handford, Kathleen. "Factors Influencing the Training Decisions of Four Women in Non-Traditional Technology Occupations." MA thesis, Queen's University, Kingston, ON, 1997.

Herd, Dean, and Andy Mitchell. "Discouraged, Diverted and Disentitled: Ontario Works New Service Delivery Model." Toronto: Community Social Planning Council, 2002.

Herring, Barbara, and Helen LaFountaine. "Marketing Non-Traditional Jobs to Girls and Women." *Women's Education des Femmes* 5, 1 (1986): 20-4.

Holder, Teresa Lynn. "Through a Brick Wall: Organizational Socialization Experiences of Women in Nontraditional Occupations." PhD diss., Ohio University, 1992.

Horsman, Jenny. *Too Scared to Learn: Women, Violence and Education*. Toronto: McGilligan Books, 1999.

Houtkoop, Willem, and Max Van der Kamp. "Factors Influencing Participation in Continuing Education." *International Journal of Educational Research* 17 (1992): 537-47.

Jackson, Nancy S., and Steven S. Jordan. *Skills Training: Who Benefits?* Downsview, ON: Centre for Research on Work and Society, 1999.

Jenson, Jane. "Redesigning the 'Welfare Mix': Policy Challenges." Canadian Policy Research Networks, February 2003.

Klie, Judy, and Eleanor Ross. "Building Together: Building Futures." *Canadian Vocational Journal* 32 (1996): 11-12.

LaRoque, Emma. "The Colonization of a Native Woman Scholar." In *Women of the First Nations: Power, Wisdom, and Strength*, ed. Christine Miller and Patricia Chuchryk, 11-18. Winnipeg: University of Manitoba Press, 1996.

Lawrence, Bonita. "'Real' Indians and Others: Mixed-Race Urban Native People, the Indian Act, and the Rebuilding of Indigenous Nations." PhD diss., University of Toronto, 1999.

–."Mixed-Race Urban Native Identity: Surviving a Legacy of Genocide." *Kinesis* (Native Women's Issue) 15 (1999/2000): 18.

–. *"Real" Indians and Others: Mixed-Blood Urban Native Peoples and Indigenous Nationhood*. Lincoln, NB: University of Nebraska Press, 2004.

Lee, Kevin K. *Urban Poverty in Canada: A Statistical Profile*. Ottawa: Canadian Council on Social Development, April 2000.

Lightman, Ernie, Andy Mitchell, and Dean Herd. *Struggling to Survive: Ontario Works Recipients Talk about Life on Welfare.* Working Report No. 1, Social Assistance in the New Economy (SANE). Toronto: Faculty of Social Work, University of Toronto, 2003.

Little, Margaret Hillyard. "Manhunts and Bingo Blabs: The Everyday Concerns, Frustrations and Rebellions of Single Mothers in Ontario in the 1990s." *Canadian Journal of Sociology* 19, 2 (1994): 233-48.

–. "The Blurring of Boundaries: Private and Public Welfare for Single Mothers in Ontario." *Studies in Political Economy* 47 (1995): 89-110.

–. *No Car, No Radio, No Liquor Permit: The Moral Regulation of Single Mothers in Ontario, 1920-1997.* Toronto: Oxford University Press, 1998.

–. "A Five-Point Plan So Single Mothers Can Hold Their Heads up High." In *Prescriptions for Canada: Memos to the Prime Minister*, ed. Harvey Schachter, 148-55. Toronto: John Wiley and Sons, 2001.

–. "A Litmus Test for Democracy: The Impact of Ontario Welfare Changes on Single Mothers." *Studies in Political Economy* 66 (2001): 9-36.

–. "The Leaner, Meaner Welfare Machine: The Harris Government's Ideological and Material Attack on Single Mothers." In *Making Normal: Social Regulation in Canada*, ed. Deborah Brock, 235-58. Toronto: University of Toronto Press, 2003.

Little, Margaret Hillyard, and Ian Morrison. "'The Pecker Detectors are Back': Changes to the Spousal Definition in Ontario Welfare Policy." *Journal of Canadian Studies* 34, 2 (1999): 110-36.

Lyon, Eleanor. "Poverty, Welfare and Battered Women: What Does the Research Tell Us?" Paper distributed through the Welfare and Domestic Violence Technical Assistance Initiative, Minnesota Center against Violence and Abuse, 1998. Online at <http://www.vaw.umn.edu/vawnet/welfare.htm> (accessed 25 September 2004).

Maracle, Lee. *I Am Woman.* Vancouver: Press Gang Publishers, 1996.

Marks, Lynne. "Feminism and Motherhood: Some Questions about Class, Race and History," *Atlantis* (forthcoming).

Marks, Lynne, and Elizabeth Vibert. Introduction to "Community Voices: Voices of Motherhood." *Atlantis* 25, 2 (2001): 73-4.

Marshall, Nancy L. "Women in the Trades: Final Report of a Survey of Massachusetts Tradeswomen." Working Paper No. 195, Centre for Research on Women. Wellesley: Wellesley Centers for Women, 1989.

Mayson, Melodie. "Ontario Works and Single Mothers: Redefining 'Deservedness' and the Social Contract." *Journal of Canadian Studies* 34, 2 (1999): 89-109.

McLean-Wilson, Clare, M. Ferguson, J. Murray, and K. Running. "A Sampling of Key Points and Best Practices to Accompany the WITT NN Retention Model." London, ON: WITT National Network, 1999.

McFarland, Joan. "Women's Access to Training in New Brunswick." Training Matters: Working Paper Series. Toronto: York University, Centre for Research on Work and Society, May 1999.

McFarland, Joan, and Abdella Abdou. *What's Happening with Training in New Brunswick.* Downsview, ON: Centre for Research on Work and Society, 1998.

McFarland, Joan, and Bob Mullaly. "NB Works: Image vs. Reality." In *Remaking Social Policy: Social Security in the Late 1990s*, ed. Jane Pulkingham and Gordon Ternowetsky, 202-19. Halifax: Fernwood Press, 1996.

McGee, Susan. "Commentary on Domestic Violence Research." School of Social Work, University of Michigan, 1997, 1-3. Online at <http//:www.ssw.umich.edu/trapped/res_coll_commentary.html> (accessed 9 September 2002).

McKinnon, Margaret, and Janice Ahola-Sidaway. "'Workin' with the Boys': A North American Perspective on Non-Traditional Work Initiatives for Adolescent Females in Secondary Schools." *Gender and Education* 7, 3 (1995): 327-39.

Messing, Karen, Julie Courville, Micheline Boucher, Lucie Dumais, and Ana Maria Seifert. "Can Safety Risks of Blue-Collar Jobs Be Compared by Gender?" *Safety Science* 18 (1994): 95-112.

Messing, Karen, Julie Courville, and Nicole Vezina. "Minimizing Risks for Women in Non-Traditional Jobs." *New Solutions* (Spring 1991): 66-71.

Michel, Sonya. "Childcare and Welfare (In)justice." *Feminist Studies* 24, 1 (1998): 44-54.

Morissette, Rene, Xuelin Zhang, and Marie Drolet. *The Evolution of Wealth Inequality in Canada, 1984-1999*. Ottawa: Analytical Studies Branch, Statistics Canada, 22 February 2002.

Mosher, Janet, Patricia Evans, Margaret Little, Eileen Morrow, Jo-Anne Boulding, and Nancy VanderPlaats. "Walking on Eggshells: Abused Women's Experiences with Ontario's Welfare System." *Final Report of Research Findings from the Woman and Abuse Welfare Research Project*. Toronto: York University, 5 April 2004.

Murray, Janet, and Mary Ferguson, "Women in Transition out of Poverty." Toronto: Women and Economic Development Consortium, January 2002.

National Advisory Board on Science and Technology. *Winning with Women in Trades, Technology, Science and Engineering*. Ottawa: National Advisory Board on Science and Technology, Canada, 1993.

National Council of Welfare. *Profiles of Welfare: Myths and Realities*. Ottawa: National Council of Welfare (Canada), 1998.

–. *Welfare Incomes, 2000 and 2001*. Ottawa: National Council of Welfare, Spring 2002.

–. *Fact Sheet: Welfare Recipients*. Ottawa: National Council of Welfare, March 2003.

New Brunswick Advisory Council on the Status of Women. *Training for Results: A Study of Women and Employment Training in New Brunswick*. Fredericton: NB Advisory Council on the Status of Women, December 1994.

Ontario. Ministry of Transportation. *Labour Market Analysis for Women in Maintenance*. Downsview, ON: Institute for Market and Social Analysis, 1988.

–. Ministry of Community and Social Services. "Welfare Fraud Control Report 2001 2002." Online at <http://www.cfcs.gov.on.ca/CFCS/en/programs/IES/OntarioWorks/ Publications/fraudReport0102.htm> (accessed 25 September 2004).

Ontario Social Safety NetWork. *Welfare Reform and Single Mothers*. Toronto: Ontario Social Safety NetWork Backgrounder OHPE Bulletin 58.1, 1998.

Ontario Women's Directorate. *Constructing Change: Dealing with Equity Issues – A Package for Apprenticeship and Skill Trainers in the Construction Sector*. Toronto: Provincial Building and Construction Trades Council of Ontario and Ontario Women's Directorate, 1995.

Ornstein, Michael. "A Profile of Social Assistance Recipients in Ontario." Toronto Institute for Social Research, York University, June 1995.

Overend, Valerie. "Proposal for the Women and Economic Development Consortium," on behalf of SaskWITT. Regina: SaskWITT, 1997.

–. "Trades Are the Ticket: Women and Carpentry Training." *Kinesis* (1998): 15-16.

–. "Regina Women's Construction Co-operative Ltd." *SaskWITT Newsletter* 5, 1, (Summer 1998).

–. *Foundation for Success: The Story of the Women's Work Training Program in Saskatchewan*. Regina: SaskWITT, 2001.

Overend, Valerie, and Denise Needham. "Concept Proposal: Women's Independent Work Project." Regina: Women's Work Training Program, 3 May 1995.

–. "Women's Work Training Program, Feb. 1996-Dec. 2000, Five-Year Funding Proposal." Regina: Women's Work Training Program, October 1995.

–. "Women's Work Training Program 1998, Phase 2." Funding Proposal to New Careers Employment Program – Community Works Work Placement. Regina: Women's Work Training Program, April 1998.

Owens, Sherry Lynn, Bobbie C. Smothers, Fannye E. Love. "Are Girls Victims of Gender Bias in Our Nation's Schools?" *Journal of Instructional Psychology* 30, 2 (2003): 131-6.

Pryor, Brandt W. "Predicting and Explaining Intentions to Participate in Continuing Education: An Application of the Theory of Reasoned Action." *Adult Education Quarterly* 40, 3 (1990): 146-57.

Ramdeen, Ken K. "Perceived Barriers to the Entry of College Women into Non-Traditional Technical and Blue Collar Training: Implications for Career and Program Planning." PhD diss., University of Toronto, 1987.

Raphael, Jody. "Domestic Violence and Welfare Receipt: The Unexplored Barrier to Employment." *Georgetown Journal of Fighting Poverty* 3, 1 (1995): 29-34.

Razack, Sherene. "Racism in Quotation Marks: A Review of Philomena Essed's Work." *Resources for Feminist Research* 20, 3-4 (1991): 148-51.

–. *Looking White People in the Eye: Gender, Race and Culture in Courtrooms and Classrooms.* Toronto: University of Toronto Press, 1998.

–. ed. *Race, Space, and the Law: Unmapping a White Settler Society.* Toronto: Between the Lines, 2002.

Resnick, Lauren. "Learning In School and Out." *Educational Researcher* 16, 9 (December 1987): 13-20.

Rodgers, Karen. *Wife Assault: The Findings of a National Survey.* Juristat, Canadian Centre for Justice Statistics. Ottawa: Statistics Canada, March 1994.

Rose, Nancy E. *Workfare or Fair Work: Women, Welfare, and Government Work Programs.* New Brunswick, NJ: Rutgers University Press, 1995.

Ross, David P., Katherine J. Scott, and Peter J. Smith. *The Canadian Fact Book on Poverty.* Ottawa: Canadian Council on Social Development, 2000.

Royal Commission on Aboriginal Peoples. Vol. 3, *Gathering Strength*, and Vol. 4, *Perspectives and Realities.* Ottawa: Supply and Services Canada, 1996.

Royal Commission on the Status of Women in Canada. *Report of the Royal Commission on the Status of Women in Canada.* Ottawa: Supply and Services Canada, 1970.

Running, Kathryn. "Women in Unions Working Towards Equality." MA thesis, Queen's University, Kingston, ON, 1987.

–. "A Focus on Retention of Women in Trades, Technology, Operations and Blue Collar Work." Paper prepared for WITT National Network. London, ON: WITT National Network, July 1997.

Sabourin, Beverly Ann, and Peter Andre Globensky. *The Language of Literacy: A National Resource Directory of Aboriginal Literacy Programs.* Winnipeg: Beverly Anne Sabourin Associates, 1998.

Saskatchewan Women in Trades and Technology, Operations, and Blue-Collar Work. "Women's Work Training Program 1997." Paper presented to Saskatchewan Government, Future Skills Bridging Program, 15 November 1996.

Schneider, Margaret. "Women in Non-Traditional Occupations: Educational Strategies that Work." *Proceedings of the International Conference Linking Research and Practice.* Vol. 2: *Education and Work.* Ed. D. Corson and S. Lawton, 40-8. Toronto: Ontario Institute for Studies in Education, 1990.

Schom-Moffatt, Patti, and Marcia Braundy. *National Survey of Women in Trades and Technology Orientation Courses.* Ottawa: Employment and Immigration Canada, April 1989.

Scott, Catherine. *The Recruitment Guide: How to Recruit Women into Trades, Technology Operations and Blue-Collar Work and Training.* London, ON: WITT National Network, 1995.

Shah, Priti. "Participating for Change." Paper prepared for the Women's Employment and Training Coalition, Drishti Consulting Service, Toronto, April 2000.

Silver, Jim, with Darlene Klyne and Freeman Simard. *Aboriginal Learners in Selected Adult Learning Centres in Manitoba.* Winnipeg: Canadian Centre for Policy Alternatives, June 2003

Shragge, Eric, ed. *Workfare: Ideology for a New Underclass.* Toronto: Garamond Press, 1997.

Skof, Karl. "Women in Registered Apprenticeship Training Programs." *Education Quarterly Review* 1, 4 (1994): 26-34.

Staton, Pat, and Joyce Scane. *Identifying Models of Successful Community School Partnerships: Co-operative Education for Young Women in Non-Traditional Careers.* Toronto: Ontario Institute for Studies in Education, 1994.

Stephen, Jennifer. *Access Diminished: A Report on Women's Training and Employment Services in Ontario.* Toronto: Advocates for Community-based Training and Education for Women, June 2000.

–. "Employing Discourses of Employability and Domesticity: Women's Employment and Training Policies and the Formation of the Canadian Welfare State, 1935-1947." PhD diss., University of Toronto, 2000.

Stewart, Jennifer, and Martin D. Dooley. "The Duration of Spells on Welfare and Off-Welfare among Lone Mothers in Ontario." Paper prepared for the Canadian International Labour Network, McMaster University, 1998.

Streisel, Sheri, and Tracy Myers. *Career Information Resources for Aboriginal People* (Saskatoon: Aboriginal Human Resource Development Council of Canada, 2000).

Strong-Boag, Veronica. "Wages for Housework: Mothers' Allowances and the Beginnings of Social Security in Canada." *Canadian Journal of Canadian Studies* 1 (1979): 24-34.

Struthers, James. *The Limits of Affluence: Welfare in Ontario, 1920-1970.* Toronto: University of Toronto Press, 1994.

Sugiman, Pamela. *Labour's Dilemma: The Gender Politics of Autoworkers in Canada, 1937-1979.* Toronto: University of Toronto Press, 1994.

Sweet, Robert, and Paul Gallagher. *Women and Apprenticeships: An Analysis of the 1994 National Apprentice Trades Survey.* Ottawa: Human Resources Development Canada, 1997.

Trainor, Catherine, and Karen Mihorea, eds. *Family Violence in Canada: A Statistical Profile.* Canadian Centre for Justice Statistics Profile Series. Ottawa: Statistics Canada, 2001, Catalogue no. 85-224-XIE, 29-30.

van Dijk, Teun A. "Discourses and the Denial of Racism." *Discourse and Society* 3, 1 (1992): 87-118.

Vezina, Nicole, and Julie Courville. "Integration of Women into Traditionally Masculine Jobs." *Women and Health* 18, 3 (1992): 97-118.

Walshok, M. *Blue Collar Women: Pioneers on the Male Frontier.* Garden City, NY: Anchor Press, 1981.

Weatherson, Rosemary. "When Sleeping Dictionaries Awaken: The Re/turn of the Native Woman Informant." *Post Identity* 1, 1 (1997): 113-44.

White, Julie. *Male and Female: Women and the Canadian Union of Postal Workers.* Toronto: Thompson, 1990.

Withorn, Ann. "'Why Do They Hate Me So Much?' A History of Welfare and Its Abandonment in the United States." *American Journal of Orthnopsychiatry* 66, 4 (1996): 496-509.

Women's Employment and Training Coalition. *Participating for Change.* Toronto: Priti Shah, Drishti Consulting Service, April 2000.

Women in Trades and Technology National Network. *Construction Technology for Women: Facilitator's Guide.* London, ON: WITT National Network, 1999.

Women in Trades and Technology (WITT) National Network, EDB Consulting, Jeroo Khodi, and Associates Inc. *Report on Employment Equity Training Needs Analysis.* London, ON: WITT National Network, 29 May 1997.

Women in Trades, Technology, Operations and Blue-Collar Work. *An Invitation to Membership: WITT National Network.* London, ON: WITT Publications, n.d.

Workfare Watch. "Women and Workfare." *Workfare Watch Newsletter* 1, 6 (1997).

Yalnizyan, Armine. *The Growing Gap: A Report on Growing Inequality between the Rich and Poor in Canada.* Toronto: Centre for Social Justice, 1998.

Zelechow, Ann, and Anne Morais. *ACTEW Survey of Employment and Training Services for Women in Metro Toronto.* Toronto: Advocates for Community-based Training and Education for Women, 1997.

Zucchino, David. *Myth of the Welfare Queen.* New York: Simon and Schuster, 1997.

Interviews Conducted

Women's Work Training Program: participants, instructors, coordinators. Interviews conducted on an individual basis, in Regina, SK, May 1998, October 1998, July 1999, and December 1999.

Women's Work Training Program: coordinators. E-mail and telephone interviews from Kingston, ON, July 2003, August 2003, September 2003, January 2004, and February 2004.

Index

Aboriginals. *See* Natives
abuse. *See* child abuse; domestic violence
accessible construction, 125
alcoholism. *See* substance abuse in Women's
  Work Training Program
Anderson, Kim, 42, 50
Anonymous Participant no. 2: 38, 41, 83
Anonymous Participant no. 4: 51, 59, 60
Anonymous Participant no. 5: 51, 52, 60
Anonymous Participant no. 6: 54, 57, 61, 79,
  81, 89
Anonymous Participant no. 7: 54, 60
Anonymous Participant no. 8: 54-5
Anonymous Participant no. 9: 55
Anonymous Participant no. 10: 56, 89, 129
Anonymous Participant no. 11: 57
Anonymous Participant no. 12: 61
Anonymous Participant no. 13: 78-9, 122
Anonymous Participant no. 14: 79
Anonymous Participant no. 15: 80
Anonymous Participant no. 16: 80-1, 99
Anonymous Participant no. 17: 82
Anonymous Participant no. 18: 99
assertiveness skills, 47, 48, 59, 69, 123-4
Audrey (WWTP participant), 58, 63

body awareness, 24, 63
Braundy, Marcia, 24, 86
bridging programs, 7, 8
building trades: acceptance of women, 123,
  130, 131; barriers toward women, 10, 16,
  20, 136
business skills, 124-8
Butterwick, Shauna, 77

Canadian Jobs Strategy, 6
career counselling, 24
carpentry retraining program, 16
carpentry skills gained in Women's Work
  Training Program, 119, 123
Charlene (WWTP participant), 48, 78
Cheryl (WWTP participant), 43, 121
child abuse: among participants in WWTP,
  51, 53; in residential schools, 50; text of
  WWTP survey on, 152-4
child raising. *See* motherhood
childcare: arrangements in WWTP, 17, 22,
  42; lack of, 5, 138-9; on-site, 141
"Choosing the Beat of Her Own Drum," 86,
  124

Chritoph, Ursule, 7
colonialism: and domestic violence, 49; and
  everyday racism, 72-4; legacy of, 50; and
  Native women, 39-40, 41-2, 75-6; at
  residential schools, 38-9
community-based organizations, 6, 7
confidence. *See* assertiveness skills; self-esteem
  problems
Consolidated Revenue Fund, 7
construction industry. *See* building trades
"creaming," 7, 101

debt problems, 59, 61, 169n87
Delphine (WWTP participant), 58
depression and abused women, 52-3
Diane (WWTP participant): effect of WWTP
  on, 119, 121; friendships, 65-6, 82;
  interviewed, 47-8, 58-9, 67; on wages, 95
domestic violence: among participants in
  WWTP, 51-6, 67-8, 132; on Native women,
  49; on poor women, 48-9; and substance
  abuse, 51-2; text of WWTP survey on,
  152-54
double-dipping, 101
driver's education, 142
drug addiction. *See* substance abuse in
  Women's Work Training Program

education: background of participants in
  WWTP, 56, 57-8; and NB Works, 9; pre-
  requisites for WWTP, 17; sacrifices for, 10
Emily (WWTP participant): interviewed,
  38-9, 50-1, 64; and S. Murray, 85-6
employment: experience of participants in
  WWTP, 56-9; of single mothers, 2-3
Employment Insurance, 7, 28, 103
equity legislation, 131
Essed, Philomena, 75
Evelyn (WWTP participant), 46-7, 60, 64, 68

federal government: equity legislation, 131;
  funds WWTP, 18, 27; and Natives, 40, 74;
  retraining programs, 5-9, 101
flashbacks, 53-4

George, Pamela, 75
Ginny (WWTP participant), 41, 64, 66, 69
Globensky, Peter, 135

Hamilton, Heather, 32

harassment: in abusive relationships, 53; of
Native women, 49, 57, 75; of participants
in WWTP, 54-5, 66
Harris, Mike, viii, 157n6
health problems of abused women, 52-3
Heather (WWTP participant): on Co-op
difficulties, 92; effect of WWTP on, 122,
126; interviewed, 48, 65, 66, 68-9
homophobia, 98-9
Horsman, Jenny, 53, 55, 62

incarceration of Natives, 75

Jackie (WWTP participant), 39, 44, 63, 64
"Judy" (WWTP participant), 39, 62-3, 67,
89

Karen (WWTP participant), 50

life goals exercise, 24
life skills education, 22-3, 25, 69, 77, 89,
121-4
Linda (WWTP participant), 96
literacy upgrading, 119
Lorie (WWTP participant), 44-5, 46, 58

"Maggie" (WWTP participant): effect of
WWTP on, 119, 123; interviewed, 57, 62,
63, 64-5, 96; on life skills, 23, 69
male work environments, 26-7, 130-1
Manpower Training Program, 5
Maracle, Lee, 50
maternity leave, 5
mathematics classes, 22
Métis, 40, 81-2
Michelle (WWTP participant): friendships,
65-6, 82; interviewed, 48, 57, 64, 96
Milarin (WWTP participant), 48
motherhood: demands of, 44-6, 47-8, 134;
need to prove abilities at, 41-3; putting
career ahead of, 46-7, 48, 69
Murray, Sharon (WWTP participant): on
being in debt, 59; on domestic violence,
51-2; as foreperson, 63, 125; hired by
WWTP, 25, 97-8; and "Maggie," 67; and
racial issues, 78, 84, 85-6

National Training Act, 5-6
Natives: baby-snatching, 39-40; birth rate,
42; conflict between reserve and urban,
82-3; domestic violence, 49-50, 51; family
relationships, 33, 39, 42-3, 59-60; non-
traditional training programs for, 18, 86;
poverty, 59-60, 75; pride in culture, 123-4;
pride in motherhood, 41-3; in Regina, 74-6;
and residential schools, 38-9; on staff of
WWTP, 84-6, 98; status, 40; substance
abuse, 50, 60, 83; success stories, 1; and
white culture in WWTP, 77-8, 128-30. *See
also* colonialism; race and racism; racism
in Women's Work Training Program
Needham, Denise: addiction issues, 87, 88-9;
author's experiences with, 11-12; background, 14, 15, 98; connects with V.
Overend, 14-15, 16; deals with racial issues,
78, 80, 83-4; "dream" training program,
141-2; frustration with Co-op women, 91,
92, 93, 94-5; on homophobia, 99-100; on
participants' problems, 55, 61, 62; on
success stories of WWTP, 67, 70
New Brunswick Works (NB Works), 8

non-traditional employment training, 7-8,
11, 18, 57, 86
North Bay retraining program, 30

Overend, Valerie: author's experiences with,
11-12; background, 15-16, 45; connects
with D. Needham, 14-15, 16; "dream"
training program, 142; frustration with
Co-op women, 91, 93, 134; funding work,
101, 102-3; on homophobia, 99-100;
importance of WWTP, 70-1, 131, 136-7; on
life-skills education, 121-2; on Native staff,
84-5

participants of Women's Work Training
Program: assertiveness skills, 47, 48, 59, 69,
123-4; background of, 36-7; communication difficulties, 77-9, 92, 122, 128-9; debt
worries, 59, 61, 169n87; domestic violence,
51-6, 67-8, 132; dreams, 62-3; educational
background, 56, 57-8; effect of carpentry
skills on, 118-22, 127; family support for,
63-5; feelings learning with men, 131;
friendship among, 65-8; health problems,
53-4, 67, 134; homophobia, 98-100; interview process, 37-8; overcoming self-esteem
problems, 55-6, 64, 68-71, 90, 119-20; past
employment, 56-9; personal crises, 33, 43,
58; pictures of, 105-17; problems with
husbands/partners, 45, 47-8, 51-5, 65;
situation after program, 120-1, 131-2, 134,
136; views on life skills classes, 23, 69, 77,
89, 122, 123. *See also* Women's Work
Training Program; Regina Women's
Construction Co-operative; substance
abuse; and *specific participants' names*
Pat (WWTP participant): after the WWTP,
120; effect of WWTP on, 45-6, 62, 69-70;
interviewed, 42, 56, 64, 65, 66, 79; as leader
of group, 66, 68, 93; racial issues, 80;
represents Co-op, 31-2
pay equity, 10, 131
physical education classes, 23-4
poverty: causes of, 2, 3; Native, 59-60, 75
prejudice: against lesbians, 99-100; against
Natives, 49-50, 57, 72-4. *See also* race and
racism; racism in Women's Work Training
Program
Proctor, Marion, 16
prostitution, 39, 74-75
provincial governments: and retraining
programs, 4-5, 7, 138; and welfare, 3-4, 8,
10. *See also* Saskatchewan, Government of

race and racism: and colonialism, 38-40,
72-4; and economic resources, 59-60;
and Native status, 40; in Regina, 74-6; in
residential schools, 38. *See also* racism
in Women's Work Training Program
racism in Women's Work Training Program:
attitudes to time and space, 80, 82, 85-6;
communication problems, 34-5, 77-9;
from customers of Co-op, 83-4; denied by
whites, 81, 84; favouritism, 79-80, 80-1;
internalized, 81-4; and lack of Native staff,
84-6
Razack, Sherene, 50
Reagan (WWTP participant), 55, 67-8
Regina, 74-6
Regina Women's Construction Co-operative:
advisory board, 32; as a business, 27-8, 31,

90, 91, 94-5, 125; develops leadership, 92, 93; difficult customers of, 83-4, 125; employee evaluations, 28-9, 92-3, 126; end of operations, 127; funding, 27; gains respect of building trade, 128, 130; management of, 91-2, 93-4, 126-7; public exposure for, 31-2; substance abuse and policy for, 87-9, 155-6; wages, 28, 29, 60-1, 95-6; weaknesses of, 91-2, 93-5, 126-7; working environment, 29. *See also* participants of Women's Work Training Program; racism in Women's Work Training Program
residential schools, 38-9, 47, 50
retraining programs. *See* training/retraining programs; Women's Work Training Program
Rhonda H. (WWTP participant): effect of WWTP on, 123; interviewed, 44, 57-8, 64, 65; left Co-op, 96, 134
Rhonda M. (WWTP participant), 43, 46, 64, 67, 121
Roxanne (Pat's sister), 65
Royal Commission on the Status of Women, 5

sabatoging success, 134-5
Sabourin, Beverly, 135
Sandy Merriman House, 88
Saskatchewan, Government of: equity legislation, 131; funds Regina Women's Construction Co-operative, 27, 101; funds WWTP, 18, 101, 102
Saskatchewan Institute for Applied Science and Technology (SIAST), 26-7, 130-1
Saskatchewan Women in Trades and Technology (SaskWITT), 19-20, 31, 131
Schom-Moffat, Patti, 86
seat purchases for training programs, 7-8
self-esteem problems: as barrier to trade job, 20; in the Co-op, 90-1, 95; and life skills, 23, 122-3; overcoming in training programs, 34, 55-6, 64, 68-71, 90, 119-20. *See also* assertiveness skills
Self-Sufficiency Projects, 9
sexual orientation, 98-100
sexualization of Native women, 50, 75
Sheila (WWTP participant): growing self-esteem, 69, 70; interviewed, 61, 62, 63, 67
Shelley (WWTP participant): effect of WWTP on, 118, 122, 123; friendships, 82; interviewed, 45, 46, 47, 65, 66; left Co-op, 96
Sherry (WWTP participant): business interest, 124, 125; growing self-esteem, 64, 70; on wages, 95-6
Shirley (WWTP participant), 40, 64, 66, 67, 69, 120
single mothers/women: public characterization of, 2-3; and training, 138; and welfare, 3-4, 8, 138; in the workforce, 139-40; in WWTP, 42
SKILTEC program in North Bay, 30
social services, 28. *See also* Employment Insurance; welfare
spousal violence. *See* domestic violence
storytelling, 12
student loans, 10
substance abuse in Women's Work Training Program: and debt, 61; and domestic violence, 51-2; by Natives, 50, 60, 83; by participants, 87-9, 134; by participants' children/partners, 46-7, 52, 132; screening

and policies for, 87-8; text of Co-op policy, 155-6
Sunshine Coast retraining program, 30
Suzette (WWTP participant), 58

Tanya (WWTP participant), 44
Thompson, Donna, 54
training/retraining programs: criteria for assessing, 13; domestic violence and, 53, 55; features of model program, 140-3; five stages of personal transformation, 133-4, 135; history, 4-7; Native problems with, 86, 129-30; in non-traditional employment, 7-8, 11, 18, 57, 86; paid for, 9-10; success stories, 11; and welfare, 8-9, 58. *See also* Women's Work Training Program

Urban Circle Training Centre, 172n8

Victoria carpentry retraining program, 88
violence: in Native lives, 49-51; participants' survey on, 37-8, 52, 53; text of WWTP survey on, 152-4. *See also* domestic violence
visible minorities, 6, 7

wage supplement programs, 8-9
war on poverty, 2
welfare: deductions, 10; dismantling of, 3-4; and domestic violence, 49; early years, 8; experiences being on, 58, 60, 96; fraud, 2, 3, 160n41; myths, 3; and single mothers, 138; and training programs, 8-9, 58; and transition to employment, 60
Women and Economic Development Consortium (WEDC), 27, 103, 133-4
women in poverty. *see* single mothers/women
Women in Trades and Technology (WITT), 6, 15, 136
women-only workplaces, 13, 20
Women's Work Training Program (WWTP): author's observations on, 11-12, 13, 68; beginnings, 14-15, 16-17; business skills gained, 124-8; carpentry skills gained, 119, 123; costs for participants, 21-2; discipline, 21, 85-6, 87-8, 94; empowering women, 31, 55-6, 62-3, 68-71, 121; end of, 118; evaluation of, 118, 120, 127-8, 132-3; flexibility, 32-4; funding, 18-20, 100-4, 144-6; hiring staff, 97-8, 100, 102, 103-4; lack of native staff, 84-6; learning methods, 24-5, 26, 34, 130-1; life skills, 22-3, 121-4; mandate, 1, 151; materials and wages provided, 21-2, 26, 28, 60-1; recruitment, 17-18; schedule and rules, 147-50; six phases of, 19, 21; success stories, 1-2, 67, 70, 136-7; supportive environment of, 20, 27, 29, 33-4, 65-8, 95, 119; tests, 25, 27, 29, 119; unique features of, 30-1. *See also* participants of Women's Work Training Program; racism in Women's Work Training Program; Regina Women's Construction Co-operative)
workfare: effectiveness of, 138, 139; and harassed women, 53; and single mothers, 4, 172n3
World War II, 5

Zena (WWTP participant), 23, 63, 69, 123